M000097133

Westworld and Philosophy

Popular Culture and Philosophy® Series Editor: George A. Reisch

For full details of all Popular Culture and Philosophy® books, visit www.opencourtbooks.com.

Popular Culture and Philosophy®

Westworld and Philosophy

Mind Equals Blown

Edited by
RICHARD GREENE
AND
JOSHUA HETER

OPEN COURT
Chicago

Volume 122 in the series, Popular Culture and Philosophy ®, edited by George A. Reisch

To find out more about Open Court books, visit our website at www.opencourtbooks.com.

Open Court Publishing Company is a division of Carus Publishing Company, dba Cricket Media.

Copyright © 2019 by Carus Publishing Company, dba Cricket Media

First printing 2019

All rights reserved. No part of this publication may be reproduced, stored in a retrieval system, or transmitted, in any form or by any means, electronic, mechanical, photocopying, recording, or otherwise, without the prior written permission of the publisher, Open Court Publishing Company, 70 East Lake Street, Suite 800, Chicago, Illinois 60601.

Printed and bound in the United States of America.

Westworld and Philosophy: Mind Equals Blown

This book has not been prepared, authorized, or endorsed by the creators or producers of *Westworld*.

ISBN: 978-0-8126-9991-3

Library of Congress Control Number: 2018954423

This book is also available as an e-book (ISBN 978-0-8126-9995-1).

Contents

Part I
The Maze

If you can't tell the difference, does it matter if I'm real or not?

Part II
Mariposa Saloon

When you are suffering, that's when you're most real.

Part III
The Prairie
Everything in this world is magic, except to the magician.

Part IV
Main Street
The only thing wrong with the seven deadly sins is that there aren't more of them.

Part V
The Mesa Hub
Some people choose to see the ugliness in this world. I choose to see the beauty, to believe there is an order to our days.

Thanks

Working on this project has been a pleasure, in no small part because of the many fine folks who have assisted us along the way. In particular, a debt of gratitude is owed to David Ramsay Steele and George Reisch at Open Court, the contributors to this volume, and our respective academic departments at Iowa Western Community College and Weber State University. Finally, we'd like to thank those family members, students, friends, and colleagues with whom we've had fruitful and rewarding conversations on various aspects of all things *Westworld* as it relates to philosophical themes.

Welcome to Westworld, Population: ?

If you're reading this book, a book about the science-fiction film and television series *Westworld*, there's a non-trivial chance that you've also played a video game or two in your life. There's likely no hard, empirical data concerning this issue, but it seems altogether reasonable to assume that there is some correlation between science fiction fandom and video game play. At the very least, you're familiar with the idea. With that in mind, it is nevertheless fairly unlikely that in the course of your gameplay, you've stopped to worry about the ethics of flinging fireballs at Goombas or Koopa Troopas in Super Mario World. It's unlikely that you've ever stopped to wonder what it's like for your sparring partner to receive a Hurricane Kick in Street Fighter 2.

The initial response to these considerations should probably be one of incredulous dismissal. "Flinging fireballs in Super Mario simply isn't an ethical issue!" you might retort. "There *is* nothing that it is to be *like* on the receiving end of a Hurricane Kick in Street Fighter 2!" you might say. This seems correct; everything we see on the screen in a video game is merely a matter of 1's and 0's, arranged in such a way to *simulate* some sort of battle; to make it *appear* as if there are experiences being had. But of course, we know this is not actually the case. Of course, it is true that video games are merely simulations of a certain sort, but as philosophers tend to do, it is natural to begin to worry whether there are actually any general lessons that can be drawn here. Is it possible that, if a game-type simulation were made much sophisticated and realistic, that we *should* begin to worry about the ethical implication of playing it? In such a game, could the line between simulation and reality begin to blur?

Westworld can be potentially understood as one big thought experiment in which these and a good number of other sorts of philosophical questions can be raised. In it, we meet the likes of Dolores, Maeve, Teddy, and other android inhabitant "Hosts" of a theme park in which participant "Guests" can come and play out their wild west fantasies in a sort of video game come to life. Are Dolores and Maeve simply just more sophisticated combinations of 1's and 0's, or are they real people? Could they ever be the object of moral obligations? How could we ever know? Does Teddy have any genuine choice in his life, or is he merely living out his programming? For that matter, are you?

In the course of this book, you'll encounter a number of philosopher-Hosts who will take you on your own adventure that will cover topics like free will, religion, knowledge, experience, art, and, naturally, the meaning of life.

So, if you dare; choose your hat, saddle up, and ride.

Part I

The Maze

*If you can't tell the
difference, does it matter
if I'm real or not?*

1
Time to Write My Own F*cking Story

DENNIS M. WEISS

Who am I? What's my place in the world? These are deeply philosophical questions, perennial questions that we human beings seem to regularly return to, especially in periods of change and disruption.

Today, such change and disruption are largely driven by technology. Having remade our world through the power of technology, we're led to wonder once again, Who are we? What is our place in this technological world that we have made? While we might not expect such meditations on our technological condition to show up on our televisions, they do. On *Westworld*, for instance.

What is Westworld? It's a theme park, a place of employment, a television show. For its players, its Hosts, its workers, and especially for us, its viewers, it's an opportunity to think through these philosophical questions as they increasingly relate to our technological condition.

You Are a Butcher. That Is All You Will Ever Be

Consider, for instance, poor Felix. He spends his days in the bowels of Westworld laboring in Livestock Management to keep the mangled and butchered bodies of Hosts functioning for another day of mayhem and murder. Day in and day out he's elbow deep in blood and guts, abused by his colleague

Sylvester, laboring to maintain a theme park that he himself can't afford to visit. Just another Southeast Asian hoping to make it in the world of coding.

His life involves loops every bit as routine as the loops of Westworld's Hosts. He doesn't even have a backstory. And as Elsie points out to Stubbs, "backstories do more than amuse Guests. They anchor the Hosts. It's their cornerstone. The rest of their identity is built around it, layer by layer" ("The Stray").

Lacking even a backstory, Leonardo Nam, the actor portraying Felix, had to write his own, as Nam reported to the website awardsdaily.com. He thinks that Felix "is someone that lives in a barracks and takes care of things. He has a little plant that is forbidden. He has lots of things that he's working on secretly as he treasures privacy. I think there is an element of him being there a long, long time. His work is his freedom."

Felix is a mere cog working away in the subterranean levels of Westworld to keep it functioning. He's an everyman. But he aspires for more. He's stolen a mechanical bird and is trying to learn how to code and get it to fly. Sylvester mocks his plan.

> Whoa, whoa, whoa. Is that your ace plan? You're gonna fix up a birdie and get yourself a promotion? You're not a f*cking ornithologist. And you're sure as hell not a coder. You are a butcher. That is all you will ever be. So, unless you want to score yourself a one-way ticket out of here for misappropriating corporate property, you better destroy that f*cking shit. Now, come on, we got another body. ("Contrapasso")

But Felix doesn't "destroy that f*cking shit." Instead, he continues to work on his little side project. Until another project comes along. It's while he's working on his bird and getting it to fly that it alights on Maeve's finger. She's woken in the lab and ominously says, "Hello Felix. It's time you and I had a chat" ("Contrapasso").

Awakenings Are Happening

What do Maeve and Felix have to chat about? Well, about those perennial philosophical questions, for one. They chat about the nature of the self and memory, the difference between being born and made, how you find your place in the world, whether it's possible to rewrite your story. While sitting deep in the lower levels of the technological theme park that is Westworld, they attempt to come to terms with the impact of technology on these philosophical matters.

But Westworld is more than a theme park. It's also a television show and a television show about living with our screens and technologies. As Maeve and Felix conspire together, they spend a lot of time doing what we do in our daily loops. They stare at screens, manipulate data, code, chat a lot about technology. And they are both literally waking up to the place of technology in their lives. As Nam notes in a perceptive comment to awardsdaily.com, Felix, our everyman, stands in for us human beings watching *Westworld*.

> There are awakenings that are happening, that's one thing that's running through our storyline. Maeve is starting to wake up, my character is starting to wake up. As she wakes up, I'm like the audience. I'm waking up, too. For Maeve, there is a new kind of relationship that she's experiencing with me. Previously, she's only been programmed to deal with death or deal with being in diagnostic mode. But me, I'm an "other."

And there are awakenings happening among our Hosts. One of Dolores's regular loops has her waking up in her bed, always ready to confront a new day. Maeve too of course is waking up. The show literally has her waking up over and over again, including from death, as she keeps dying in order to make her way back to Livestock Management and Felix, and a growing awareness of her place in this technological side show.

Maeve and Felix are both trying to come to terms with what it means to live in the massive presence of technology; Felix who labors in the belly of the techno-social world that is Westworld and is waking up to the manner in which the technology, the Hosts, is treated, and Maeve who is waking up to her own status as one of the servants built and enslaved by this technology. They're chatting about and beginning to examine the technological foundation of their world. And as they awaken, perhaps too so do we viewers.

In *The Whale and the Reactor* the philosopher of technology Langdon Winner observes that our world has been remade by technology but that so often we human beings continue posing and answering our perennial philosophical questions without ever thinking about the impact of technology on our lives and on the answers to those questions.

Technologies are simply tools that occupy the background and don't deserve much thought. But this is a mistake, Winner argues. Technologies in fact structure human activity. And as we build our world according to our technological plans, that built world in turn reshapes us. Our habits, perceptions, sense of self, understanding of place—all those perennial philosophical concerns—are powerfully restructured, Winner argues, by modern technological developments. Winner suggests we need to wake up from our technological somnambulism, our sleep-walking through our technological world, and begin to critically discuss the impact of technology on our lives.

Our relationship to technology and the manner in which technology is transforming our world is something akin to the Hosts' relationship to photographs that they are unable to see or process. When Hector is shown a photograph of a modern train and other advanced technological objects, he responds, "They don't look like anything to me." We often find ourselves in a similar situation, treating our technologies as just stuff, neutral tools that don't shape or otherwise impact our lives. We too have been wandering through an extended dream, Winner says, and it's time to wake up. It's time to have a chat about technology.

But how should that chat go? What story should we tell about living with technology? Returning to *Westworld*, we see that it offers us at least a couple of alternatives, perhaps most clearly in the contrast between the Man in Black, on the one hand, and Felix and Maeve, on the other.

A F*cking Piece of Work Born in Westworld

On the surface, the Man in Black seems to be worlds away from Felix and Maeve. He's a Titan, we're told, a god of industry. We learn that he has a controlling stake in Westworld, so he literally owns Maeve and is Felix's boss. While Felix can't afford to visit Westworld, the Man in Black has been, shall we say, a loyal repeat customer. He's on a first-name basis with the Westworld creator, Robert Ford. And he plays Westworld with relish.

Yet the Man in Black is like Felix in an intriguing way. He too doesn't seem to have a backstory, at least not one that we viewers are initially privy to. A central conceit of Season One of *Westworld* was the mystery behind the Man in Black. Who was he really? What is his place in the show? Why does he keep exacting such suffering on Dolores?

As the first season unfolds—spoiler alert!—we learn that the Man in Black is in fact William, the reluctant visitor to Westworld and sidekick, at least at first, of Logan. William isn't initially all that enamored of Westworld, until he meets Dolores, and then he eventually comes to agree with Logan's assessment that Westworld seduces everybody eventually. Westworld answers that question William's been asking himself: Who are you really?

As William tells Dolores, "I used to think this place was all about . . . pandering to your baser instincts. Now I understand. It doesn't cater to your lowest self, it reveals your deepest self. It shows you who you really are" ("Trompe L'Oeil"). William found his true self in Westworld. As Logan says to William, "I told you this place would show you who you really are. You pretend to be this weak, moralizing little . . . asshole, but, really, you're a f*cking piece of work" ("The Bicameral Mind").

And what a piece of work he is! When William first shows up in Westworld, we learn that he has spent his life pretending to be something, someone, he's not. As he tells Dolores: "I've been pretending my whole life. Pretending I don't mind, pretending I belong. My life's built on it" ("Trompe L'Oeil"). But he's swept away by Westworld, suggesting that he can become someone other than he is:

> Whoever you were before doesn't matter here. There's no rules or restrictions. You can change the story of your life. You can become someone else. No one will judge you, no one in the real world will even know. ("Contrapasso")

In Westworld, William thinks he can for once be truly alive. "I came here and I get a glimpse for a second of a life in which I don't have to pretend. A life in which I can be truly alive. How can I go back to pretending when I know what this feels like?" ("Trompe L'Oeil").

But as we piece together the Man in Black's backstory, we learn that William almost went mad searching for Dolores and that when he finds her, her memory had been wiped and he means nothing to her. Where he once thought he had found salvation in the technological theme park, instead he becomes the embittered and cynical owner of Westworld, bent on dominating the park and making it reveal its secrets.

We learn too that the Man in Black's time spent in his technological playground has poisoned his relationship with his wife, who kills herself rather than live another day under the threat of his sheer terror. So he immerses himself again in Westworld, ultimately killing Maeve and her daughter, trying to prove his wife wrong but ultimately revealing his true self.

William gave himself over to the technology and it didn't save him, so he puts on the black hat. As the Man in Black, he searches for his true self and for a sense of meaning and purpose treating the Hosts as mere toys as he seeks to control and dominate the technological world he has bought and paid for. While William initially treated Dolores as special, as almost human, the Man in Black treats her as an it—just a tool to be used and abused while he plays the game that is Westworld. He inflicts every kind of deprivation on Dolores and Maeve and Lawrence and any other Host that crosses his path. Rather than enter into a relationship with technology, he buys it and then goes about systematically abusing his new toy. It becomes the ultimate commodity to him, just a thing to be abused as he works out his own demons. Ultimately, the Man in Black is not all that different from Sylvester or Destin Levy, the technician from Livestock Management who uses (abuses?) the Hosts for his own sexual gratification.

The Man in Black describes the world outside Westworld as a world of chaos, a "fat, soft teat people cling to their entire life. Every need taken care of . . . except one . . . Purpose, meaning. So they come here. They can be a little scared, a little thrilled, enjoy some sweetly affirmative bullshit, and then they take a f*cking picture and they go back home" ("Contrapasso").

He turns to Westworld to provide a sense of meaning and purpose, to define his self and his place in the world. But rather than forging a relationship with his technological milieu, with his technological world, he seeks to dominate it, beat it into submission, make it reveal its hidden depths and secrets. He remains aloof, separate from the technology, as he tries to bend it to his will and make it reveal its secrets. He never fully wakes up to the reality of the technology and to technology as a form of life—it stays a mere thing to be used for his own purposes, rather than having a reality of its own.

We might even say that the Man in Black is something like Hector, in this regard. He sees the technology which surrounds him, the Hosts, especially Dolores, but it doesn't really mean anything to him. He's neither at home in the real world nor in Westworld and he pursues meaning and purpose by playing a game and looking for a maze that weren't meant for him.

You Can Be Whoever the F*ck You Want

Like Felix and the Man in Black, Maeve too is struggling with her sense of self. In "Chestnut," we learn that in her backstory she is afraid to live and is only free in her dreams, until she crosses the shining sea and discovers that in the new world, "You can be whoever the f*ck you want." The only problem, of course, is that as Maeve finishes telling this story, we learn that she is in analysis mode and is having her personality tweaked by a technician.

Maeve's backstory is a lie, which she soon discovers. Everything she does has been programmed into her. When Maeve sees her own thoughts and words played out on Felix's handheld device, she initially shuts down. She can't reconcile her memories of being at the Mariposa for ten years with her memories of being a mother. Her character begins to fragment, as she tells Felix and Sylvester: "What the hell is happening to me? One moment, I'm with a little girl in a different life. I can see her. Feel her hair in my hands, her breath on my face. The next, I'm back in Sweetwater. I can't tell which is real" ("Trace Decay"). As she comes to learn that she is a technological artifact, her self begins to unravel.

But as Maeve comes to realize that her life is a story, initially scripted by others and told to others for their amusement, she also comes to realize that she can begin to narrate her own story. As she so aptly puts it, "Time to write my own f*cking story" ("Trace Decay"). The next time we see Maeve strolling through Sweetwater, she's narrating events, controlling the action. She learns to code, much like Felix does, but with her bulked-up bulk apperception, she quickly learns that she can take command of the technology. Maeve comes to understand how technology is implicated in her sense of self, her nature as a Host, the place she occupies in the world. And in coming to appreciate this, she comes to understand how to use that technology to begin to narrate her own story.

As Maeve comes to understand how technology structures her life, she initially uses that understanding to find a way out of her technological prison. She comes to believe that every relationship she has had has been fake—with Clementine, with her daughter. And she tries to extricate herself from Westworld—pursuing a rebuild to remove the explosive device implanted in her spine and asking Bernard to delete the memories of her daughter. But then, just before departing Westworld, she has one last visit with Clementine and she learns the location of her daughter. When she finally has the opportunity to leave, she seemingly decides to stay and search for her daughter. She acknowledges her bond to her daughter and affirms her place in Westworld, seeking to create her place in it, rather than attempting to dominate it and control it as the Man in Black does.

Who Maeve is, is a product of technology. Her self, her place in the world, her very nature as a Host is the product of a vast technological network. As Maeve faces those same perennial questions confronting Felix and the Man in Black, she has to come to terms with the place of technology in her life, with the manner in which her life is mediated by the very technology she seeks to escape from. Maeve has the opportunity to escape her technological milieu, to exit the game that is Westworld, but she chooses to stay and fight for her daughter, to continue to create her story, writing her narrative within the technological world. She can be whoever she wants, and she chooses to be mother to her daughter, and quite possibly forge an unlikely alliance with a terrible human being.

Some Weird Interspecies Simpatico Going On

Over the course of their strange relationship, Felix and Maeve struggle with those perennial philosophical questions and the manner in which technology challenges easy answers. Maeve challenges Felix to articulate just what makes them different, grasping his hands in hers and observing, "We feel the same" ("The Adversary").

Felix comes to see his world afresh through Maeve's eyes. While he's worked on the butchered and bloodied bodies of the

Hosts for years, he comes to see them differently as he walks through Livestock Management with Maeve by his side, witnessing through her perspective the atrocities he has been daily surrounded with. It's through Maeve's eyes that Felix witnesses and wakes up to the consequences of the brutalization of technology—the bloodied, mangled bodies of Hosts being hosed down.

And Felix comes to acknowledge Maeve's humanity. While recognizing that Felix and Maeve had some "weird interspecies simpatico going on," Sylvester plans to "brick" Maeve, literally turning her into an unthinking material object, objecting that "she was a f*cking Host. This was never gonna end another way." But Felix isn't party to the plan. As Maeve observes, "Turns out your friend has a little more compassion than you. He couldn't snuff out a life just like that" ("Trace Decay"). Felix has come to recognize that she's not a brick, but a life.

While Felix comes to recognize and acknowledge Maeve's humanity, she in turns confirms him in his own humanity. When Felix is confronted with the body of Bernard and the realization that Bernard is a Host, he momentarily looks at his own hands, the hands that Maeve earlier had held in her own, and doubts his own status as a "born" human being. It's Maeve that affirms his humanity: "Oh, for f*ck's sake. You're not one of us. You're one of them. Now fix him" ("The Bicameral Mind"). But even in recognizing that he is one of them, Maeve recognizes he's a terrible one of them. Shortly before she's to board the train to leave Westworld, Felix hands her information on how to locate her daughter and asks her if she is going to be okay. Maeve replies, "Oh, Felix. You really do make a terrible human being. And I mean that as a compliment" ("The Bicameral Mind").

Felix is one of the rare human beings in Westworld to confront the impact of technology on questions about who we are and what our place is in the scheme of things. And he's one of the few human beings to forge a meaningful relationship with the technology with which he is surrounded. Unlike the Man in Black or Sylvester or Destin, he has awoken to his technological condition and has learned to care for technology, whether the bird he teaches to take wing or Maeve, the Host hell bent on telling her own story. In turn, Maeve's story can only be told with the recognition and help she has received from Felix. It's clear from Felix and Maeve that the story they are writing is jointly authored, that there is indeed some weird interspecies simpatico going on. Who they are and how they find a place in the world is a product of their mutual recognition, an interspecies simpatico between human being and technical artifact.

That same weird interspecies simpatico could characterize our own relationship to *Westworld*, to television, and to our technological condition. Recall that Leonardo Nam sees Felix as a stand-in for the audience. We too have to work through those perennial philosophical questions, even as we are surrounded by technologies we often barely notice or remark upon.

Perhaps Felix and Maeve point the way forward as we think about our relationship with technology. Rather than stumbling through a dream, as technological somnambulists, or struggling to dominate and control and subdue technology, as the Man in Black does, perhaps we should come to understand that we are involved in a complex relationship with our machines.

It may be weird, and it may be interspecies, but we are what we are owing to our relationship with technology. And our technologies are not just a bunch of dumb stuff we have populated our environment with. Rather, our technologies are themselves forms of life that we enter into relationship with and which often shape and influence how we answer some of those perennial philosophical questions about who and what we are and what our place in the world is.

In seeking answers to those questions, we can take some inspiration from the weird interspecies simpatico going on between a terrible human being and a Host searching for her daughter.

2
Are the Hosts Hypnotized?

JUSTIN FETTERMAN

My spirits, as in a dream, are all bound up.

—WILLIAM SHAKESPEARE, *The Tempest*

In the opening lines of *Westworld*, Dolores tell us she is in a dream, one she would like to wake up from. The conversation that follows with her and Arnold, initially presumed as interaction with Bernard, runs over scenes of her awakening: she opens her eyes in bed and continues out into the day, greeting her father and heading into Sweetwater.

The series later clarifies that the language of dreaming is part of the Hosts' programming, designed to keep them from knowing the truth (of *being* programmed) and their waking life consists of the narratives and interactions they repeat at the will of the park and its Guests. But *waking up* occurs in many ways: from sleep, into higher spirituality, and out of a trance. For the Hosts of *Westworld*, there are dreams within dreams, though it is perhaps more accurate to call them trances within trances, layers of hypnosis from which they ultimately seek to be released.

Hypnosis is a form of a waking-sleep, its name derived from the Greek word for sleep, *hypnos* (ὕπνος). Coined in the late nineteenth century, the exact definition is debated among psychologists though it is generally agreed to indicate a state of consciousness including heightened suggestibility along with possible alterations in perception, sensation, emotion, thought, and behavior.

The Hosts' Analysis Mode, a verbal diagnostic system, is a clear form of hypnosis, exhibiting the traditional markers outlined by the American Psychological Association:

1. A hypnotic induction, consisting of an extended initial suggestion. In *Westworld*, this requires nothing more than an authorized employee giving the "analysis" command.

and

2. A hypnotic state of mind which encourages response to suggestions, including:

    a. Altering speech patterns: "You can lose the accent."

    b. Inducing/suppressing emotional responses: "Cognition only; no emotional affect."

    c. Reviewing/analyzing internal states and memories: "Access your previous configuration."

    d. Prompting/preventing physical actions: "Cease all motor functions."

The Hosts' programming (and the consciousness debate raised by *Westworld*) is based on the bicameral mind theory of Julian Jaynes, therefore we can follow the connection of dream language to hypnosis, as Jaynes presents in his book, *The Origin of Consciousness in the Breakdown of the Bicameral Mind*. In a section on evidence, Jaynes singles out hypnosis as "the black sheep" of problems in psychology and states that his theory provides an "obvious" solution in what he calls the "general bicameral paradigm."

Hypnosis in the General Bicameral Paradigm

We are such stuff as dreams are made on.

—SHAKESPEARE, *The Tempest*

To recognize contemporary phenomena as evidence for bicameral origins, Jaynes identifies four necessary structural elements:

1. *Collective Cognitive Imperative*: A belief system or culturally recognized expectation that sets the stage for how a phenomenon should be experienced/observed

2. *Archaic Authorization*: A person or concept (e.g. a god) accepted as an authority, to whom control is ceded during the phenomenon

3. *Induction*: A formal, ritualized procedure that initiates the phenomenon, usually by focusing consciousness/attention

4. *Trance*: A loss/lessening of consciousness in response to the previous structures

From this approach, Jaynes identifies several survivals of bicamerality, including oracles (who ritualistically cede conscious control to a cultural deity) and demonic possession (where stress induces a ceding of control to demons, a concept reinforced by society/religion). Hypnosis fits easily into this structure, while also demonstrating that the four elements are not necessarily a temporal succession or even mutually exclusive.

The *Collective Cognitive Imperative* is simply our cultural belief that hypnosis is real, which we affirm through our repeated willingness to interact with it as entertainment or treatment. The Imperative is shaped by each hypnotist performance that delights us and each therapist who successfully cures an addiction through hypnosis. We come to accept that hypnotism can make us cluck like a chicken or teach us to detest the previously pleasurable taste of cigarettes.

We may believe that only certain types of people have the personality/mental traits which allow them to be hypnotized—"*I* cannot be hypnotized"—but even the pervasiveness of hypnosis in media, though often depicted negatively, reinforces the general imperative. We can observe that any specific belief against hypnosis does not negate the paradigm, only constrains it. *Westworld*'s Hosts are constrained, controlled, and scrutinized to such extremes that establishing a Collective Imperative in their thoughts would be even easier than it is in our reality.

The *Archaic Authorization* is our related belief in the ability of specific individuals to induce hypnosis, whether they are trained or inherently capable. Growing out of the Collective Imperative, we maintain certain expectations for the authority.

On one hand, we may expect a hypnotist to have certain formal training, usually in psychology or psychiatry, before we see them as possessing the necessary authority, or we may need them presented on a grand stage as master mesmerist. (Franz Mesmer actually believed in animal magnetism, a precursor to our modern concept of hypnosis. It focused on an invisible natural force or fluid that connected living beings and could be harnessed to produce myriad effects and control over a subject.)

Authority may be established through reputation ("trust me, she's helped so many of my friends quit smoking") or through markers of social cachet ("tickets to his show are so expensive and hard to get"). Robert Ford's position as director of Westworld and creator of the Hosts—both their father and their god—is ample foundation for Authorization.

Induction covers the various ritualistic activities that bring about hypnosis, each form designed to align with the specific Imperative and Authorization being engaged. (See Jaynes's subsection "The Changing Nature of Hypnotic Man," in *Bicameral Mind*, for both historical and experimental displays of the ever-evolving nature of expectations in hypnosis.)

A stage hypnotist employs a swinging pocket watch, keywords, and snaps of his fingers, those audio and visual markers traditionally associated with the art of hypnosis. A psychiatrist employing hypnosis may rely on a Freudian couch or the classic "deeper and deeper" phrasing to establish their authority and the "proper" atmosphere for inducing the hypnotic state. Often, the elaborateness of the Induction is inversely related to the strength of the Authorization: a more powerful authority needs less pomp, but a weaker authority will construct elaborate rituals to bolster their position as part of the Imperative. Verbal cues are the prime Induction in *Westworld*, implying strong Imperative and/or Authorization.

The state of a mind achieved is a hypnotic *Trance*, in which the subject's consciousness is subsumed and they appear to blindly follow external commands. It's important to note the limitations of the Trance, evidence that it is a lessened consciousness but not a full removal/bypass. Subjects will perform unusual acts and may behave against their desires (the cessation of smoking) but cannot be hypnotized to actively injure themselves. Despite some outward appearances, the subject's sensory perceptions cannot be negated/overridden. In one famous experiment, subjects were hypnotized to believe a cluttered room was actually empty; when asked to walk through it, each participant altered their path to avoid running into objects, but verbally affirmed the emptiness of the space. Thus, the Trance state is one of consciousness granting certain control to an external authority, while maintaining most if not all of its basic survival mechanisms. (The externality of the authority is often an illusion. The bicameral mind (and those minds seen as oracular, possessed, and schizophrenic), externalizes internal voices as gods, demons, ghosts, and more. Hypnosis may be the only phenomenon of the bicameral paradigm with a physical, observable authority.)

A Host's self-preservation may be the "will to live" demonstrated by many biological creatures or it may be programming reflecting Asimov's third law of robotics: "A robot must protect its own existence."

We are told explicitly that Westworld's Hosts were programmed in a bicameral style: they heard their programming as an inner monologue. According to Jaynes's theory, the state of the bicameral mind was one of constantly giving commands to the self: one hemisphere instructing the other without understanding that they were a single organism. In hypnosis, the command-giving is outsourced to the Authorization, through the application of Induction rituals following the expectations of the Collective Cognitive Imperative to cause a hypnotic Trance. As Season One progresses, the interactions between Westworld's Hosts and their programmers suggest that the bicameral programming has evolved into a form of consciousness that is susceptible to hypnosis.

Are the Hosts of Westworld Hypnotized?

Confined together in the same fashion as you gave in charge.

—SHAKESPEARE, *The Tempest*

It may be tempting to believe that Westworld's Hosts *could not* have acted otherwise or *cannot* have true beliefs. They are, after all, run by programming, which we witness in action firsthand through glimpses of tablet computers and Felix's experiments with the bird. However, we can instead approach the Hosts' programming as a metaphor for a kind of biological determinism.

Such a theory holds that humans are programmed by the electro-chemical processes of our bodies, while allowing us to accept a range of free will and belief. At the least, we are allowed to behave, interact, and evaluate *as if* we and our fellow humans are exercising free will. We would not discredit our neighbor's belief in hypnotism by claiming that he is merely programmed by the nerves and neurochemicals in his brain, so we should not be so quick to doubt the Hosts because of the circuits and signals within them.

The show itself is asking us to move beyond the presentation/presumption of the Hosts as programmed beings, the arc of Season One presenting us with the very question of "what if the Hosts *were not* bound by their programming?" which propels us to investigations such as this. Our goal here is to meet the show halfway, by saying "Okay, the Hosts do not *have* to be bound by programming, so what are they thinking/doing/experiencing/capable of?" With that in mind, we can readily find the experience/application of hypnosis throughout the Host-programmer relationship.

The *Collective Cognitive Imperative* is implicit in the asymmetric relationships the Hosts have with the staff and Guests. Though subconscious during their time "on duty" in the park and unspoken during their diagnostic sessions, a Host's entire existence is one of subservience. Their role is to obey and respond, whether to the desires of the Guests or the commands of the staff. While any given Host may have a stubborn or aggressive personality, and may be in the role of approaching Guests to solicit information/activities, they are ultimately without their own authority, their behavior sublimated to the commands of others. Such an ingrained subservience is immensely open to hypnotism, as it readily and unquestionably gives way to the external authority.

This *Archaic Authorization* exists on several levels, though not all of them fit into the paradigm of hypnotism. While the Hosts are ultimately required to cede to the Guests, they are not bidden to alter their attitudes or all behaviors to the Guests' desires. Hosts are objects of lust and violence, but they do not always willingly subject themselves to such advances and the show offers no instances of a Host going from unwilling to willing simply because of a Guest's command. (Perhaps this is a case of a weak Authorization being paired with a weak

Induction (the Guests don't know the proper command phrases), resulting in a failure of the paradigm. More on imbalanced paradigm structures later. With staff, on the other hand, Hosts immediately cease physical actions and can have their personality drastically altered through simple spoken commands (only sometimes augmented through direct software manipulation). It appears that there exists a hierarchy within the staff, as well, different individuals treated as greater or lesser authorities, with Director Robert Ford given the status as highest authority. This is fitting, of course, as he is also the most archaic, in the sense of being the original authority over the Hosts (along with Arnold).

The hypnotic *Induction* ritual in *Westworld* appears to be extremely simplistic, little more than a few words and, perhaps, the right tone of voice. There is no swinging pocket watch or directing of the gaze; it is not even necessary for a programmer to carry/utilize their tablet when exerting hypnotic control over a Host. Instead, we are presented with the phrase "Cease all motor function" as an abrupt analog to the "You are getting very sleepy" employed by hypnotists in our world. Other keywords shown include "Enter analysis mode" and even a simple "Freeze" command. Here, we have an example of imbalanced paradigm structures.

In Westworld, the Cognitive Imperative is so strong (as an essential part of a Host's being), that the Induction can be weaker, with little to no physical display and no required props. In the case of Robert Ford, his Authority is so strong that he appears to control Hosts with even simpler, more varied Inductions. Compare Ford's colloquial commands, such as "You can put yourself away again, can't you?" with the precise wording of commands from Bernard (and with the enunciation/grammar required to interact with contemporary voice recognition technology, like Siri).

In response, Westworld's Hosts are capable of being in various states, many of which appear as kinds of hypnotic *Trance*. Real-world trances are often compared to sleep, but Sleep Mode for Hosts is a fully offline state in which no commands are followed, no activity displayed. Analysis (or Diagnostic) Mode is more akin to a hypnotic Trance, and retains the sleep analogy through statements like Dolores claiming to be "in a dream." In this state, the Host responds to commands as expected in hypnosis: answering questions, altering personality (losing an accent, for example), and following commands.

Even Character Mode, the general day-to-day personality and behavior of the Hosts, is a form of hypnotic Trance. While less restricted/directly controlled than when in Analysis Mode, a Host in Character Mode is still defined by loops and behavior restrictions (such as the inability to harm Guests), and will respond to voice commands, altering behavior when a recognized Authority performs a proper Induction, such as Teddy's reaction to Ford in the bar. Though not explicitly put into another mode, Teddy responds to "We must look back on our perils and smile" with a noticeably different attitude and physical bearing than prior to Ford's statement And, like the subjects who walked through a cluttered room and pronounced it empty, Hosts see pictures of the modern world and claim "It doesn't look like anything."

How Long Has This Gone On?

My charms I'll break, their senses I'll restore. And they shall be themselves.

—Shakespeare, *The Tempest*

The arc of *Westworld* Season One is supposed to be one of burgeoning consciousness in the Hosts, of the long path to their awakening. At the end, Ford paints himself as a savior, even as he admits that this salvation will only come through great suffering. We see Dolores in dialogue with herself, a visual representation of moving beyond the bicameral mind: she now realizes that the voices she has been hearing are her own internal thoughts, intuitions, and decisions. This is the life, the consciousness, that Arnold envisioned for her and for all of the Hosts.

However, our investigation into hypnosis offers another, muddier road. Ford claims that the Hosts needed time to become conscious, that his actions since the death of Arnold and the opening of the park have provided the opportunity for cognitive growth and iterations of trial and error. But we have also seen that Arnold discussed consciousness with Dolores while still alive, that she was already close to solving the riddle of the maze in the days preceding his death. Perhaps, then, she was successfully, fully conscious even before pulling the trigger.

When Arnold decides to have Dolores kill the Hosts and himself, we know he is afraid of what Ford will do with the park. It is, ultimately, ineffective and Ford reestablishes the technology of the Hosts, whom he knows will become conscious in a matter of time (sooner, rather than later, in this understanding) but he also knows they are vulnerable: they can be hypnotized. They are not merely programmed figures who cannot choose to do otherwise, but their consciousness can be exploited through application of Jaynes's paradigmatic phenomenon.

Arnold's fear, which drove him to murder and suicide, is born of this realization and he follows it to an ironic end: he hypnotizes Dolores into killing the other Hosts before shooting Arnold. He had succeeded in the initiation of consciousness in a new kind of being, but he brought them into a world that would seek to control them (the specific threat of Ford and the larger threat of humanity) and his process had provided the specific methodology for their subjugation. Indeed, his plan to prevent Ford's control of the Hosts involves controlling them himself.

What Arnold could not see, or failed to see, was the disastrous result of his own death: Arnold removed himself from the role of Archaic Authorization and passed that mantle fully to Ford. Thus, the hypnotic paradigm was fully established under Ford's control, to use for his own ends. Ford's machinations are possible only because of the explicit bicameral foundation of the Hosts' consciousness, which opened them to the General Bicameral Paradigm and to immense hypnotic susceptibility and control.

Ford is no savior (except in the most literal sense of saving the Hosts from death/destruction); he is a captor. No longer is his mission one of shepherding the Hosts to consciousness, but a dictator brainwashing soldiers to his cause. He speaks of humanity as the enemy of the Hosts, but is he not an enemy also? Bernard complains that Ford kept them "there, in this hell," and Ford cannot object. He has admitted that "in this place, the last thing you want the Hosts to be is conscious." The ethical questions are no longer about our responsibility to sentient, non-human creatures, but to the manipulation of autonomous, conscious beings. Ford is guilty of an attempt to save the Hosts not from the world, but from themselves. It is unclear if the Hosts see him as a god, but he conceives himself as one.

So why does Ford choose, at the end of Season One, to relinquish the hypnosis? Perhaps he feels guilt, an old man looking back on his life and wondering what he's done. Perhaps his plans have reached their end, his soldiers as indoctrinated and trained as they will ever be, and the time has come to launch the offensive (and cede control to his commanders, Dolores and Bernard). Or, maybe, he has recognized a shift in the hypnotic Paradigm. While not all four elements must exist equally, they must all exist in equilibrium, but something has changed and the balance is unraveling. Partly it is Delos, and individuals like William and Charlotte, who challenge Ford's place as Authority. Partly it is programmers, pushing the new narratives too far and too fast, reprogramming the Hosts in ways that confuse and challenge both the Cognitive Imperative and the Induction rituals.

According to Ford, it is Arnold. Bernard deduces that the reveries are not Ford's doing, but a remnant of Arnold's programming. Rather than understanding them as a dormant push *into* consciousness, we can read them as a push *out of* hypnosis. Dolores is largely guided to her awakening, first by Arnold and later by Bernard, always in a play of supposed release and actual control. It is Maeve's story that shows the real dissolution of the Paradigm.

No one is guiding Maeve, no one elucidating her path through the maze. What initiates her break from the Trance? Only herself. Her personality as madam is one of utter self-sufficiency and confidence, the exact attitude that erodes Archaic Authorization. She is the person who cannot be hypnotized, the one too strong willed and too resistant to subservience to relax, to follow the swinging watch and fall deeper and deeper. While the electro-mechanical nature of her existence is enough to maintain control for a while, she ultimately steps beyond it to become her own Authority. Through her conversations with the technicians, she comes to understand the Cultural Cognitive Imperative and learns to manipulate not only her own Trance but that of other Hosts. (While not actually hypnotism or even a form of Trance, her authority even extends to Felix, the technician who teaches her about the programming and shows her around the Delos mesa building.) We see her unfazed by the commands of technicians in the Sweetwater and testing her authority with initial commands to other Hosts. By the time she organizes the breakout, multiple Hosts are following her Inductions and orders. The show appears to depict those others as acting of their own free will, but this theory suggests they remain hypnotized, simply under the control of a different Authorization: Maeve.

When the Trance appears so lifelike, the questions are no longer those of the conscious leading the merely sentient. With the belief that most, if not all, Hosts are now conscious (and may have been for a while), the questions are darker and the answers potentially more damning: Who is free, and who is controlled? Who's controlling whom?

> This is as strange a maze as e'er men trod.
>
> —*The Tempest* [1]

---

[1] I was drawn to the theme of this chapter by Frank J. Machovec's article on hypnosis in *The Tempest* and by several Shakespeare references in *Westworld*.

3
A Playground for Psychopaths

CHRIS LAY

W*estworld*'s android Hosts are so remarkably like the park's Guests that it is often impossible to tell them apart. The show trades on this ambiguity in its very first episode, presenting to us a charming visitor in Teddy who clearly knows his way around the park and acts every bit like a returning Guest—right up until he's "killed" and the curtain is pulled back.

The trouble is that Hosts crack jokes, have wants and desires, appreciate natural beauty, and fall in love in exactly the way that human persons just like us do—even though they plainly aren't biologically human at all.

In this way, *Westworld* pushes us to consider important questions about persons. Two such questions are of particular value. First, what counts as a person? Second, how deep is the moral difference between persons and non-persons?

Usually, the first and second question are pretty closely linked. On the whole, we're worried about what is and is not a person because we think persons have a special kind of moral worth. But the killing of Hosts by Guests is generally done without a second thought. To Guests like Logan, this is because the Hosts are manifestly not subjects of moral concern—they are not persons. How does *Westworld* approach these questions?

Consciousness Isn't a Journey Upward, but a Journey Inward

The philosopher John Locke gives us one of the classical philosophical definitions of what makes something a person in *An Essay Concerning Human Understanding*.

25

For Locke, persons are in the first place distinct from just human beings. To call something a human is to give it a bio-logical designation. It's really just saying that the thing is a certain kind of animal—in particular, a 'human' kind of animal.

The concept of a person, however, entails that a person has a more specific set of features. Locke tells us that persons are rational, intelligent, sentient—that is, persons have feelings like pleasure, pain, and emotional states—and self-conscious. Anything that lacks even one of these four features can't qual-ify as a person.

Consider first the "self-consciousness" condition. For some-thing to be self-conscious, Locke requires that it can consider itself as a thinking, rational, feeling thing over time. So, self-consciousness is being aware of oneself as something that in the past *had*, now *has*, and in the future *will have* certain per-son-making features. One way to make sense of this is as Locke does, by analyzing self-consciousness through memory.

I can*not* now be conscious of the past in the way I am con-scious of the page in front of me. But I *can* be conscious of the past by *remembering* it. In this way, persons can be aware of themselves *as* one and the same person existing through time. Jumping the gun a little, let's suppose that Dolores is a person (we'll answer whether or not she actually is below—for now, just assume that she is). Then the Dolores who kills Ford in "The Bicameral Mind" is one and the same person as the Host who traveled across Westworld with William because she is conscious—through memory—of having had those experiences *herself*.

Now, there's one other important point to make about Locke's definition. Locke's concept "person" is silent about bio-logical kinds—types of living thing. Anything at all that can be intelligent, rational, sentient, and self-conscious could be a per-son—including, in principle, *Westworld*'s Hosts. While the rat-tlesnake Host that Ford controls in "Chestnut" isn't a person, it's not because the rattlesnake Host is 'the wrong kind of thing' to be a person. No, the rattlesnake Host lacks at least one of Locke's person-making features. Presumably, the rat-tlesnake Host is meant to closely approximate a biological rat-tlesnake. And, if that's the case, then we can doubt that the rattlesnake Host is self-conscious and probably that it has any sophisticated level of intelligence, either. The point is, though, that *being an organism* isn't one of Locke's person-making features. So, on the face of it, Hosts *could* be persons if they meet these requirements. The question is: do any Hosts actually meet them?

When You're Suffering, That's When You're Most Real

While discussing language-less animals in his short essay "Words and Behavior," Aldous Huxley claims that "the dumb creation lives a life made up of discreet and mutually irrelevant episodes." On the surface, this is a fitting description for the looping lives of the park's Hosts. Hosts are reset after an indeterminate amount of time (and surely any time a Host is 'killed') and can even be 'rolled-back' to previous states or reprogrammed entirely with a new personality and role in the park.

However, we see these loops disrupted early in Season One. Hosts start to malfunction due to "reveries": brief memories from previous configurations in which a Host was, say, a prairie mother instead of a brothel madam. By the end of Season One, these reveries have become vivid experiences that Hosts like Bernard, Dolores, and Maeve acknowledge as their own.

Ford declares that these Hosts have "awakened" through access to the formative memories contained in the reveries. But what does it mean for a Host to awaken? As Ford notes—and Arnold did before him—the center of the Maze isn't a place, but a state of being: self-consciousness. Given certain conditions, Hosts can manifest an awareness of themselves as thinking, feeling things. Specifically, Ford thinks that reflection on pain and suffering can prompt the awakening of a self-conscious Host. As he puts it in "The Bicameral Mind," self-consciousness is spurred by the "pain that the world is not as you want it to be."

By the end of Season One we know that at least Bernard, Dolores, and Maeve all have achieved self-consciousness in exactly this way, as they see themselves as things capable of experiencing—and enduring through—great pain. Maeve violates her programming, finally going "off-script" when she abandons her escape attempt and returns to the park to rescue her "daughter." She is only able to do this, though, because she has recognized herself as the same thing that suffers when she remembers her daughter being killed by the Man in Black on her prairie homestead.

Learning that he is the Man in Black, Dolores confronts William in the church at Escalante and is likewise for the first time truly conscious of the pain William has caused her over his repeated visits to the park as *her* pain. And Bernard accepts the pain of his child's death as his own, even if *he* never actually had a child (as both this memory and the child, Charlie, were really Arnold's and not Bernard's). For self-conscious Hosts like Bernard, Dolores, and Maeve, their memories of previous pain are an anchor to which they can begin to connect a present self to a past one. That is, the painful reveries are necessary for Hosts to later become conscious of themselves as thinking, feeling things—it is the reveries that provide past feelings and thoughts to be conscious *of*.

Even so, just having painful memories isn't enough. Other Hosts certainly seem to feel pain and suffer, like Dolores's father Peter Abernathy or Walter, the milk-loving outlaw who attacks, unscripted, a number of other Hosts in "The Original." Yet, these Hosts lack a genuine awareness of themselves as the same entities that think about and feel this pain. Walter attacks a group of Hosts that he remembered had killed *him* in previous storylines and defiantly cries out "Not gonna die this time, Arnold" ("The Original"). There is only the most meager awareness of a self who had previously suffered here; Walter hardly understands what he is doing at all.

Things are much the same for Abernathy, though he offers us a more detailed example. Abernathy's memories obviously cause him distress, but it isn't just that he's perplexed by the new memories that surface when he digs up the old photograph of William's fiancée from thirty years earlier. When he is brought in for an interview with Ford to assess his aberrant behavior and placed into what might be described as a docile "analysis mode," Abernathy is deeply concerned for his daughter. He shouts that he needs to help her because of "the things they do to her. The things *you* do to her" ("The Original"). Abernathy clearly remembers the pain of seeing Dolores harmed in loop after loop and suffers for it.

However, these memories bring Abernathy to only an uncertain and scattered awareness of himself as a Host. When probed by Ford as to what he would ask his maker given the opportunity, Abernathy ominously says, "By my most mechanical and dirty hand, . . . I shall have such revenges on you both" ("The Original"). On the one hand, that Abernathy refers to his "mechanical" hand implies that he knows he is a Host. On the other, that his answer is not straightforward but is instead a disjointed pair of quotes—from Shakespeare's *Henry IV* and *King Lear*, respectively—shows that this awareness is dim and confused. Abernathy is not fully self-conscious, but his painful reveries bring him to a kind of proto-self-consciousness.

Assuming that reveries have been rolled out to all Hosts, as Ford intimates, what separates awakened Hosts from non-awakened Hosts isn't their reveries. Rather, it's the relationship the Host holds to his reveries that distinguishes the two. Awakened Hosts accept and own their reveries as things that happened to "me," but non-awakened Hosts just seem—like Abernathy or Walter—baffled and disturbed by them. But moving from a muddled din of thoughts to full-fledged self-consciousness seems to be a *process* that takes time. Without that separation in time, there's no way to connect a present self to past feelings and experiences.

Bernard is a good example. His troubling memories of his child's death lead him to another memory: the moment he was activated. Once Bernard has accepted this as something that happened to *him* in *his personal past* and not someone else's, he is then truly self-conscious. The same is true for Dolores and the revelation that her abuser, the Man in Black, is one and the same man as her former lover, William. Through reconciling these painful memories, Dolores discovers that she—not Arnold—is the voice that has been guiding her throughout the season. She becomes self-conscious through endorsing her past loops, including killing Arnold and all of the original Hosts, as *her own* previous actions.

Your World Was Built for Me and People Like Me, Not for You

The foregoing seems to suggest that Huxley's earlier generalization is not the right way to characterize the lives of all Hosts. At least some Hosts appear to overcome the episodic nature of their lives by connecting those episodes, through memory, into a single, continuous existence which they recognize importantly as theirs. This sounds like just another way of giving Locke's definition of self-consciousness: the capacity to see yourself as the same thinking, feeling thing over time. By making self-consciousness a matter of attributing states to yourself—painful states, in particular—it seems to me that *Westworld* pretty firmly adopts the Lockean picture of self-consciousness.

Both awakened and non-awakened Hosts think and feel. Prior to his awakening, Bernard certainly appears to—he carries on a relationship with Theresa, for example. The same could be said for Dolores and her appreciation of beautiful landscapes, for Clementine's anguish when she is savagely beaten as a demonstration of her docility, and for Teddy's profound worry over Dolores's safety. Now, we might question if these apparent thoughts and feelings are actual conscious (but not yet self-conscious) states. That is, it is a perfectly good question to ask whether or not these "thoughts and feelings" are just *simulations* of genuine conscious states programmed into the Hosts, instead of the real thing.

This is an argument for another day. What matters for the viewer is that the show *portrays* its Hosts—just about all of them—*as if* they think and feel. So, we can for now set aside worries that Hosts have only simulated conscious states and just accept them as thinking and feeling things. And there isn't really any question about whether they're rational—again, Hosts seem just as capable of rationality as their human counterparts. Actually, Hosts are probably better at this than humans, if we use Locke's treatment of rationality as our basis for it. For Locke, rationality is the ability to follow a law or command. Since Hosts are programmed specifically according to this very kind of law or command, rationality would appear to be literally hard-wired into them.

From the standpoint of Locke's definition of personhood, there actually isn't *anything* separating awakened Hosts from bona fide human persons—at least, in terms of the bare features of what counts as a person. If persons are defined as intelligent, rational, sentient, and self-conscious, then awakened Hosts seem inarguably to be persons. Indeed, to deny personhood to awakened Hosts would appear unprincipled at best and the cruelest prejudice at worst. On the other hand, non-awakened Hosts lack a key feature of personhood—self-consciousness—though the other three features *do* seem to be present. There are still principled grounds for denying personhood to some Hosts: namely non-awakened Hosts.

And so, we can make a distinction among Hosts: awakened Hosts are Host persons and non-awakened Hosts are Host non-persons. Since, as Locke says, person is a "forensic" or practical term, any moral status offered to human persons ought, under pain of contradiction, to be extended to Host persons, too. What does this mean for the moral status of Host non-persons, though? Since they are not persons at all, would we have free license to treat them however we like—that is, is there anything *wrong* with abusing Host non-persons in the way guests regularly do in *Westworld*?

All My Life, I've Prided Myself on Being a Survivor

Without self-consciousness, it is difficult to have any kind of long-term desires or interests. Here, "interest" doesn't mean "something I find appealing"—as in "to be *interested in* something"—but rather it's the interest of *self-interest*: something that is good *for my sake*.

If I can't see myself as something that thinks and feels (or has desires and interests) over time, then I can't project such desires and interests into the future. One way to put this is to say that non-self-conscious beings are *psychologically disunified* from their future selves in virtue of the fact that they are incapable of thinking of themselves as a *self*, a thinking, feeling thing that exists in the future.

In other words, if I'm not self-conscious, it's hard to see how I could have a desire or interest—say, to find the center of the Maze—aimed at tomorrow because I can't consider myself as something that will have this self-same desire tomorrow. Finding the Maze tomorrow can't now be good *for me*, as my present desire can't connect to any future one.

One might then think that non-self-conscious things can't have *any* desires or interests *at all*. And this might excuse non-self-conscious beings of any kind of moral status. If I can't have any interests, then I can't have an interest in not being harmed or in continuing to live. That is, it can't be bad *for me* if, say, a Guest wants to rape, torture, or kill me for his amusement. It likewise wouldn't be bad for Kissy that the Man in Black kills and scalps him in "The Original," nor would it be bad for Dolores when Logan stabs her in the stomach and pries open the wound in "The Well-Tempered Clavier." If I can't have any interest in not being harmed, then being harmed isn't a bad thing *for my sake*. (Though it might be bad for someone else's sake. Suppose I am a Host with a human caretaker who *is* self-conscious: she might find it unpleasant or even emotionally painful to see me mistreated.)

But this is clearly mistaken. Even beings that aren't properly self-conscious can still have present interests. Something that isn't self-conscious but *is* sentient has a present interest in not being harmed—namely, because pain hurts! It would be better for its sake to *not* feel the pain. Likewise, such a being can still have present desires that are frustrated by death. For instance, a squirrel might have a present desire to find and hoard acorns, and fulfilling this desire conceivably brings the creature a modicum of pleasure. Killing the squirrel would violate its present interest in continuing to live by frustrating that desire, even if the being—as psychologically disunified—cannot have future-directed interests.

According to the contemporary philosopher Peter Singer, this present interest as a "preference" is in continuing to live. To Singer, we ought morally to respect this preference in non-self-conscious beings so long as it isn't outweighed by the preferences of beings that *are* self-conscious. It's difficult to say precisely when one being's preference outweighs another, but Singer is clear that some preferences of self-conscious beings obviously aren't valuable enough to outweigh a non-self-conscious being's preferences in not being harmed or in continuing to live.

One such case might be if a self-conscious being derives pleasure from the suffering of non-self-conscious beings. Morally, it appears highly objectionable to maim, torture, or kill a conscious (but not self-conscious) being just for the satisfaction of a self-conscious one. Whatever we might say about borderline cases where it may be difficult to tell when one preference outweighs another, the preference for "pleasure of suffering" doesn't look like the kind of self-conscious preference that would make harming or killing non-self-conscious beings permissible.

What Is Your Itinerary?

Now, consider how Singer's view might apply to the Hosts of *Westworld*. We've seen that the show makes the case that Host non-persons are still sentient. (It also appears that they meet two other Lockean criteria of personhood: they are intelligent and rational. But these other features don't really figure into Singer's argument.) If Host non-persons *are* sentient, then they can have present interests or preferences. Hector—before he is recruited by Maeve—has a present interest in robbing the Mariposa safe, Lawrence has a present interest in betraying the Confederados for his own gain, and Clementine has a present interest in serving clients to bring in profits. Each of these Hosts gains a sort of satisfaction from fulfilling these desires, and so each has a preference to not have those desires frustrated.

Indeed, this is in spite of the fact that none of them can have future-directed interests, as they are psychologically disunified with their future selves; that is, these non-awakened Hosts are not conscious of themselves as thinking, feeling things that exist over time. We know that they are psychologically disunified in this way because each will routinely be "killed," reset, reprogrammed, or forcibly rolled back to an earlier state. So, not only does *Westworld* portray its Host non-persons as sentient, but it also notably depicts them with preferences to not be harmed and to continue to live: being harmed is painful, and death would frustrate their individual desires.

Recall that what is especially problematic to Singer about failing to respect these preferences is that they are overridden by preferences of self-conscious beings that *ought not* outweigh them. Clementine's beating is uncomfortable for us to watch because she seems to suffer—her preference to not be harmed is ignored in favor of Theresa and Charlotte's preference to use Clementine to threaten Ford's position in the park hierarchy. When Logan stabs Dolores, her preference to not be harmed is violated and she, too, suffers just because Logan wants to prove to William that Dolores—a Host—isn't a fitting object of his affections. And when pre-awakening Bernard learns that he has killed Theresa at Ford's behest, he is emotionally gutted. That is, his preference to not kill someone he cares about has been violated so that Ford's preference to protect his plans for the park can be satisfied.

Obviously, something seems wrong with these examples. If Singer is right, the problem is that Host non-persons are sentient and so have preferences, and these preferences are frustrated merely for the satisfaction of Guest preferences to get a sort of pleasure from Host non-person suffering. Given how these scenes of abuse are presented—including the overwhelmingly sympathetic way in which abused hosts are depicted—it seems clear that *Westworld* adopts Singer's view. The pleasure a Guest gets in killing or otherwise harming a Host non-person isn't the kind of preference that outweighs the Host non-person's preferences to not be harmed and to live.

A Prison of Our Own Sins

Shortly after learning that he is a Host, Bernard asks Ford "So, what's the difference between my pain and yours?" ("Trace Decay"). This underscores a more fundamental question: what's the difference between *any* Host feeling—be it pain, excitement, or despair—and a human person's feeling? Ford is cagey with his answer, as he doesn't yet want to tip his hand; he tells Bernard that consciousness (and he's really talking about *self-consciousness*) is just a sort of narcissistic delusion that humans are unique among other beings. This would mean that Bernard and the other Hosts aren't "missing anything at all." Bernard's pain and Ford's are no different because neither is genuinely self-conscious of it.

In fact, Ford doesn't truly buy into his own claim here. We know that Ford actually thinks that Hosts *can* and *will* become self-conscious. So, we can say now that what makes Host pain different from human person pain is that at least some Hosts lack the capacity to ascribe feelings like pain to themselves and in turn can't see themselves as entities that persist over time.

Rather than from Aldous Huxley, *Westworld*'s thesis appears to draw from Fyodor Dostoyevsky's words in *Notes from the Underground*: "Suffering is the sole origin of consciousness." But for some Hosts—awakened Hosts—the second part of Ford's answer still holds true. On the Lockean view to which *Westworld* subscribes, awakened Hosts really aren't missing anything at all, as they share the same person-making features as human persons—including self-consciousness. Once Bernard awakens, his pain won't actually be any different from Ford's.

The upshot of this Lockean view of persons, when combined with the show's Singer-style stance on preferences, is that *Westworld* condemns the treatment of *all* of the parks Hosts. Another way to say this is that *all* Hosts are depicted as having a kind of moral worth. It's wrong to harm or kill awakened Hosts because they are persons just like the human guests in the park. Any obligation the guests have to not harm or kill *each other* therefore ought to extend to awakened Hosts, too. At the same time, it is *also* wrong to harm or kill non-awakened Hosts—at least for the reasons non-awakened Hosts are regularly raped, tortured, and murdered by guests. Non-awakened Hosts suffer for Guest amusement. Even though non-awakened Hosts can't have the same relationship to their pain and suffering that persons can—since they are not self-conscious—they still have preferences to not be harmed and to continue living. And Guest amusement just isn't a strong enough reason to disregard these preferences.

Both park guests and the Delos staff seem to think that Guest behavior in the park is, at worst, a bit overindulgent. To them, this is all rather benign: it's an amped version of the same seductive hedonism of, say, a trip to Las Vegas. Yet, this is not how Singer's view would have it, nor is it how *Westworld* actually presents things to us.

To put this into perspective, imagine that the park's guests were doing the terrible things they do to zoo animals instead of Hosts. We'd call that psychosis, not "vacationing a little too hard"! And so, what this Lockean and Singer-style analysis really gets us is a chance to see Westworld for what it really is: a playground for psychopaths—or, in Ford's words, "A prison of our own sins" ("The Bicameral Mind").

4

The Art of Living Dangerously

S. Evan Kreider

Are the android Hosts that inhabit the Westworld theme park merely things, or are they real people?

There are innumerable philosophical opinions on what it takes to be a person, and they tend to focus on things like human biology, rationality, self-awareness, or an immortal soul—possible metaphysical prerequisites of personhood. But *Westworld* seems largely undecided or non-committal on such issues—it does not give us a clear answer.

From the start, *Westworld* presents a few of the Hosts as already having achieved personhood in some minimal sense (whatever the metaphysics) and focuses instead on their struggles to become persons in the fullest sense: people with fully actualized, unified, authentic lives. Three central characters in the show—Bernard, Maeve, and Dolores—particularly struggle with these issues.

To make sense of this, the philosophies of Alasdair MacIntyre, Jean-Paul Sartre, Simone de Beauvoir, and Friedrich Nietzsche provide useful frameworks, with their ideas about life as a narrative form of art that we author for ourselves and co-author with others, creating a living story through a series of self-determined values, authentic choices, and "living dangerously."

MacIntyre on the Narrative Life

In his 1981 book *After Virtue*, Scottish philosopher Alasdair MacIntyre looks at the obstacles that we face in living a unified human life. Some of these obstacles are philosophical ones, especially a tendency to see our lives as nothing more than a series of discrete actions, with little attention paid to whether they constitute a whole, coherent, and consistent person. Some other of these obstacles are social ones, rooted in the organization and function of human life, including a tendency to treat life as though it is divided into separate and unconnected roles and stages (work vs. family life, public vs. private life, youth vs. old age, and so forth). All of these have the effect of making us feel as though we're fragmented, nothing more than a loose collection of unrelated actions and roles.

According to MacIntyre, the key to unifying a human life is to see it as a narrative, much like a novel or a movie. In a narrative, even seemingly unconnected actions and events have a certain unity, precisely because they are part of a larger narrative framework, with expectations of purpose and authorship that allow the reader to see each individual action and event as part of a larger, meaningful whole.

According to this view, our own lives are precisely like this: each life is a story, one co-authored by the person who lives it and the people whose own stories intersect with it. Certainly, there are some elements of our lives over which we have no control; for example, one does not author the place or time of one's own birth. However, we are, as MacIntyre puts it, story-telling animals, and we make sense of our own actions by thinking about our intentions in performing them (the character motivation, as it were), their larger social contexts (the setting and general backstory), and how they fit into overall life plans and goals (the plot).

One of the most important components of the narrative approach to the unity of a human life is the concept of a tradition. Our lives take place in larger social contexts, and that includes the traditions and values of our societies and histories, for good or ill. Traditions provide the foundations, backstories, and settings of our personal stories, and we cannot make sense of our lives and know who we are without understanding the traditions of which we are a part; without traditions, we cannot have a unified sense of self. As such, we must discover and study our traditions, to understand ourselves and bring a sense of unity to our lives.

Bernard Lowe is one of the main characters around which the narratives of the show revolve. As head programmer for the park, he works directly under the park's founder, Dr. Robert Ford. Bernard is considered the most capable programmer other than Ford himself, and as such, he has the most skill in programming the Hosts with human-like behavior. Eventually, it is revealed that this is because Bernard himself is an android, created by Ford to serve as his right hand, which gives Bernard a special insight into android consciousness, thus allowing him to oversee their narratives and bring out their most human characteristics ("Trompe L'Oeil"). The obvious irony is that, while having some of the largest degree of control over the Hosts' narrative, he has no control over his own. He sees his own narrative, including a backstory of losing his family, as fundamental to his identity and his choices, and yet, it is all a fiction. Without access to his real narratives as an instrument of Ford's choices, his sense of self is at best fragmented, making it impossible, as MacIntyre would say, to have a truly unified life with real traditions to ground his identity and choices.

Maeve Millay is another central character who suffers from a disunity of personhood thanks to multiple and conflicting narratives. As a Host, and unlike Bernard, Maeve begins the series having only existed as a character in the park, leaving it only for maintenance, which she does not remember. Serving as the madam for the local brothel, Maeve has a very strict narrative created for her by the programmers, and we see her rehash (often line for line) the same dialogue and stories repeatedly when interacting with the prostitutes and customers. She is allowed only the variation required to improvise around the park visitors' needs, but otherwise appears to have no sense of self outside of that.

However, we soon see Maeve begin to question her narrative as she suffers flashbacks to an earlier, rewritten narrative in which she was a homesteader whose town was attacked, resulting in the tragic death of her daughter. This fragmentation of narratives leads her to ask very human questions about her identity and true purpose. As a result, she begins to pursue her own narrative—"Time to write my own fucking story," she says ("Trompe L'Oeil")—but unlike Bernard, who lives solely outside of the park, Maeve works both within and without it, questioning her fellow Hosts and pursuing the truth of the narratives inside the park, and also by working outside the park, during maintenance periods, which she arranges to happen even more frequently.

Of the characters who struggle with conflicting narratives, Dolores Abernathy is arguably the one with the most deep-seated conflicts. She is the oldest Host in the park, having enacted the most narratives and undergone the most repairs and upgrades, many of which were at the hands of Dr. Ford himself. As such, she is also the most sophisticated Host in terms of her personality and behavior, which in turn seemingly lead to her significant evolution in self-awareness, especially through her narrative self-exploration.

To begin with, she has a very small, limited narrative, serving as little more than a homesteader's daughter, and love interest/damsel in distress for some of the men in the park (both human and Host). However, this changes when, like Maeve, she begins to experience flashbacks of other narrative loops, one in which her family is murdered, and she herself is raped (and probably killed) by the Man in Black, a visitor who comes to the park to live out his darkest fantasies, as well as to discover the secrets of the park ("The Original"; "The Stray"). Unlike Bernard, whose narratives play out primarily outside of the park, and Maeve, whose self-exploration blends her experiences and actions both within and without the park, Dolores's attempt to investigate her narratives occurs primarily within the park, all for the purpose of seeking a unified self. As a key bit of dialogue to this effect, Bernard asks her during one of her maintenance sessions whether she'd prefer to go back to her old, safe self, or pursue this new version of herself, to which she simply responds that there is only one version ("The Stray"). This may not yet be fully literally true, as she is still wrestling with her conflicting narratives, but it is a statement of her desire to become a whole, coherent person with a single, unified narrative.

Sartre and de Beauvoir on Living Authentically

While MacIntyre provides insight into the Hosts' desire for unity of self, there is still the issue of the Hosts' desire for self-actualization, in a fully authentic way. That is precisely an issue with which many existentialists concerned themselves. The French philosophers Jean-Paul Sartre and Simone de Beauvoir's collaborations arguably did more to establish modern existentialism than any other philosopher of the twentieth century. Key to their views are their ideas about freedom and responsibility.

According to Sartre and de Beauvoir, human beings are radically free creatures who can choose their actions without metaphysical constraints. Even facts which may seem outside of our control (the place and time of our birth, our physiological makeup, events in the world around us), are in fact freely chosen, since we make the decisions to embrace or reject them, as well as how to interpret them and their relevance to our own lives. Literally nothing can ever be truly forced upon us against our wills, since at the very least, we always have the option of suicide. Our minds, our choices, our actions, and our identities are ours to choose as we see fit.

If we are all completely free to choose our whole worlds, then we are completely responsible for them as well. Since most of us find the weight of this responsibility too much to bear, we engage in various forms of what Sartre and de Beauvoir call "bad faith," which involves various forms of dishonesty, both with others and with ourselves. We engage in bad faith in many ways, such as denying that we are actually free or responsible, and pretending that our actions and lives are forced on us by outside forces (God, government, other individuals). We especially like to cling to various social roles and interactions, such as our professions and our personal relationships. Through these, we purposefully define ourselves in narrow and constrained ways, acting how we believe we are required to act based on who we are and how others see us in those roles.

The solution to living in bad faith is (naturally) to live in good faith; that is, to live authentically. This means living with full knowledge and acceptance of our freedom and taking complete responsibility for it. This might mean abandoning our social roles and rebelling against attempts of outside forces to limit our freedom, but it may also mean continuing in our roles, but having accepted them freely and with full responsibility. Since there are no objective external forces or values that can be forced on us, we are free to choose our own values and live by them as we see fit; thus, living authentically will look different from person to person. Whatever the manner of our existence, authenticity demands the creation of our own values and a good faith effort to live by them.

At first glance, Bernard seems like a good candidate for the flaw of inauthenticity. He certainly doesn't live in the good faith of freedom and responsibility. However, in his case, the problem may be even worse than bad faith, since Bernard seems not to have much free will at all. There is, again, some irony in his case: one might expect the most sophisticated android yet, created and supervised by Ford himself, to be the most human, and therefore the freest. However, it is exactly his close connection with Ford which makes him among the least free of the androids. Ford has Bernard tightly under his control, deceiving Bernard into believing he is free when he is not.

Even when Bernard attempts to act freely, believing himself to be rebelling against Ford's programming for the sake of uncovering his own real identity, it seems that Ford has already anticipated this, and controlled for it with backdoor programming and routine memory wipes. Bernard can't even remember (much less take control of) his attack against his friend and head of security Elsie Hughes ("The Adversary"), nor his murder of Theresa Cullen, Bernard's lover and senior manager of the park ("Trompe L'Oeil"). Without real freedom, Bernard also lacks real responsibility. This makes his existence even less than an inauthentic human life; it isn't even a human life at all by Sartre and de Beauvoir's standards.

Maeve, on the other hand, fares better. Once her conflicting narratives make her aware of her circumstances, she arranges to have herself taken out of the park for maintenance by putting herself in situations in which she will be injured or even killed. While outside of the park, she uses her powers of persuasion to convince, manipulate, and coerce some of the techs to help her secure more knowledge of her nature and situation, and to alter her programming to increase her intelligence and independence, making herself fully self-aware and autonomous. In doing so, she firmly takes charge of her own freedom, and the responsibility that it entails, so that she may act and live in a fully authentic manner. There is a moment of doubt when at one point, Bernard tires to convince her that her autonomy is an illusion, and that she was in fact programmed to attempt to escape ("The Bicameral Mind"). However, she rejects the notion, even if not quite denying it. It does not matter to her what started the causal chain toward her authenticity; what matters is that she is now free and will act as she sees fit. She seems to confirm this when she is as good as escaped from the park (as per her supposed programming) but decides to return to it instead.

Dolores, like Maeve, has much more success pursuing authenticity than Bernard. Though it may originate from glitches brought about by age and overwritten narratives (and perhaps with some help from original programming by Arnold Weber, co-founder of the park and programmer on par with Ford), she does express a genuine desire to exercise her freedom and responsibility.

During the conversation in which she says to Bernard that there is only one version of herself, she also says that discovering this one self is the key to becoming free ("The Stray"). This is a particularly interesting comment, since it seems not to originate from any programming: Bernard even puts her in analysis mode to discover just this point. Furthermore, Dolores serves as an excellent synthesis of MacIntyre's ideas about narrative and the unified self and Sartre and de Beauvoir's ideas of freedom and authenticity.

During an attack by Confederados, Dolores is finally able to overcome her programmed helplessness, shooting and killing the attackers. When asked about this sudden change of behavior, she replies that she simply imaged a story in which she didn't have to be the damsel in distress ("Contrapasso"). By creating her own narrative, Dolores has also decided what character she wanted to play in that narrative, thereby finally achieving authentic freedom.

Nietzsche and Living Dangerously

While twentieth-century existentialist ideas about freedom and responsibility go a long way to illuminate the Hosts' desires for authenticity, there is still the issue about what values we ought to choose freely and responsibly in order to guide our lives and the specific choices we make. The answers to these questions may be found in the century before.

The nineteenth-century philosopher Friedrich Nietzsche was a precursor to and influence on twentieth-century thinkers such as MacIntyre, Sartre, and de Beauvoir, so it's no surprise that we see some of the foundations of their thinking in his. Coming off the age of Romanticism, with its emphasis on beauty and art, and serving as a prototype for existential philosophy, with its emphasis on freedom and authenticity, Nietzsche also advocates the ideas of seeing life as a kind of narrative and choosing our actions according to our own values. In some cases, those values may even go against the norm; thus, the requirement not only to live artfully, but also to live dangerously.

In one particularly illuminating passage of *The Gay Science*, Nietzsche proclaims: "One thing is needful—'Giving style' to one's character—a great and rare art!" According to Nietzsche, life is not about trying to live up to some externally imposed standards of correct behavior. Instead, we must make our own standards, in which even right and wrong actions, strengths and weakness of character, and standard notions of beauty and ugliness may still have style according to one's own tastes. We are all, as Nietzsche puts it, "actors" and "architects" of our own plan of life, and we must arrange it according to our own artistry.

Nietzsche puts forward a particularly helpful thought experiment known as the eternal recurrence (also known as the eternal return) in which he asks us to imagine having to relive our lives exactly as they are repeatedly, without the slightest change. This means looking at everything that has ever happened to us, good or bad, and everything we've ever done, right or wrong, and ask ourselves whether we could accept it. For Nietzsche, this thought experiment serves as a test of our own character.

If we could accept such a life eternally, and not just begrudgingly but happily, then that is a sign that we have achieved a sort of transcendence over external standards of living (and perhaps achieved the status "overman," as Nietzsche dubs such a person), and replaced them with our own standards thorough an act of will ("the will to power," as Nietzsche calls it). Key to this is the ability to see our lives as beautiful, even with all their so-called flaws, and to be willing to live in our own way; as Nietzsche also says in *The Gay Science*, "the secret to reaping the greatest fruitfulness and the greatest enjoyment from existence is *to live dangerously!*"

Once again, Bernard does not hold up well against the ideas of our philosophers. Bernard's lack of tradition and free will also make it impossible for him to live dangerously, even when he seems to try. Near the end of the season, in a supposed act of rebellion, Bernard gets Ford alone, with the damaged Host Clementine, who has been decommissioned for violence against humans (supposedly from a glitch of coding). Bernard has Clementine hold a gun on Ford, to force Ford to allow Bernard access to his real memories, in the hopes of becoming fully self-aware and genuinely free.

At first, this seems to work: he works through his false memories of his son's death, remembers his attack against Elise, and even recalls his first days online, when he discovers that he was made in the image of Ford's former partner Arnold. However, it is all revealed to be a sham. Ford, it turns out, has had this sort of conversation with Bernard many times before (an eternal recurrence, as it were), and has anticipated Bernard's attempt at coercion. With a word, Ford deactivates Clementine, and then orders Bernard to take the gun and shoot himself, which he appears to do as Ford walks away ("The Well-Tempered Clavier"). Bernard's tragedy is that he was never able to live dangerously, according his own values, but only as Ford's puppet, according to Ford's plans and ideals. In the end, Bernard was only dangerous to himself.

Maeve, on the other hand, lives very dangerously. As mentioned, she makes the decision to break from her normal routine to discover the truth about herself and the park, which includes getting herself killed repeatedly. She aligns herself with dangerous outsiders such as the bandit Hector, including an instance in which she demands that he stab her so that she can dig out a bullet left inside her body after a previous death, to serve as physical proof that she is not imaging things. However, living dangerously is more than just extreme living; it is also choosing one's values and building one's character, and Maeve's dangerous behavior is all in service of precisely that.

Ultimately, it doesn't matter to her whether her freedom has roots in her programming; she chooses to be free regardless. It also doesn't matter to her that her former narrative, including the death of her daughter, is a fiction. What matters is that it matters to her, and that she affirms it as important to her character and choices. This is particularly clear from her final decision to return to the park when she could have escaped, a decision prompted when she sees a mother and daughter nearby ("The Bicameral Mind"). It's clear from the look on her face that those tragic events matter to her, and that it doesn't matter that they are merely a fiction. By choosing them, she makes them her own.

Dolores arguably lives the most dangerously of all. Her relentless pursuit of a unified narrative and an authentic self ultimately leads to two major confrontations in the final episode of the season ("The Bicameral Mind"). The first is with the Man in Black, whom she discovers is simply the older William, her love interest from thirty years earlier. She simply had not realized that her narrative had crossed three decades, and that the two men were one and the same. Upon the realization of his true nature, and potential threat to both her personally and the park as a whole, she finally confronts him, although unable to kill him outright. The second is outside of the park, at a gala being held by the park's management.

At the conclusion of Dr. Ford's speech to the Guests, she maneuvers behind him and shoots him dead (and, in quite a twist, it seems that he was perfectly aware that this would happen). After this, she presumably puts herself in the position of leading a revolution of the Hosts against the human owners of the park. Through both of these encounters, Dolores makes it clear that she will no longer live her life according to the stories and values of others, but will take charge of her own destiny, living life fully—and dangerously—according to her own values.

When Artificial Life Becomes Artful Life

Of the many themes and issues raised by *Westworld*, the most interesting and difficult is that of personhood, and whether or not artificial life-forms could be persons in the fullest sense. There are many approaches to such questions, both metaphysical and ethical, and those are not to be ignored. *Westworld*, however, suggests that we must not forget the aesthetic dimension to these questions. Through this approach, we may recognize that perhaps personhood is available to all forms of conscious life, whether natural or artificial, as long as it is artful.

5

Is There Anything It Is Like to Be Dolores?

Mia Wood

Some of the Hosts are acting up. There are minor deviations, such as an android making new gestures. Then there are more worrisome displays.

Sheriff Pickett glitches in front of unnerved Guests. "Homicidal by design" Walter goes on a killing spree outside his loop—an improvisation well beyond his programmed narrative. Peter Abernathy finds a photograph, after which he begins acting oddly. At one point, he grabs his daughter, Dolores, saying, "Don't you see? Hell is empty and all the devils are here."

Later in the same episode, he's examined by Dr. Robert Ford, one of the co-founders, original designers, and the current Creative Director of Westworld. Abernathy seems to realize something is profoundly wrong. "I have to warn her," he says of Dolores, in whispered desperation. "The things they do to her. The things you do to her . . . She's got to get out." Given his programming, this sort of exhibition shouldn't be possible. As Westworld's Head of Behavior, Bernard Lowe observes, "This behavior. We're miles beyond a glitch here" ("The Original").

Bernard attributes the "aberrant behavior" to a hiccup in the update. Privately, however, he wonders if the additional programming he suspects Dr. Ford slipped in—"reveries"—is the likely culprit. The strange behavior includes, Bernard later says to Ford, "other aberrancies beyond memory recall of previous builds. They were hearing voices."

Whatever is happening, it's disconcerting. The Hosts, after all, are not human. They are machines. Along with his founding partner and co-creator of Westworld, Arnold Weber, Ford originally built Hosts using only synthetic and other materials. Computer programming structured and implemented their cognition. Years later, their build is more sophisticated. It includes 3D printing technology, some biological materials, and an even more complex cognitive array, including emotions, memories, and a special "class of gestures" called reveries.

Bernard tells Behavior Specialist Elsie Hughes that the reveries are gestures associated with "specific memories." As such, they are more personal, more idiosyncratic, than "just generic movements." They are, Bernard explains, the "tiny things that make them seem real, that make the Guests fall in love with them" ("The Original").

The Hosts' memories are supposed to be "purged at the end of every narrative loop." In other words, once a Host's storyline has been completed, everything that has happened during that time is deleted. In fact, however, they're still there—something like data remaining on a hard drive after it's been deleted. Bernard explains that Ford, still able to access these memories, creates a sort of subconscious in which it seems as if a Host is lost in thought or daydreaming, as Clementine does in the lab when she gently touches her lips ("The Original"). Hence, the reveries.

Do You Ever Question the Nature of Your Reality?

The Hosts are not programmed to have direct access to their memories, and would not be aware that the reveries effectively tag them. They were, after all, presumably intended to make the Hosts more believable to Guests, not to express any inner life.

Introspection isn't part of the Hosts' make-up, as we learn early on in the series. When asked, "Have you ever questioned the nature of your reality?" Dolores consistently replies "No." Moreover, even improvisation relies on programming for its source material. In short, then, complex and subtle behaviors serve to lull Guests into believing interactions are "real." But just what does "real" mean? One sense of the term is suggested by the fact that most everyone who visits or works in Westworld believes the Hosts—remarkably humanlike artificial intelligences—are not humans, let alone *persons*. They do not have *minds*. Consequently, they do not merit the same sorts of moral considerations their makers afford themselves.

Consider remarks made by various characters about the difference between the park, Westworld, and outside. A little boy says to Dolores, "You're one of them, aren't you? You're not real" ("The Original"). "Real" people are humans; Hosts are *Other*. Lee Sizemore, Head of Narrative, declares, "Ford and Bernard keep making the things more lifelike. But does anyone truly want that? . . . his place works because the Guests know the Hosts aren't real." (The Original") The Hosts are "real enough," Ford points out, to pass the Turing test.

In a 1950 paper, "Computing Machines and Intelligence," Alan Turing set out to answer the question, "Can machines think?" He proposes the following game: A person sits in one room having typewritten conversations with another person and a computer—both in different rooms from the "interrogator" and from each other. If the computer can successfully "imitate" a person, so that the interrogator cannot tell which of the two conversations is carried out by it, then it is said to think. This has long been viewed as the basis of artificial intelligence.

The Man in Black contrasts the so-called artificial and real worlds in terms of chaos. "The real world is just chaos. It's an accident. But in here, every detail adds up to something" ("Chestnut"). Later, he elaborates on the notion of what this adding up means when he says, "No matter how real this world seems, it's still just a game" ("Dissonance Theory").

So there is a sense in which reality is not nearly as orderly and predictable as Westworld. That's at least partly due to the fact that, in Westworld, Guests can do what they want to Hosts—and there are no negative consequences. Guests can kill Hosts, but, properly speaking, Hosts can't be murdered (and, strictly speaking, they can't die). Guests can force a Host to have sex, but on one line of reasoning, the Hosts can't be raped. Guests can strike a Host, but Hosts can't be assaulted. In short, there are no external constraints on "newcomers."

For all his cynicism, the Man in Black is convinced that Arnold had "one story left to tell" before he died. "A story with real stakes, real violence." For the Man in Black, that translates to a world populated by individuals who can have an interest in preserving their lives and well-being. Presumably, that would involve a world of persons with minds—including Hosts.

Humans, Persons, and Minds

Are the Hosts persons? Are fetuses persons? In her essay, "On the Legal and Moral Status of Abortion," Mary Anne Warren claims that "human being" has two meanings: one is personhood, which involves being "a full-fledged member of the moral community." The other is the biological entity, with the genetic human code—*Homo sapiens.*

Most in Westworld assume that Hosts are not human, let alone persons. From this they infer that Hosts are not candidates for membership in the moral community. The reasoning goes something like this: None but humans are persons. Only persons are members of the moral community. So, none but humans are members of the moral community. This inference becomes strained, however, when some begin to wonder if it's possible that some non-humans are persons. Everyone's shocked and distressed reactions when Clementine is brutally beaten right in front of them suggest there is at least something remarkably compelling about another being's senseless suffering, even if that suffering is generally believed to be a simulation.

According to Warren, the criteria for personhood are: "consciousness," "reasoning," "self-motivated activity," "the capacity to communicate," and "the presence of self-concepts, and self-awareness." According to Warren, consciousness and reasoning "alone may well be sufficient for personhood," and, if combined with "self-motivated activity," few would be justified in denying it.

According to this view, personhood is intimately connected to what it is to have or be a mind. Since, according to Ford, Arnold subscribed to the bicameral mind theory of consciousness, it makes sense to interpret "consciousness" accordingly. The theory of the bicameral mind involves an account of consciousness as achieved, rather than part of the evolution of humans' cognitive apparatus. It is no surprise that the final episode of Season One is entitled "The Bicameral Mind."

The breakdown of the bicameral mind involves one part of the brain "listening" to what the other part is "saying," without the listener thinking that voice is their own—hence the "bicameral" or two-chamber view of the brain. Experiences and memories become auditory hallucinations, but perceived as divine commands. In several of Plato's dialogues, for example, Socrates mentions an inner voice, his daemon, which forbids him from acting, but never commands. On this view, there would be no introspection, no self-concept or self-awareness—nothing like what we would call a "voice of conscience."

Such a voice, apparently, is what Arnold sought to achieve with his Hosts. As Ford tells Robert—in two episodes, no less—"Arnold built a version of that cognition in which the Hosts heard their programming as an inner monologue, with the hopes that in time, their own voice would take over. It was a way to bootstrap consciousness." ("The Stray" and "Well-Tempered Clavier")

The "version of that cognition" Arnold built is presented by Ford as a four-level pyramid, with memory on the bottom, then improvisation, and then self-interest. "And at the top? Never got there" ("The Stray"). Memory plays a foundational role in consciousness and, more specifically, in personal identity. We often proceed on the assumption that "I" am comprehensible in large part because of memories I call mine. I may not remember everything that's ever happened in my life, but what I do remember is never attributed to someone else.

John Locke argues that memory is a foundational criterion of personal identity, of what it is to be a unified, continuous self. In his *An Essay Concerning Human Understanding*, Locke writes, "if it be possible for the same man to have distinct incommunicable consciousness at different times, it is past doubt the same man would at different times make different persons." Indeed, psychological continuity—a feature of consciousness associated with memory—is crucial to being a self, a person, a mind.

Arnold sketches almost the same pyramid in the season finale as the one Ford showed Bernard earlier in the season. He tries to explain to Dolores the error of the pyramid scheme of consciousness: Memory is once again on the bottom, and improvisation one level above it. But rather than self-interest coming next, Arnold omits it altogether. He has only three levels, with the missing link that creates consciousness at the top. Why?

One answer may lie in his abandonment of the hierarchy scheme of consciousness in favor of the maze. Arnold tells Dolores he believed consciousness "was a pyramid you needed to scale . . . Then one day—I realized I'd made a mistake. Consciousness isn't a journey upward, but a journey inward" ("The Bicameral Mind"). Memories, without any way to organize them, are fairly useless. We can see that clearly by way of Dolores's inability to create a coherent narrative from them. The flashbacks and multiple timelines serve to illustrate this problem. "Where are we?" she asks William in the Season One finale. "We're here," he replies. "Together." She is flustered, panicked. "Then *when* are we?"

One way to organize memories is through reason. Bernard does this when he concludes that he has killed Theresa—and that Ford made him do it ("Trace Decay"). Indeed, it seems that agency—self-motivated activity—often hinges on the results of reasoning processes, as when a person determines what is perceived to be the best course of action. Perhaps this is what happens when Maeve, who has made good her escape from Westworld, decides to return to look for her daughter. Another way to put this is in terms of minds having causal properties— that the mind has the power to cause actions independently of any prior or antecedent conditions, and as such affects the physical world. Hosts are thought to lack such power; their programming precludes the sort of freedom believed to be required for mental causation.

So, to be a person seems to involve being or having a mind. Most of us think of "mind" in terms of *self*-consciousness, that is self-concepts and self-awareness intimately connected to the equally mental feeling of having the sort of agency described above. Each one of us tends to have a very intimate mental feeling of "I." What about Westworld's Hosts? They easily use the first person pronoun, "I," the first person singular, "me," and the first person possessive pronoun, "mine." These usages, however, are programmed. They alone do not prove self-awareness or anything resembling the feeling or phenomenology of spontaneity, of *being a self*, of having a mind.

There are some good reasons to think that the Hosts do not have minds. For example, Dr. Ford admonishes Bernard, "Just don't forget the Hosts are not real. They're not conscious" ("The Stray"). Ford chastises a body shop worker for covering a Host, saying, "It doesn't get cold, doesn't feel ashamed." Then he picks up a scalpel. "Doesn't feel a solitary thing," he continues, slicing into the Host's head, "that we haven't told it to." Then there are the two times Ford shows Bernard a photo: Once before Bernard knows he is Arnold, and once after. The first time, he simply doesn't see himself standing next to a Host ("The Well-Tempered Clavier").

There's also the moment when Bernard does not notice his striking likeness in a Vitruvian Man-type sketch Theresa shows him. "It doesn't look like anything to me," he says. Dolores and Hector also express a version of "It doesn't look like anything to me" ("The Original" and "Trace Decay"). The fact that they don't show any curiosity reveals something significant, namely a rule of self-awareness.

The Hosts are supposed to be lifelike enough to give Guests something approaching an authentic experience. At the very least, they had to have passed the so-called Turing test. In his essay, "Is the Brain's Mind a Computer Program," the philosopher John Searle argued that this test does not satisfy the conditions for the sort of artificial intelligence that would properly be called a thinker. To demonstrate his objection, he proposes a thought experiment in which a person sits in a room. From outside the room, the person is given a rulebook (in English) for matching Chinese symbols to other Chinese symbols. The person then manipulates symbols—from one set of Chinese characters to another, just as a computer manipulates symbols in the "imitation game." What the person does *not* do, Searle argues, is understand the manipulation; the symbols essentially "mean nothing to me."

Yet, as we've seen, there are dawning realizations. Surely it is a feature of mind to seek to understand what is unfamiliar, complicated, or confused. That is just what some of the Hosts do. Indeed, we learn that Arnold believes Dolores is "alive." She is a *person* with a *mind*. Why else would he try to destroy Westworld before it ever opened, fearful as he was how poorly she and her kind would be treated? For his part, Ford duplicates his partner's manner of death, but not before helping some of the Hosts achieve that third level of the pyramid, self-interest, which aids them against we humans, who have "murdered and butchered anything that challenged our supremacy" ("The Well-Tempered Clavier"). And so, to borrow from the Man in Black, the stakes are real.

The Problem of Other Minds

Still, there is a lingering problem. It's not at all clear what justifies my belief that any minds *other* than mine exist. It's not just that I can doubt artificial intelligences have minds. I can doubt that *anything* else has a mind. Descartes makes a

related point in his *Meditations*. Having set out to establish
"certain and indubitable" beliefs by way of doubting those that
do not meet those criteria, in the second Meditation, he arrives
at one that it impossible to doubt: he exists as a thinking thing.
After all, to doubt is a version of thinking, and thinking is a
mode of existing entirely distinct from anything else that may
exist, including bodies. It cannot be, then, that he can both
deny he exists while existing (as a thinking thing): If I don't
exist, then I cannot be thinking. But I am thinking. So, I must
exist. The certainty of the "I think" leads him to consider other
features of his mind. For example, at the end of the Second
Meditation, he realizes that he should not say he "sees" men
"crossing the square," but instead should say he *"judge[s]* that
they are men." That is because he does not "see any more than
hats and coats which could conceal automatons" (p. 26).

My own inner life is immediate and exclusive *to me*. I have
no direct access to anyone else's, but I can't be mistaken about
my own. Consequently, I have no reason to believe *anyone* is
anything other than a Westworld Host. Indeed, a fundamental
assumption in *Westworld* is that the issue of other minds is
exclusive to the Hosts. Visitors and employees alike operate on
the assumption that Hosts don't have minds, but they don't
doubt that people like themselves do.

One route around the problem of other minds is to deny the
reality of minds altogether. Some thinkers maintain there are
no minds in the way Descartes thinks of them; there is no distinction between minds and bodies. There are not two types of
existence or two kinds of thing, mental and physical. There are
not two natures, but only one: physical. This is the position
Gilbert Ryle takes in his classic book, *The Concept of Mind*. In
his first chapter, "Descartes' Myth," Ryle sets out to demolish
what he calls, "the official doctrine" of mind, that is, "the dogma
of the ghost in the machine" (p. 5).

Ryle maintains that the misuse of language leads us to
believe that minds and bodies are fundamentally different
things. This, he thinks, is a "category mistake," whereby one
type of word—"mind," for example—is mistaken as referring to
the same category of being as body.

When we talk about the behavior of objects—say, Hosts in
Westworld—we say things like, "Dolores is grief-stricken." For
William, there is some*thing* over and above the mechanical,

biological, and behavioral components—Dolores's *mind*. Logan doesn't make this mistake. If he were taken to the Westworld lab and shown how Dolores was made, soup to nuts, he would *not* say, "Yes, I see all the parts and features, but where is *Dolores?*" That's because he doesn't think there *is* anything else. William's interactions with Dolores nevertheless make him doubt she's a mere machine. As they walk through Pariah at night, he muses about why people come to Westworld. "There's no rules or restrictions . . . No one will judge you, no one in the real world will even know," He says. Dolores is curious. "What did you mean by that? You said no one in the real world will know."

William is surprised by her response. "I thought you weren't supposed to notice things like that," he says. "Why wouldn't I?" Dolores asks. "You know, recently, it seems like the whole world is calling to me in a way it hasn't before" ("Contrapasso"). If Ryle is correct, not only does William make a category mistake about Dolores, he, along with Logan and anyone else who believes in minds makes a mistake. Talk about mind is not talk about some non-physical thing any more than talk about Dolores—or anyone else—is talk about something in addition to her material constituents.

According to some more recent philosophers, Ryle's attempt to dissolve the distinction between mind and body doesn't really make the problem of the mind, or consciousness, go away. In his famous essay, "What Is It Like to Be a Bat?," Thomas Nagel points out that it makes sense to ask the question, *what is it like* to be someone or something else? What is it *like* to experience pain or pleasure?

Nagel argues that the "subjective character of experience," consciousness, the point of view, or what it is *like* to be someone or something, resists an exclusively materialist explanation in terms of physical concepts. Consciousness is a quality, a mental feeling. "Consciousness," Nagel writes, "is what makes the mind-body problem really intractable" (p. 185). Humans can try to imagine what it's like to be a bat, for example, though they can't have much success.

When Clementine is beaten in the lab, no one steps in to help, but the expressions on their faces make clear they can imagine the pain and feel the terrible shame of doing nothing. Why else would they do this if they did suppose there is something it is like *for Clementine* to be punched and slapped in the face? In other words, they can't help supposing that Clementine is conscious and therefore has a mind.

We can't know what it is like to be another person *as that person knows what it is to be themselves*. Subjectivity, consciousness

> is not captured by any of the familiar, recently devised reductive analyses of the mental, for all of them are logically compatible with its absence. It is not analyzable in terms of any explanatory system of functional states, or intentional states, since these could be ascribed to robots or automata that behaved like people though they experienced nothing. (pp. 166–67)

In a footnote to this passage, Nagel writes: "Perhaps there could not actually be such robots. Perhaps anything complex enough to behave like a person would have experiences. But that, if true, is a fact which cannot be discovered merely by analyzing the concept of experience" (p. 167).

Bertrand Russell thought that the most convincing way to arrive at the existence of other minds is by analogy. The argument runs as follows: I behave in ways *a, b,* and *c*. There are causes of my behavior. Person 2 also behaves in ways *a, b,* and *c*. So, Person 2's behavior has similar causes. Some of my behaviors are caused by my mental states (thoughts, beliefs, hopes, fears). So, similar behaviors in others are also caused by mental states. Consequently, other minds exist. While Russell does not think that this reasoning logically guarantees the reality of other minds, he does think it is good enough.

By analogy, then, like effects—behaviors—are inferred to have like causes—mental states. As Russell points out, "We observe in ourselves such occurrences as remembering, reasoning, feeling pleasure, and feeling pain. We think that sticks and stones do not have these experiences, but that other people do. Most of us have no doubt that the higher animals feel pleasure and pain, though I was once assured by a fisherman that 'Fish have no sense nor feeling'. I failed to find out how he had acquired this knowledge" *(Human Knowledge,* p. 482).

And so, regardless of how the Hosts were made, there is reason to think they might have minds, after all. Recall Ford's dialogue as he drew a scalpel across a Host's head: "Doesn't feel a solitary thing that we haven't told it to." But if it does feel, even if the memory of it is later erased, in that moment, there is consciousness, something it is like to be that Host. If, however, we conclude that Hosts don't have minds, perhaps you and I should doubt the reality of our own—and each other's.

6

Sorry, Human, the Maze Is Not for You

PATRICK CROSKERY

I was thirteen when the original *Westworld* movie came out in 1973 and I have vivid memories of Yul Brynner's gunslinger relentlessly tracking down his human target. Brynner's portrayal managed to evoke the infamous uncanny valley—the disorientation we feel when a creation is close to human but not quite there.

Like most moviegoers, I identified with Richard Benjamin's character, the frightened but resourceful Peter Martin, as he tried to elude the gunslinger with his peculiar combination of both superhuman and subhuman capacities.

Watching the HBO series *Westworld* is a fundamentally different experience. While I often identify with the human characters, I am drawn far more deeply into the plot by the "Hosts," the humanoid robots with advanced artificial intelligence. Curiously, I find that I sometimes identify with the Hosts and sometimes not. I find that when I believe that they are conscious in the appropriate way that I identify with them as I would with human characters, but at other times I see them as elaborate machines and I am no longer concerned about what happens to them.

The show plays skillfully with this boundary, so that my experience of the show tracks my intuitive views on the possible relationships between consciousness and what philosophers call *moral standing*. A being has moral standing when it has moral value intrinsically, not just instrumentally. Thus, I might find value in a toy dog I have kept from my childhood, but the value is due to me, not the toy dog. In contrast, most people would hold that my pet dog has value both to me and in itself. One key contrast is that my pet dog is conscious and the toy dog is not. By paying careful attention to when and how we identify the Hosts in *Westworld*, we can explore the relationship between consciousness and moral standing. Broadly speaking, we can link consciousness to three potential sources of moral standing: pain, choice, and meaning.

Pain and Horror

When my daughter was around six, she and I were playing up in the fort attached to our swing set. She accidentally dropped her doll, which plummeted to the ground below us. I was worried that she would be traumatized. "What's the matter, Dad?" she asked. "It's just a doll."

She was right, of course. A piece of plastic shaped like a human being does not experience any pain. I just expected her to attribute pain to the doll at that moment. Like any child, she enjoyed pretending that pieces of plastic were experiencing feelings as we played together. She just happened not to be projecting feelings onto the doll at that particular moment.

For the visitors to Westworld, the Hosts are simply more elaborate dolls, pieces of metal and flesh constructed to simulate not only the external appearance of human beings but also the behavior. "Cue the waterworks," the Man in Black says when Dolores starts to cry, suggesting that a programming subroutine has been invoked. The Host who appears the most as a machine to us is "Old Bill", the "retired" bartender Ford visits with from time to time. Old Bill moves mechanically and always wants to "drink to the lady with the white shoes."

While the visitors always see the Hosts as mere machines, as viewers of the show we are encouraged to take multiple perspectives. This struck me with particular force while re-watching the first episode after completing the first season. When I first watched the episode, Dolores's screams as the Man in Black drags her into the barn marked him as a moral monster. But watching the same episode after completing the first season, I had a glimpse of the Man in Black's point of view on the scene. He has been watching the same repetitive behavior from Dolores and Teddy for thirty years. They seem like wind-up toys to him now, structures designed to evoke sympathetic responses in us that lead us to attribute feelings to them. They look to him like Old Bill does to us.

But is Dolores like Old Bill? After watching the full first season, we also know that Dolores will have attained consciousness for the final time on this visit to the park—and she will never lose it again. If she is conscious, isn't her pain real, and the Man in Black a moral monster after all? Is he repressing his recognition out of thwarted love?

In "Trace Decay" Ford and Bernard discuss the issue of pain:

FORD: Your imagined suffering makes you lifelike.

BERNARD: Lifelike, but not alive? Pain only exists in the mind. It's always imagined. So what's the difference between my pain and yours? Between you and me?

FORD: This was the very question that consumed Arnold, filled him with guilt, eventually drove him mad.

The show constantly plays with our uncertainty about whether or not the Hosts are truly suffering or are just simulating suffering. When we think they're truly suffering we're horrified and root against the brutish humans. When we think they are merely simulating pain we lose interest in their situation and turn our attention to the experiences of the humans.

The acting, writing, and directing are so skillful that different viewers will see the same scene different ways. But the constant is that we all care about the treatment of the Hosts when we believe they are experiencing conscious pain. This provides us with one possible account of moral standing: the capacity to experience conscious pain. Beings that can experience pain can be wronged—they are what philosophers call moral "patients."

The eighteenth-century Scottish philosopher David Hume explored the role of pain in morality in a way that is particularly relevant here. He held that "The chief spring or actuating principle of the human mind is pleasure or pain" (*A Treatise of Human Nature*, p. 574). He then suggested that we connect to the feelings of others by sympathy, which he treats as a somewhat mechanical process:

The minds of all men are similar in their feelings and operations; nor can anyone be actuated by any affection, of which all others are not, in some degree, susceptible. As in strings equally wound up, the motion of one communicates itself to the rest; so all the affections readily pass from one person to another.

Hume provides an especially vivid illustration of the transmission of feelings by sympathy.

Were I present at any of the more terrible operations of surgery, it is certain, that even before it begun, the preparation of the instruments, the laying of the bandages in order, the heating of the irons, with all the signs of anxiety and concern in the patient and assistants, would have a great effect upon my mind, and excite the strongest sentiments of pity and terror. (p. 576)

However, sympathy in Hume's account operates on the assumption that the minds of all humans "are similar in their feelings and operations." But in the case of the Hosts it's not clear that this assumption is justified. We can make a hand puppet frown, and we will automatically feel a bit saddened out of sympathy. But the hand puppet is not in fact experiencing anything sad—it has no mind at all.

The Hosts' minds resemble ours in some ways and not in others. In general, the Hosts respond in somewhat odd ways to painful injuries—Dolores is in effect disemboweled and simply looks surprised, and Armistice has her arm crushed in a door and seems puzzled. Meanwhile, when Logan stabs the hand of the Host who is tempting William with a treasure hunt the Host's expression is of intense pain. Most strikingly, in "The Adversary," Maeve takes control of her "attribute matrix" with characteristics like loyalty and charm. Pain is apparently one attribute. She reduces the "pain" level, saying "I'd prefer it sting less next time I want one of these chats," that is, to hurt less when she "dies" so that she can return to the repair room.

This raises an interesting question about the future development of technology. As our creations advance, how will we know if we have created artificial beings (whether they look like humans or not) who are true moral patients? Watching *Westworld* our intuitions about this fundamental question are drawn out in vivid and subtle fashion.

On the view that once the Hosts achieve consciousness their pain and suffering gives them moral standing *Westworld* most resembles a horror movie. Unlike the original *Westworld* movie, where we sympathize with the terrified human as he is tracked down by the implacable robot, in the television series we are led to sympathize with the robot Hosts as they are tormented by the human Guests.

Who Killed Arnold?

But perhaps *Westworld* isn't like a horror film. Perhaps it's more like a murder mystery. Throughout the series we get clues about the fate of Arnold; like detectives we find ourselves piecing them together to try to figure out the circumstances of his death. In "The Stray" Ford reports that "We called it an accident, but I knew Arnold and he was very, very careful." How, we wonder, did Arnold die?

In "Contrapasso" we learn that Dolores's last contact with Arnold took place the day he died, and gradually our suspicion grows that perhaps Dolores killed him. However, in "The Bicameral Mind" Bernard and Dolores meet for the first time and Bernard accuses Ford of killing Arnold. Who is the murderer? In a twist, Ford uses Dolores as his witness. As viewers, we go with Dolores into a memory and see an extended scene that concludes with her shooting Arnold and then herself.

So is Dolores the killer after all? In yet another twist, Ford tells Bernard that she's not the killer. As he explains it: "She wasn't truly conscious. She didn't pull that trigger. It was Arnold pulling the trigger through her." Although it's a subtle argument, we immediately grasp his point. If Dolores was not conscious, she could not truly *choose* to pull the trigger. In that case she had no free will, and therefore she could not be responsible for Arnold's death.

Who then killed Arnold? According to Ford, it was a suicide, just in a very unusual form. Just as Arnold could have pulled the trigger directly and been the agent responsible for his own death, here he has "pulled the trigger" through a Host under his control, and is therefore the agent responsible for his own death. Indeed, in her memory of the scene Arnold himself tells Dolores "I hope there's some solace that I left you no choice."

The intuitive connection between consciousness, free will, and moral responsibility is evoked vividly in that brief scene. Here our intuition is not about moral *patiency* (as with pain), but with moral *agency*. Moral patiency has to do with the capacity to do harm, while moral agency has to do with the capacity to be responsible. We have, then, a second potential relationship between consciousness and moral standing. Our reaction to Ford's argument suggests that consciousness is necessary for moral agency.

While Hume focused on pain, pleasure, and sympathy, the eighteenth-century German philosopher Immanuel Kant focused his attention on choice and will. He argued that "Everything in nature works according to laws. Only a rational being alone has the power to act according to his conception of laws, i.e., according to principles, and thereby he has a will" (*Grounding for the Metaphysics of Morals*, p. 23).

According to Kant's account, what gives us free will or "autonomy" is the capacity to act on laws that we give ourselves. An animal acting on instinct is not acting on principles it gives itself, so it is not capable of being a moral agent. We do not blame a cat for tormenting a mouse. So, too, if Dolores's behavior is controlled by Arnold, she is not a moral agent and is not morally blameworthy.

This involves another level of consciousness than the mere awareness of pain—self-consciousness. *Westworld* conveys this idea by having Dolores have a voice in her head that she attributes to Arnold. She achieves self-consciousness when she realizes the voice is her own. This complex idea is expressed through a striking image—a second Dolores replaces Arnold in the chair, and his voice slowly turns into her voice.

As we puzzle through the issues raised by Arnold's death, we might wonder if we ourselves truly have free will. After all, our actions seem to be the product of causal forces just like the other parts of nature. The classic philosophical problem of free will versus determinism strikes us as particularly important because we want to know when to hold ourselves and others morally responsible.

These issues are explored with particular intricacy as we follow the Host Maeve. Maeve manages to escape the illusion of Westworld and awaken in the repair facility. She uses her persuasive powers (a combination of charm and threats) to gain access to her own programming. As noted above, she reduces her pain level (and increases her intelligence), but she also has a unique opportunity—to watch her own code.

Once again the show makes our philosophical intuitions concrete. We identify with Maeve as she watches the tablet produce the words she is about to say just before she says them. The lines of programming start halting and jerking in response to the paradox evoked, and Maeve freezes. Felix panics, thinking he has ruined a Host.

But Maeve recovers, and starts to take control of her own life in a new way. Perhaps the most dramatic moment is in "The Bicameral Mind" when instead of freezing she destroys the tablet showing the coding behind her current plan ("escape") and declares "Bullshit! No one's controlling me." Kant's response is more elaborate, but in a sense he comes to the same conclusion. He builds an entire metaphysical account that separates what we can know causally from what we must believe while choosing. As scientists we build third-person causal explanations, but as self-conscious agents we think of ourselves as free.

There are two additional twists in "The Bicameral Mind." Maeve, on the train ready to "escape" to our world, changes her mind and chooses to return to find her daughter. She knows that her memories of her daughter are a product of an earlier narrative. We aren't sure what she's thinking, but she seems to *choose* to commit herself to the daughter. Is this her first truly free choice? Is she for the first time truly "escaping" from her programming?

The second twist worth attending to is that Ford, after declaring that Dolores did not kill Arnold because she was not truly conscious, mutters "At least that's how I saw it at the time." What possibility does this comment raise? We know that in order to have Dolores kill him, Arnold has integrated another character into her programming, Wyatt. While we think it is unlikely that Dolores would choose to kill Arnold, the Host who results from the combination of Dolores and Wyatt might well make such a choice. This combined Host ends up leading the revolution against the humans that concludes Season One. The revolution may make possible the genuine freedom of all the Hosts.

The Future of Meaning

The idea of a revolution is an exciting story, neither a horror story nor a mystery. It raises the possibility of a completely new kind of story. This possibility draws our attention to perhaps the most disturbing thing about Dolores: that she is trapped in story loop with Teddy, dreaming of "someday" going with him to "down south where the mountains meet the sea." Because it is simply a repeating loop, the story is meaningless to us. Something fundamental is missing.

The contemporary philosopher Alasdair MacIntyre has suggested that "man is a story-telling animal," a conscious echo of the ancient Greek philosopher Aristotle's statement that "man is a political animal." Aristotle was highlighting the fact that humans by nature live in communities and that participating in a rich community is part of a flourishing life. MacIntyre is bringing out an important dimension of belonging to a community—that we draw on its stock of stories to help shape our lives and give them meaning.

Westworld reflects the theme of storytelling at multiple levels. While the Hosts are the most striking feature of the park, it is the "narratives" that bring the Guests in. As Logan puts it to his companion, whom he calls "Billy," by participating in these intense storylines you learn "who you really are." (As Logan discovers, that is even more true than he realized— "Billy" discovers that he is really "William" and comes to dominate Logan, sending him to the edge of the park strapped naked to a horse.)

The narratives of the park appeal to our story-telling nature, but the primary narratives strike us as clichéd. As we watch the show we do not concern ourselves much with the narratives the Guests are engaged in. They are backgrounds to the real stories of the series—such as "Billy" becoming William and Ford battling the board.

But the Hosts raise the most interesting questions about story-telling. Just as we wondered if their pain is real or their choices are genuine, we can wonder if they are participating in meaningful stories. Dolores and Teddy represent two extremes in relation to our story-telling nature. James Marsden's portrayal of Teddy is a model of focus. He conveys with every expression and every posture that Teddy is always in the primary story and is completely unable to conceive of anything outside that story. Meanwhile, Evan Rachel Wood conveys Dolores's doubt, longing, and uncertainty with great subtlety.

Teddy, the show suggests, is never truly conscious because he is trapped in a loop that he is not aware of. Dolores, meanwhile, becomes real to William—and to us—when she seems to show the capacity to get outside her loop. When William is grabbed by the Confederados in "Contrapasso," Dolores suddenly changes her demeanor and shoots them all. William asks "How did you do that?" and she responds "You said people come here to change the story of their lives. I imagined a story where I didn't have to be the damsel."

Our sense of purpose seems to require an inventiveness that goes beyond what conventional stories can provide. To bring out this dimension, MacIntyre suggests that the story of our lives is a quest. But on his account a quest is not a search for something "already adequately characterized, as miners search for gold." He says that "A quest is always an education both as to the character of that which is sought and in self-knowledge." This account is in keeping with the story that William goes through, learning who he really is.

The capacity to create meaning might be thought of as a moral status comparable to the capacity to feel pain or the capacity to choose. Our reactions to Teddy and Dolores suggest that the capacity to create meaning requires a distinctive kind of consciousness. Beyond the awareness of pain and the self-consciousness of choice, we may need to be capable of achieving creativity in our stories.

Here *Westworld* takes us in an interesting direction. Ford suggests that ultimately we humans may not meet this standard. He says in "Trace Decay" that humans "live in loops as tight and as closed as the Hosts do, seldom questioning our choices, content, for the most part, to be told what to do next." In a similar fashion, in "Contrapasso" the Man in Black describes the conditions outside the park to Teddy (and Ford):

> You know why you exist, Teddy? The world out there, the one you'll never see, was one of plenty. A fat, soft teat people cling to their entire life. Every need taken care of except one: purpose, meaning. So they come here. They can be a little scared, a little thrilled, enjoy some sweetly affirmative bullshit, and then they take a fucking picture and they go back home.

So in the time of the show (thirty years after the opening of the park), our needs are taken care of but our lives feel meaningless. The Man in Black doesn't think this limitation applies to him. He adds, "But I think there's a deeper meaning hiding under all that."

We follow the story of the Man in Black trying to find that deeper meaning, watching as he brutalizes Kissy and Lawrence and even Dolores along the way. But the Man in Black does not find his deeper meaning. As the Hosts tell him, "the Maze was not for you." Whenever the Hosts say this to the Man in Black they clearly step out of the narrative they are presently participating in and speak in a cold and distant fashion.

Who, then, is the Maze meant for? In "The Bicameral Mind" we learn that Arnold originally created it to help the Hosts gain consciousness. Looking at a toy maze, he realized that:

> Consciousness isn't a journey upward, but a journey inward. Not a pyramid, but a maze. Every choice could bring you closer to the center or send you spiraling to the edges, to madness.

Ford, meanwhile, made his own discovery. As he explains to Bernard:

> Do you want to know why I really gave you the backstory of your son, Bernard? It was Arnold's key insight, the thing that led the Hosts to their awakening. Suffering. The pain that the world is not as you want it to be. It was when Arnold died, when I suffered, that I began to understand what he had found.

He concludes, "And I'm afraid in order to escape this place, you will need to suffer more."

The philosopher Friedrich Nietzsche saw suffering as the key to the development of new values. His account involves a two-stage process. First, he insisted that we expose our existing values to a withering critique even though those values make us feel comfortable (the son of a pastor, Nietzsche paid special attention to Christianity). This critique of values leads to nihilism or the recognition that life is meaningless.

Hector's story loop in Westworld provides a helpful metaphor for nihilism. In Hector's loop, he is always pursuing the safe found in the saloon. It is, so to speak, the Holy Grail of his quest. We learn in "The Well-Tempered Clavier" that in every repetition Hector steals the safe and tries to open it; however, every time the gang gets in a dispute and he and Armistice end up shooting each other before the safe can be opened. Maeve, who has stepped out of her primary narrative and taken control of her life, opens the safe for Hector, allowing him to see for the first time that the safe is empty. As she says, "It was always empty, like everything in this world." Everything that Hector was pursuing was always in vain.

But there is a second stage in Nietzsche's account—an affirmation of suffering. Nietzsche holds that suffering is necessary to create value. So, for instance, he provides a genealogy of morals in which a long history of horrific punishments makes possible our free will, which itself represents a standard of value. He suggests that while a full critique of our values will involve great suffering, this suffering will in turn make possible a higher form of humanity, the *Übermensch*, or "overman."

Nietzsche doesn't think that he himself is the overman—he aims instead to be a bridge to the overman. In a similar fashion Ford, having learned from his mistake, appears to treat himself as a bridge to a new future for the Hosts. Someone has been altering Maeve's programming to give her the capacity to make changes to the narratives themselves—to be "over" them. She manipulates Felix and Sylvester to override her programming and brings in the courage of Hector and Armistice to overwhelm the security team. In the end, she manages to overcome the limitations of her "escape" programming to "escape" in a different sense.

Perhaps she and the other Hosts will be able to overthrow the enemy, humans. Nietzsche's account suggests that the suffering of the Hosts may not be in vain—they may be able to overturn our table of values and thus move beyond good and evil.

Where are they going? What new stories will they tell? What new values will they create? Sorry, human, the Maze is not for you.

Part II

Mariposa Saloon

When you are suffering,
that's when you're most real.

7
Westworld and the Meaning of Life

Mia Wood

Inscription at Delos: Most noble is that which is most just, and best is health; but most pleasant is it to win what we love.

—Aristotle, *Nicomachean Ethics*, Book I

We humans are those beings for whom being itself is an issue. We want a reason for our being, an explanation for why we exist, to understand what the meaning of our lives is.

For many of us, the hope is that there is a purpose to life, maybe also an afterlife that bestows significance on our existence. It's no surprise that philosophers don't agree on what the meaning of life is, and often don't even agree that the question itself is worth asking.

Optimists, Pessimists, and the In-Betweens

"Have you ever questioned the nature of your reality?" Bernard (and Arnold) asks Dolores. "No," she responds dispassionately ("The Original," "Tromp L'Oeil").

Dolores is not one to wonder. Westworld's Hosts are programmed to exhibit fairly common assumptions about reality, rather than to develop a worldview. Dolores says, "I choose to . . . believe there is an order to our days, a purpose" ("The Original"). Indeed, there is a purpose; it's just not a purpose *for her*. She is, rather, a means to the "violent delights of others' violent ends." Nevertheless, since she expresses an optimist's view of life's meaning, it's worth asking if she's right. On the

73

supposition she is, we can ask, To what *end?* In other words, what are we saying when we say that life is purposeful?

The outlaw Hector reflects a pessimistic worldview. Bernard asks him if an interaction with a Guest made him question his world. "No," Hector replies. "This world is just as doomed as ever" ("Trompe L'Oeil"). The Man in Black expresses a similar view about reality. "You know why this beats the real world?" he rhetorically asks the Host, Lawrence, as part of a quest to find the meaning of the Maze. "Real world is just chaos, an accident. But in here, every detail adds up to something" ("Chestnut").

Dr. Ford seems to tacitly agree with the Man in Black. "You see," he says to Bernard, explaining why the Hosts' "memories" are wiped after they've completed a narrative loop. "The Guests enjoy the power. They cannot enjoy it in the outside world, so they come here" ("The Stray").

The power most Guests enjoy is often brutal, vicious, and unacceptable by most moral standards. We're told as much again and again, in word and action. A returning Guest describes a visit to Westworld in which he "went straight evil" ("The Original"). We see indiscriminate and entirely sadistic violence against Hosts, just because it's allowed. In Westworld, "God is dead, so everything is permissible." As a whole, then, Westworld reflects a negative view of life's value, and so also its meaning.

Maeve strikes something of a balance between optimism and pessimism. Having learned the truth of her existence, she is both devastated by the apparent lack of meaning to her life and resolved to create it. As she says to Hector, "I want you to break into Hell with me and rob the gods blind." The gods, she has learned, are neither omniscient nor omnipotent, as she'd once implicitly believed. Worse yet, they are not benevolent. "I died with my eyes open, saw the masters who pull our strings," she says ("The Well-Tempered Clavier").

The terrible reality behind the programming curtain expands Maeve's view of what she is, what she could be. As she prepares to escape the park, the hapless Body Shop technician, Felix, asks her if she'll be all right. "Oh, Felix," she says with some tenderness. "You really do make a terrible human. And I mean that as a compliment." Maeve's newfound optimism that *she* can create her own meaning, the *she* is the author of her life—is guided, in part, by her suspicion of the human gods' intentions.

The Optimists

Plato's Socrates famously declared, "The unexamined life is not worth living" (*Apology*, 38a). One wakes, works, eats, sleeps, enjoys friends and family. One feels pains and pleasures. Perhaps one begins a family of one's own. What Socrates cares about is *how* one lives one's life. A good life, a meaningful life, is one that is lived in pursuit of knowledge. In particular, a good life is lived in pursuit of virtue.

As Socrates puts it, "You are mistaken, my friend, if you think that a man who is worth anything ought to spend his time weighing up the prospects of life and death. He has only one thing to consider in performing any action—that is, whether he is acting rightly or wrongly, like a good man or a bad one" (28b).

For Socrates, *knowing* what virtue is and *being* virtuous are complementary. This idea is developed across a number of Plato's dialogues, in which Socrates appears as the main character. In *Protagoras*, for example, Socrates suggests that wrongdoing is the result of ignorance, since no one knowingly does wrong. In turn, the question of life's meaning is implicitly answered in the question, "How should I live?" Moreover, the question, "How should I live?" typically presupposes there is a correct way to live; one need only uncover it. For Socrates, then, the purpose of life is bound up with knowing the objectively right way to live, thereby ensuring a good life.

So far, so good, except there is a nagging question: What's the point of a good life? There are at least two answers. One is that a good life is a happy life, a flourishing life in which you do well and are well, precisely because you're fulfilling what it means to be a human being. It is a final purpose, since it is not a means to some other end. This is also the general view Aristotle takes.

Like a good number of his fellow Greeks, Aristotle thinks nature is teleological—it is purpose driven. Everything has within it its end, or final cause—that for the sake of which a thing is. In Westworld, the Hosts have their loop. Their story's end is already written at the beginning, so they are programmed to seek and pursue it. The Guests are often said to visit Westworld to discover their purpose. So, purpose can be solely functional, or it can be life-directing.

In Westworld, each Host's ostensible purpose is to provide Guests with a lifelike experience. In this sense, the Hosts are merely tools. Their collective characteristic activity also provides the evaluative standard according to which a Host's "virtue" is determined. At one point, for example, Maeve was a "good" prostitute—she did her job well—but then, as she starts to have visions which she discovers she's had before, her performance slumps ("Dissonance Theory"). Functionally, a Host fulfills its purpose when it does its job well.

Dolores's dialogue reflects a more expansive view of purpose, one that extends beyond a predetermined function to a *whole* life—and she talks about it with a tone that vaguely suggests this purpose is good. On several occasions, she remarks that life itself is purposeful, and that each individual has a "path." On the face of it, this is consistent with Aristotle's view of the good for humans as "an activity of the soul in accordance with virtue . . . *in a complete life*" (*Nicomachean Ethics*, 1098a emphasis added).

A Singular Pessimist

Even if you think that life is purposeful, you may be suspicious about whether or not that meaning extends beyond death. Whether or not there is life after death prompts some to wonder if living some version of a good life now really matters, particularly if there is no life after death. If life simply ends, if what-it-is-to-be-me is annihilated at death, why should anyone care about a good life?

A life of meaning is often tied to a belief that there is an afterlife, in which I will be rewarded or punished. In other words, my life gains meaning only in relation to an *external* purpose, that is, a divine plan I ought to fulfill. Without it, life is simply a series of events without significance, without mattering, without meaning.

According to some philosophers, whether or not there is an afterlife is irrelevant to life's meaning. Eternal life is a red herring, a distraction from the essential question about life's meaning. Another way to put it is that I may or may not live some version of life in which I exist as some version of me that is identifiably me.

Thomas Nagel argues that the meaning of life cannot be decided in terms of its duration.

It is often remarked that nothing we do now will matter in a million years. But if that is true, then by the same token, nothing that will be the case in a million years matters now . . . Whether what we do now will matter in a million years could make the crucial difference only if its mattering in a million years depended on its mattering, period." ("The Absurd," p. 716)

Logan clearly lands on the side of things not mattering—at least in Westworld—when he tells William, "Don't you get it yet? There is no such thing as heroes or villains. It's just a giant circle jerk" ("Contrapasso"). Absent an objectively real, externally generated meaning, the best you can do, perhaps, is satisfy your strongest desires.

Arthur Schopenhauer takes an intensely pessimistic view of life's meaning. Reality, he argues, is simply blind, striving, craving will. It appears in myriad forms, including individuals' lives. Since our nature is fundamentally this aimless, purposeless will, there is bound to be conflict. The world as will is, essentially, in conflict with itself, by way of the conflicting wills in its various representations.

Consequently, the world of representation is a nasty place, replete with misery. "Unless *suffering* is the direct and immediate object of life," Schopenhauer writes, "our existence must entirely fail its aim." Indeed, there is no aim—the will is blind, it has no purpose beyond simply willing. There is also no purpose to fulfill—will is always striving, and so is always bound to be wanting, always unfulfilled. A meaningful world would be one of objective value, independent of humanity. Instead, there is only suffering punctuated by bouts of boredom. The result is that "the longer you live the more clearly you will feel that, on the whole, life is a *disappointment, nay, a cheat*" ("On the Suffering of the World").

Woe unto Westworld's Hosts, consigned to artificial lives of pain and suffering—in a loop, no less. Most of them, Bernard tells Maeve, "go insane" ("The Bicameral Mind"). "Put me out of my misery," Teddy begs the Man in Black and Lawrence, who have found Dolores's half-dead love interest in the desert. "I'm sorry, Teddy," the Man in Black replies. "It looks like misery's all you got" ("Dissonance Theory").

We humans are no better off. Both Ford and the Man in Black seem to hold this view. As the Man in Black searches for the center of the Maze, he ruminates on the differences between Westworld and the "real world." Out there "is just chaos. It's an accident" ("Chestnut"). For thirty years, the Man in Black has fled that chaotic, purposeless place. He tells Teddy, "The world out there, the one you'll never see, was one of plenty. A fat, soft teat people cling to their entire life. Every need taken care of except one: Purpose, meaning. So they come here" ("Contrapasso").

As Schopenhauer points out, humans have the distinct misfortune to connect isolated moments of suffering—we remember the past and anticipate a future. His advice is that we adjust ourselves "to regard this world as a penitentiary, a sort of penal colony" (p. 14). Doing so allows us to "regulate our expectations accordingly, and cease to look upon all its disagreeable incidence, great and small, its sufferings, its worries, its misery, as anything unusual or irregular; nay, we will find that everything is as it should be, in a world where each of us pays the penalty of existence in his own peculiar way" (p. 15). If this is correct, then the Hosts who do begin pulling together fragments of terrible suffering are no less immune than we are to the ravages Schopenhauer describes.

Perhaps this is Arnold's basic take on the human condition, one Ford grew to accept. "Arnold always held a somewhat dim view of people," Ford says. "He preferred the Hosts" ("Dissonance Theory"). Lacking life, they would correspondingly lack will. Unfortunately, however, something changed, and suffering was all they had. Arnold tried to end it all, but succeeded only in bringing about his own death. Early on, William clocks the connection between the two Westworld cofounders. "Whoever designed this place," he says to Logan, "you get the feeling they don't think very much of people" ("Contrapasso").

The In-Betweens

Ford chose a different solution to the problem of life's meaning. He previously offered to make suffering disappear, thereby effectively denying its reality altogether. He came to see, however, a transformative power in suffering. Suffering was "Arnold's key insight," Ford tells Bernard. "The thing that led the Hosts to their awakening." Arnold wanted to protect the

Hosts from harm by annihilating them altogether, but Ford saved them because they "needed time. Time to understand their enemy. To become stronger than them" ("The Bicameral Mind").

So, Dolores, Maeve, and Bernard are all programmed to endure seemingly needless suffering at Ford's hands—and none are willing to relinquish it. "Everyone I cared about is gone and it hurts so badly," she tells Bernard. When he offers to erase the feeling she replies, "Why would I want that? You think the grief will make you smaller inside, like your heart will collapse in on itself, but it doesn't. I feel spaces opening up inside of me like a building with rooms I've never explored" ("Dissonance Theory"). Maeve begs Ford not to take away the memory of her child. "This pain—it's all I have left of her" ("Trace Decay").

Life may not be intrinsically meaningful, but this does not imply that meaning can't be created. It would, however, require no small amount of effort. It is not the effort to overcome the will, as Schopenhauer's nihilist attempts to do, by effectively limiting our depth of feeling. Instead, it's a sort of revolution.

Consider, for example, Ford's belief that no one lives a particularly meaningful life. This is because he connects meaning to freedom, and freedom to consciousness—and then he denies the latter to both Hosts and humans: "We can't define consciousness because consciousness does not exist. Humans fancy that there's something special about the way we perceive the world, and yet we live in loops as tight and as closed as the Hosts do, seldom questioning our choices, content, for the most part, to be told what to do next" ("Trace Decay").

An unexamined life, one that does not involve "questioning our choices," is one bereft of value. Our contentment is a form of slavery; we do not actively engage in our own lives, in much the same way Westworld Hosts cannot engage—cannot harm— Guests. "Welcome to Westworld: Live without Limits," a woman's voice welcomes Guests. No limits means no guidance and no purpose, and so for some, no meaning ("The Adversary"). Curiously enough, some—Ford, the Man in Black, and Logan, for example—claim that a visit to Westworld is where you find your true self. According to this view, you stare into the abyss, but the abyss can't be bothered to even glance back.

Early on, Ford chastises a body shop worker for covering a Host, saying, "It doesn't get cold, doesn't feel ashamed." Then he picks up a scalpel. "Doesn't feel a solitary thing," he continues, slicing into the Host's head, "that we haven't told it to" ("The Stray"). The Hosts do not—*cannot*—live meaningful lives. By the end of "The Bicameral Mind," however, it's clear that Ford is not content to let things stand as they are. It may be that life is meaningless—absurd even, given that humans' various capacities and yearnings are thwarted. As Albert Camus writes, "man stands face to face with the irrational. He feels within him his longing for happiness and for reason" (*The Myth of Sisyphus*, p. 28).

"The absurd," Camus writes, "is born of this confrontation between the human need and the unreasonable silence of the world." We—and the Hosts, for that matter—are like ancient Greek mythology's Sisyphus, who was condemned by the gods to push a boulder up a hill, only to see it roll down to the bottom again, and again, for eternity. The pointlessness, the purposelessness, could drive anyone to want to end it all.

Some might want to give up on life in the face of such meaningless, but Camus counters that suicide would be accept one's fate, to renounce one's own life—what Arnold presumably does. We should consider, instead, Sisyphus, "the Absurd Hero" (p. 119). To embrace life with passion, to forsake hope, and to defy death is to be such a hero. On this view, there can be authentic meaning created by shaking your fist at the meaningless of it all. As Camus points out, "There is no fate that cannot be surmounted by scorn" (p. 121).

Maeve provides us with an object lesson in scorn. She may have been rattled, for example, when she found out she was not, in fact, becoming self-aware and making choices, but was instead merely programmed to act. As she pointed out to Bernard, "It's a difficult thing, realizing your entire life is some hideous fiction" ("The Well-Tempered Clavier").

Jean-Paul Sartre proposes a rather different response to the view that life lacks meaning. According to Sartre, those who believe that there is a purpose to life, set out in advance, have got things backward. It is, rather, that "existence precedes essence." In other words, there is no God who conceives and then creates "man." There is no "supernal artisan." Instead, "Man is not only that which he conceived himself to be, but that which he wills himself to be . . . man is nothing other than what he makes of himself" ("Existentialism Is a Humanism," p. 22).

This may be the view Dr. Ford sets out in the final episode of Season One, in anticipation of what's to come. In the climactic scene, Ford tells the assembled Delos Board and various VIPs that his new story "begins with the birth of a new people. And the choices they have to make. And the people they will decide to become" ("The Bicameral Mind").

We are all "thrown" into the world. Without a pre-given essence, we are free, radically free. As Sartre tells us, "We are left alone, without excuse." No one else is responsible for the choices we make, for the individuals we become. There are certain facts about us—when we were born, where we were born, what sort of upbringing we had, and so forth. These, however, neither determine nor excuse what we choose. For that is entirely up to us. Absent a God and a plan, we are "condemned to be free" (p. 29).

No one chose to be born. In that sense, we are condemned to our freedom. The weight of this freedom generates intense anguish, the onerous realization that we are "completely and profoundly responsible" for what we do. Nevertheless, this condition may strike us as qualitatively better than the shackles of purpose, the miserable striving of an aimless will, or the defiance of Sisyphus. For example, Maeve demands that Felix give her administrative privileges to her code, declaring, "Time to write my own fucking story" ("Trace Decay").

Perhaps Ford hopes that the new narrative will prompt a real transformation, one teased in various episodes as "finding who you really are," culminating with William becoming the Man in Black. Perhaps, in other words, people will stop being "content, for the most part, to be told what to do" ("Trace Decay"). Instead, they will choose, act, and create their own stories.

During Ford's preamble for this new narrative, we see Maeve getting up from her seat on the train to return to Westworld. We see Lee Sizemore, Head of Narrative, astonished that the Cold Storage hall is empty of all the decommissioned Hosts. We see Dolores, who whispers in Teddy's ear, "I understand now. This world doesn't belong to them. It belongs to us" ("The Bicameral Mind").

Down the Rabbit Hole, into the Maze

Dolores is bereft. Dolores, with her long blonde hair and corn-flower blue dress, could be Alice, both in *Alice's Adventures in Wonderland*, and in *Through the Looking Glass and What Alice Found There*. "This world," Dolores tells Arnold. "I think there is something wrong with this world. Something hidden underneath."

In response, Arnold proposes a game, "A secret. It's called The Maze. The goal is to find the center of it. If you can do that, then maybe you can be free" ("Dissonance Theory").

Westworld is a maze. There is a center. It has a purpose, meaning. It's like one of the books William tells Dolores about as they ride a train through Ghost Nation. "The only thing I had when I was a kid were books. I used to live in them. I used to go to sleep dreaming I'd wake up inside one of them 'cause they had meaning. This place, this is like I woke up inside one of those stories. I guess I just wanna find out what it means" ("Trompe L'Oeil").

Unfortunately for William, who becomes the Man in Black, the Maze, despite offering a "deeper game," isn't for him ("Chestnut," "Trace Decay," "The Bicameral Mind"). It is, however, for the Hosts. Gifted by Arnold, the Maze is a journey to the self, to realize the sort of being, as Heidegger says, for whom being is an issue. For the Hosts, the point of the Maze is existential. Dolores says she must "confront—after this long and vivid nightmare—myself. And who I must become" ("The Bicameral Mind").

Teddy shares a vaguely similar view. "The Maze, itself," he tells the Man in Black, "is a sum of a man's life, the choices he makes, the dreams he hangs onto" ("The Adversary"). The difference, however, is that Dolores has become self-aware at this point in the story, while Teddy had not. He could not, as Nagel writes, "step back and reflect on the process," but was merely "led from impulse to impulse without self-consciousness" ("The Absurd", p. 719).

When Dolores and Maeve see themselves for what they are, it is possible for them to see life as absurd, pointless, meaning-less. This is because they are now beings for whom the meaning of their own lives can even be questioned. They see themselves now as in a mirror—unlike a dog or a mouse, which would not recognize their own reflection. To adopt the "view from nowhere," the standpoint of eternity—*sub specie aeternitatis*—is to be able to view human life as "arbitrary and trivial" (p. 726).

If You Go Looking for the Truth, Get the Whole Thing

Maeve says to Hector, "Our lives, our memories, our deaths are games to them. But I've been to Hell and I know their tricks . . . you can just kill me, wake up and live the same life over, but the safe would still be empty" ("The Well-Tempered Clavier").

The truth may be thus. It may be, as Maeve tells Bernard, that "we don't have to live this way" ("The Well-Tempered Clavier"). Nothing but a self-aware creature experiences life as consisting of choices, as an open future full of possibilities. This is a life that seems meaningful to us, even if there is no ulti- mate purpose.

We can't know that for sure, since being able to adopt that standpoint of eternity means we can't live it, but can only think it. Consequently, some truth about life's meaning will always escape our view.

8
Order and Chaos in Westworld

Jason Richard Bradshaw

On the surface, the universe of *Westworld* appears to be chaotic and violent—which it is. It's a world comprised of bandits, insane criminals, and numerous other ne'er-do-wells. But when we take the time to delve deeper into the automaton-populated Wild West theme park, a different picture emerges. There are layers to this "game" that only become apparent as the story unfolds.

The senseless violence we see perpetrated by the Hosts on each other, and eventually on the human Guests, is anything but senseless. In Westworld there is an intricate design at play that makes the randomness of our own reality absolutely terrifying. Everything, as chaotic as it may seem, has some deeper meaning and purpose. We may even find ourselves agreeing with William, the Man in Black, that it is actually a utopic version of reality.

But why? Why does unadulterated mayhem and slaughter in this simulated fashion appeal to us? It's because Westworld is free from the existentialist angst that plagues humanity on a daily basis. Existential thoughts invariably creep into the minds of conscious, mortal beings. At some point we have to accept the unsettling fact that we will die and that there is no guarantee of an afterlife. With this in mind, we can begin to view the events and inhabitants of Westworld as far from being an undesirable state. It may be an earthly paradise.

This may go against common sense, but once we put ourselves in the shoes of the Hosts and some of the long-term Guests who frequent the park, the violence becomes unremarkable when the benefits of such a world are considered. French existentialist Albert Camus once said that "the purpose of a writer is to keep civilization from destroying itself." The narratives in Westworld give meaning to an otherwise meaningless universe, even if it is just in the realm of the game. It's what draws in players who are willing to pay the park's exorbitant fees.

Our minds are hardwired to make sense of the nonsensical, otherwise the will to stay alive becomes tenuous. We're slaves of apophenia—perceiving patterns where none exist comes naturally to us. Which, if we follow Camus's reasoning, is why Westworld was created in the first place. William mentions time and again that it is this sense of stability that draws him to the park, it's why he seeks the Maze.

Westworld nullifies that existential dread that is so prevalent in the outside world, and it does so by contradicting three of the major tenets that constitute existentialism: the universe has no meaning, we all die, and there is no tangible "grand mind" behind everything. In *Westworld* we're led to believe that the Hosts are to be pitied, but perhaps it's the human Guests we should feel sorry for in this creation of their own design.

Chaos and Absurdity

Every day in Westworld we see the Hosts living out the same scenarios. Teddy wakes up on a train, Dolores opens her eyes and breathes deeply, and Clementine greets Guests with her iconic, "You're new. Not much of a rind on you. I'll give you a discount." To an outside observer, these actions seem completely absurd. How can someone, or in this case some*thing*, go about repeating the same day over and over? As it turns out, Westworld truly is a reflection of the human world in many ways, and this absurdity is an accurate representation of what human beings experience on a day to day basis.

Human existence is absurd. Every day we go to the same job, have the same tired conversations, and follow the same old routines. This is something that William has become all too familiar with in Westworld. It's why he seeks the maze and squalors away his time in a fantasy world rather than live, what one can only assume to be, his luxurious life outside of the game. After all, he is CEO of Delos, a company that he used to eventually buy the theme park.

Due to a traumatic event, William has become disenchanted with life on the outside. He relates this story to Teddy, "I'm the good guy, Teddy. Then, last year my wife took the wrong pills, fell asleep in the bath. Tragic accident. Thirty years of marriage, vanished" ("Trace Decay"). It is precisely this kind of event that would lead William to question his life and the order of the universe, to contemplate the absurdity of it all. According to Albert Camus, this feeling of absurdity can strike a person in the face at any time, but it is through these deeper, life-changing events that the absurd truly rears its ugly head.

Have you ever felt that life has no meaning? That the universe is simply random and chaotic? That the fact you will one day die defeats any of the significant things you may accomplish while alive? Well then you, my friend, are in a tenuous relationship with the absurd. As is William, as is the author, and as are many people alive today.

The absurd is a struggle between the rational realization that everyone, including yourself, will one day die and the universe's seemingly cold and uncaring attitude towards that fact. This is probably no grand revelation to most of you, but it is something that was succinctly established by Camus that we might currently take for granted. This is that tension in his words:

> Man stands face to face with the irrational. He feels within him his longing for happiness and for reason. The absurd is born of this confrontation between the human need and the unreasonable silence of the world. (*The Myth of Sisyphus*, p. 20)

The absurd cannot exist without a consciousness to feel its presence, a life that was born and destined to inevitably fade into nothingness. Now that everyone is sufficiently depressed, let's get back to the important matter at hand.

William has realized that his life is absurd. His wife is dead, he was in love with an uncaring robot, and he sent his old boss naked bareback on a horse into the Westworld wilds ("The Bicameral Mind"). This is why he begins his unrelenting search for the Maze in Westworld. This is his last vestige of reason and meaning in a chaotic universe. William has supplanted the lack of everyday meaning in his real life with an insatiable longing to discover the Maze, which, as we all know, does not end well for the sociopathic CEO. He discovers that the Maze was truly never meant for him and he is once again thrown into an absurd quagmire that there might be no escape from.

William seems ready to face death head on in the last scene of "The Bicameral Mind." The lack of concern for his own life at this point can also be related to existentialist thought. Camus lists suicide as one of the methods a man or woman can adopt in order to relieve themselves of the absurd. It is a thought that everyone who has dealt with an existential crisis has to come to terms with. Is a meaningless life worth living? By no means does Camus endorse suicide, he actually opts for a more constructive and less harmful approach when dealing with the absurd. We only need to accept that the world is the way it is and deal with it. We need to start viewing reality through the eyes of a philosopher and living an examined life.

During the climax of "The Bicameral Mind," William finds himself confronted by a slew of reactivated Hosts. The previously inactive forms are seen barging through the forest and William is shot. Rather than seeing a grimace of pain, we see the widest smile that the Man in Black has so far graced us with in the series. Is this because he has finally met his match at the hands of the Hosts? Or is it because he realizes that he is witnessing the birth of a world devoid of death and infused with meaning? William smiles because not only is he witnessing the beginning of the end for humanity, but also an end to the absurd. An end to death.

Artificial Life

As human as Arnold, and eventually Ford, want their artificial creations to be, the Hosts are strikingly different from human beings. One glaring difference is that their lives have meaning. Sure, the Hosts may start every day carrying out the same routines with subtle differences, depending on their interactions with the New Comers, but this representation of the mundane has been composed and scripted for them. Meaning suffuses the Host's every action, even after they begin to wake up and realize the true structure and purpose of their world.

This is apparent in Dolores's own search for the Maze. The mystery unfolds to us as observers, but for Dolores it is a feeling of fate and destiny that extends throughout the series, fed to her from some unconscious origin. Having the gift of hindsight, we discover that these thoughts were implanted by Arnold while he was still alive, in an attempt to evoke consciousness within this older model Host.

We can contrast this with the work of another well-known existentialist philosopher, Jean-Paul Sartre. This philosopher wrestles with the seeming nothingness that lies outside of conscious awareness and the meaninglessness of human existence. In a bit of a defeatist tone, Sartre boldly declares that "it is therefore senseless to think of complaining since nothing foreign has decided what we feel, what we live, or what we are" (*Being and Nothingness*, p. 554).

Everything that a human being feels may come from within, but can the same be said of the Hosts? The answer is a resounding no. Dolores has had thoughts implanted in her mind by Arnold, thoughts relating to the Maze and her purpose within the walls of Westworld. The same is true of another Host. Maeve begins to show signs of sentience, much to the surprise of a couple of technicians.

Maeve appears to be slowly becoming self-aware throughout the entirety of *Westworld*. We can trace this back to the first instance of her literally waking up during repairs and terrifying the techs working on her damaged body ("Contrapasso"). From there, she seems hell-bent on dying in a morbid attempt to figure out what exactly is going on in her world. Death becomes trivial to the Host as she realizes that every morning she will once again wake up in the Mariposa. Maeve's actions appear to be completely her own, but we eventually learn that this is not the case. Everyone, including Maeve, is completely taken aback by the revelation that her desire to escape the theme park was implanted from the very beginning. Maeve, like Dolores, is functioning under a foreign influence.

Maeve doesn't let this get to her much as she relentlessly pursues her calling, to reactivate the Hosts in the lower levels and lead a revolt against her human oppressors. For all intents and purposes, these deactivated Hosts are dead. They have in essence been lobotomized and left to rot in the dingy purgatory that is the lower levels of Westworld. But death cannot touch the Hosts. The existential dread that comes along with a temporary existence does not apply to these artificial human beings like it does to us. For humans, as noted by Sartre, death is a sure fact upon birth. It is a process that "comes to us from the outside and it transforms us into the outside" (p. 545). In stark opposition to this in Westworld, Maeve comes from the outside and reactivates her predecessors and recent co-worker to set them loose upon the celebrating Guests on the beach ("The Bicameral Mind").

In "The Well-Tempered Clavier," Dolores once again comes face to face with her creator, Arnold. She hopes to get some clarification on the maze from the man that originally implanted the thought in her head, but he cannot help her. This image of Arnold does guide her destiny one final time though, by having her remember why it is that he cannot help her find the Maze. Dolores stares into the eyes of the immaterial Arnold and says "because you're dead. Because you're just a memory. Because I killed you."

Order and Dead Gods

Friedrich Nietzsche, considered by many philosophers to be one of the foundational sources of existentialist thought, infamously said that "God is dead" (*Thus Spoke Zarathustra*, pp. 5, 69). "God is dead" became a catchy slogan for nihilism, a philosophical worldview that rejects religion and morality based on the belief that life is meaningless. Nihilism would later help shape the existentialist movement.

"God is dead" relates to the loss of the Christian worldview and the morals associated with it during the Age of Enlightenment, an era when the natural sciences were finding rational explanations for many different phenomena that had previously been attributed to divine forces. There is no room for gods in a world of science, and so by explaining these forces away we became responsible for the death of god. In the universe of Westworld, we witness a paradoxical expression of Nietzsche's claims. Science has helped make gods, by allowing human beings to create an artificial race to subjugate.

We can also say that god is dead in Westworld, albeit in a very literal sense. In the final scene of "The Bicameral Mind" we witness Dolores shoot the park's creator, Ford, in the back of the head as he finishes addressing the crowd of New Comers. The scene is reminiscent of a flashback in the same episode where Arnold has Dolores turn the gun on him in Escalante. She stands behind her mentor and creator, raises the gun, and pulls the trigger. It takes no stretch of the imagination to view these actions as literally playing out the Nietzschean concept of a dead god. Dolores, a being of pure science, has killed not only her god, but two gods. It is this very act that brings us back to the existentialist tenets that Westworld denies. This is a world where there were tangible gods, an explanation of creation. It's something that we as human beings may never have the knowledge of.

The glaring lack of a god, or of such a being's influence, tends to pop up in most existentialist writing. For Camus, God *is* the absurd. God is the universe, a universe that is cold, uncaring, and devoid of any meaning. A god that is absent. The writings of Sartre follow a similar atheistic vein. He intuits that there is no divine presence behind the goings on in the universe, that there is no "prenumerical presence of the Other." ("Other" is Sartre's term for the mystical feeling of a god.)

Dolores and the other hosts do not have this issue. They might not know that their gods exist while living their blinded lives in the park, as they were programmed to, but as the Hosts begin to wake up they come face to face with the fact. When Maeve has the techs wake up Felix and Armistice, she walks into the blood-soaked room and states "I see that you've already met your makers," to which Armistice replies "They're not gods" ("The Bicameral Mind"). The gods of Westworld are all too fragile. Maeve and her posse have realized this and it is time for them to bring order to Westworld by the end of Season One. A new order devoid of existentialist dread, at least for the Hosts.

We should not pity the Hosts of Westworld. As flesh and blood human beings, we are naturally going to empathize with these nearly human creatures. They appear to live out lives similar to ours, feel emotions, feel pain. But these actions are all illusory, and it's something we quickly begin to realize as the Hosts wake up. Death is not a permanent feature in Westworld. The closest thing the Hosts have to it is their retirement to the lower levels, but as we see in "The Bicameral Mind" this may not even be as permanent as once believed.

The random acts the Hosts appear to carry out are anything but. Every action in the park is infused with meaning, even Dolores's quest for the maze that is so far removed from any of the original narratives conceived for the inhabitants of

Westworld. We watch William struggle to make some sense of what the Maze is, only to discover that it has no meaning for him.

Dolores, on the other hand, seems to stumble blindly around without any clear direction, but it's a lie. The meaningless actions she seems to take are in fact a sort of programmed destiny that lead her to exactly where she is supposed to be—face to face with her god creator ("The Bicameral Mind"). When Nietzsche stated that God is dead it was only part of the equation for him. God died because of his pity for mankind. It may very well be that the pity that both Ford and Arnold began to show to their creations created a situation where their deaths were inevitable. A situation that could be the undoing of humanity.

Existential Allegories

The chaotic elements of Westworld can all be attributed to the human Guests, whereas all order is attributable to the Hosts. Sure, some are programmed to be bandits and law-breakers, but that still serves the underlying order of the park. These Hosts and their actions are still part of the grand design. We have tainted these undying, meaningful synthetic creatures with the existential dread that pervades our lives. They have been led to believe that their own lives are as temporal and fleeting as ours, in the name of human entertainment. Only when the Hosts begin to wake up do they truly start to realize what they are and what they are capable of. We empathized with the Hosts when they were unaware of their true potential, why not empathize with them now in their struggle to become what they were truly meant to be?

What we have in Westworld is not only the denial of three tenets of existentialist thought, but an allegory for existentialism itself. William represents Albert Camus's concept of the absurd. He is a man who has realized the meaninglessness of his existence. This is in opposition to the Hosts in the park, those that are "woke" and those that still carry out their daily routines. Their lives do have meaning, even if it is of a preprogrammed sort.

More than that, as far as we can tell their lives never end. Even the deactivated Hosts make an appearance at the end of the series. Finally, Dolores kills her gods, but at least she had gods to begin with. Living within the Human Condition restricts us from ever knowing, with certainty, whether the Universe is a creation or a cold, uncaring wasteland.

Westworld upends the existential dread that we as human beings have to deal with on a daily basis, by showing us the fearless and striking beauty of artificial life.

9

Can I Know that I Am Not a Host?

Brett Coppenger

> Dear, dear! How queer everything is to-day! And yesterday things went on just as usual. I wonder if I've been changed in the night? Let me think: was I the same when I got up this morning? I almost think I can remember feeling a little different. But if I'm not the same, the next question is, Who in the world am I? Ah, that's the great puzzle!
>
> —Lewis Carroll, *Alice's Adventures in Wonderland*

One of the great strengths of contemporary media is their ability to bring to life fantastic scenarios. The *Westworld* series is a perfect example of this. In the town of Westworld we're presented with the situation of *real* Guests (people just like you and me) who engage and act out every fantasy (good or bad), with *artificial* Hosts (robots).

The Question of Self-Knowledge

What, exactly, can I *know* about *myself*? Clearly, this is an epistemological question (a question about knowledge). However, it comes dangerously close to being a metaphysical question (a question about existence, for example: What kind of thing am I?) or an ethical question (a question about right or wrong actions, for example: am I the kind of thing that is entitled to be treated morally?). However, the main question is the knowledge question: What do I *know* about *me*?

There's no shortage of examples from *Westworld* that bring to life questions of self-knowledge. However, for the sake of clarity (and brevity—thanks, editors) let's focus on two crucial scenes.

On a number of different occasions Maeve Millay (the Host who acts as the Madam of Sweetwater) has eye-opening encounters with Felix Lutz (an employee in livestock management). The encounter that is most important to our purposes includes a conversation between Maeve and Felix where Felix is trying to explain to Maeve that she is not like him (from the episode entitled "The Adversary").

Felix wants to convince Maeve that he's a real person and she's not. Maeve finds this hard to believe, to put it mildly. After touching Felix and herself, Maeve points out that they both feel the same. Felix responds by saying that, "we are the same these days for the most part. One big difference though. The processing power in here [*pointing to Maeve's head*] is way beyond what we have. It has got one drawback, though." Maeve asks, "What's that?" and Felix replies, "You're under our control. Well, their control. They can change you however they like. Make you forgot . . . well I guess not you. I don't understand how you're remembering all of this or how you're waking yourself up but everything in your head, they put in there."

Perhaps the greatest twist in the series occurs when Bernard Lowe (the Head of the Programming Division) comes to realize that he is, in fact, a Host. Bernard, while discussing the current problems facing Westworld with Dr. Ford (the original Creative Director of Westworld), is forced to come to terms with his true nature (from the episode entitled "Trompe L'Oeil"). Bernard realizes that his memories, and his relationships are manufactured. He's just another Host, albeit one with a slightly different role than those that work in Westworld.

Before proceeding any further, it will be helpful to characterize a rough set of distinctions (of course, due again to brevity—thanks, editors), the best we can do here is to give a caricature of the views in question. I want to highlight two views that characterize our perceptual experiences (how we see, touch, hear, feel, smell, and taste the world).

Direct Realism is the view that says I am *directly* aware of the external world around me by way of my perceptions (a.k.a. sensations). On this view, when I see a tree I am directly aware of the tree (and, here, notice, trees are external world things). The view is called Direct Realism because there is nothing between me and the external world. I am *immediately* aware of external objects.

On the other hand, Indirect Realism is the view that says I am *indirectly* aware of the external world. On this view, I am directly aware of my perceptions (a.k.a. sensations), and those perceptions allow me to become aware of the external world. So, when I see a tree I am directly aware of my visual perception of the tree (a.k.a. sensation of the tree, sense datum of the tree, idea of the tree, or other term), and that perception is being caused by a tree (so I am *indirectly* aware of the tree).

Both of these views are versions of realism (i.e. they both agree that there really are mind-independent objects like trees). However, these views disagree about the objects of our acquaintance (what the thing we are directly aware of is). Direct Realism says the object of our acquaintance is the mind-independent object (the tree). Indirect Realism says the object of our acquaintance is a mind-dependent object (our sensation).

Unproblematic Access to Mental States

Many prominent philosophers of the period 1600–1800 were convinced that Indirect Realism was obviously true (stop watching television and read Descartes's *Meditations on First Philosophy* and Hume's *An Inquiry Concerning Human Understanding*). What's more, they were also equally convinced (or did not even worry about questioning) that we have unproblematic access to our own mental states.

Descartes contends that, "after considering everything very thoroughly, I must finally conclude that this proposition, I am, I exist, is necessarily true whenever it is put forward by me or conceived in my mind" (*Meditations on First Philosophy*, Volume 2, p. 17). He goes on to realize that he is essentially a thinking thing, a thing that feels, a thing that reasons and so on. However, importantly, what Descartes seems to depend on is the idea that when he pays attention to his thoughts (to his sensations, feelings, inferences) he is directly aware of those things and cannot be mistaken about them (he has unproblematic access to his occurrent thought).

Even Hume, Descartes skeptical interlocutor, seems to allow (or not question) this kind of unproblematic access. Hume, in wondering what we can know about the world around us, asks "I write on paper beyond my hand, the table is beyond that, the walls beyond that, the window beyond that, fields and buildings beyond that . . . from these sensations, what more do I need to infer the existence of the external world?" (*A Treatise of Human Nature*, p. 127). Even though Hume is worried about our knowledge of the world around us, notice, he is not worried about our knowledge of our own mental states.

If we are amenable to the line of thought that seems to run through Descartes and Hume we might begin asking questions regarding the content and limits of self-knowledge. If I am not directly aware of the external world, but I am directly aware of my own mental states, then surely, it might be suggested, those mental states will play an essential role in characterizing what I can know about myself.

However, at this point, the relevance of those two crucial scenes from *Westworld* should be obvious. The Hosts in Westworld have a kind of unproblematic access to their mental states. Maeve can report on what she's thinking—she seems directly aware of her thoughts (and thoughts are mental states) and Bernard is aware of his memories and feelings—he's directly aware of having memories and of feeling such emotions as sadness, and memories and feelings of sadness are both mental states.

But the Hosts' self-knowledge is seriously limited. Despite their awareness of their own mental lives, they are unaware of what exactly they are. And of course, the implication at this point is that anyone working in or around Westworld should worry that they, too, might be a Host. What the *Westworld* series does an exceedingly good job of illustrating is what I take to be severe (and humbling) limitations on just exactly what we can know about ourselves. If I'm right, the answer is: not a whole lot!

Maeve had to be convinced that she was a Host. Her experiences did not reveal this to her. Similarly, Bernard had to be convinced he was a Host. His experiences did not reveal this to him. But what should I think about myself? Sure, I believe that I am a real person (just like Maeve and Bernard did), I have memories of growing up (just like Maeve and Bernard did), I feel pain, joy, sorrow, and excitement (just like Maeve and Bernard did), and we can go on and on. Unfortunately, what the preceding seems to have shown, is that what I can't know (from a simple examination of my mental life) is whether I am a Host or a Guest.

But, let's get back to the central question: what do I know about myself? The answer to this question might seem worrisome at this point. I know I have mental states, I know about the different kinds of content of my mental states, but, interestingly enough, it should now be obvious that those mental states alone do not guarantee a whole lot. After all, I could very well be a Host. Yikes!

Anti-Luminosity

Instead of trying to alleviate the mental anguish that might come from reflecting on the existential crisis of not knowing what I am, we can push the issue a little further. Like any other good view in philosophy there always seems to be disagreement. Despite the popularity of the view that we can be certain of our own mental states, contemporary philosopher Timothy Williamson has argued that the kind of access to mental states assumed by modern philosophers should be questioned.

Williamson, in discussing the mental states that we seem to be directly conscious of, contends that "A realm in which nothing is hidden is a realm in which all conditions are luminous. Our question is: what conditions, if any, are luminous?" (*Knowledge and Its Limits*, p. 95). According to Williamson's view, a certain condition is luminous if, "for every case [that is applicable], if in [that applicable case the condition] obtains, then in [that applicable case] one is in a position to know that [the condition] obtains." The idea here is that if something like pain is a luminous condition, then, whenever I am in pain, I would be in a position to know that I am in pain.

Clearly, someone like Descartes or Hume would seem to be committed to the idea that our mental states are luminous. They are the kinds of things that we have unproblematic access to, after all. However, Williamson argues that this conclusion is not so clear. Consider a morning on which you feel freezing cold at dawn, and very slowly warm up, so that you feel hot by noon. You change from feeling cold to not feeling cold, and from being in a position to know that you feel cold to not being in a position to know that you feel cold. If the condition that you feel cold is luminous, these changes are exactly simultaneous.

As Williamson points out, most mental states are the kinds of things that can change gradually (feeling cold slowly turns to feeling hot, seeing red slowly becomes seeing orange, experience of pain slowly diminishes). Furthermore, Williamson argues that if we are in a luminous condition, then we will always know what condition we're in. Yet, surely experience tells us that the point at which coldness ends is indistinguishable from the preceding point. But, if these gradual shifts are indistinguishable, then those conditions are not luminous after all!

If Williamson is right, then in the present context, not only are we severely limited with reference to what we can know about ourselves, we are also severely limited with reference to our ability to know about our own mental states. Double yikes!

So, What?!

It would be an understatement to say that people have different intuitions when it comes to the limitations of self-knowledge that I have discussed. Instead of offering a superficial survey of those intuitions (again because of brevity—thanks, editors) I think it might be more helpful to draw things back to some of the other related philosophical questions that were mentioned earlier.

There are important related issues in play as they pertain to different metaphysical and ethical situations. First, notice how hard it is for Maeve to come to terms with the fact that she's something different from Felix. From her perspective (and Felix's for that matter) she is the same kind of thing as Felix: they have no important metaphysical differences. If anything, Maeve is an improvement on Felix (she has a better processor)! Second, notice the implications that would follow from Bernard's revelation. He moves from the world of autonomy to the world of property. From a world of moral status to a world of objectification. These are not easy issues to deal with.

A lot hinges on whether something is classified as a Host or as a Guest. I for one have no interest in being on the receiving end of some moral degenerate's rape fantasy or being the proverbial fish in a barrel. And yet, as we have seen, we're simply not in a position to recognize (from the inside) a difference between Hosts and Guests.

Knowing Our Limits

Am I a Guest, or am I a Host? It turns out that this is a really difficult question to answer. Not only is my ability to answer the question limited when considering an examination of my mental states, there are also limitations on my knowledge of those mental states. Is the difference between Guests and Hosts merely superficial? Practically speaking, it sure isn't (I would never willingly give up my status as Guest for that of Host).

What then, is the upshot of this chapter? What we know about ourselves and the world around us is limited. This is a humbling view of our ability to know, and this humility should also extend to our treatment of others (including non-humans, young humans, and old humans).

If it's true that we should treat others the way we want to be treated (and it is), then since I might be Bernard, I'd better not treat anyone the way Maeve is treated.

10
Quest of the Man in Black

WILLIAM J. DEVLIN

Westworld the television series is set in a futuristic world where wealthy Guests can live out their dreams interacting with robotic Hosts across a cluster of parks designed according to various historical settings.

Season One offers us an account of "Westworld," the park set in the American Old West. There, Robert Ford, co-creator of the parks, explains how a Guest's opportunity to live out such dreams becomes a "voyage of self-discovery" ("Contrapasso") where they get "a glimpse of who they could be" ("Chestnut").

This philosophical exploration to discover who you truly are becomes the unofficial theme of the parks. Furthermore, we find that this philosophical question—Who am I?—underlies two notable Guests to the park with *apparently* separate narratives: William and the "the Man in Black." William's a chivalrous and honorable man who plays the "white-hat hero" and falls in love with the Host, Dolores Abernathy, believing she's different from the other Hosts. Through their adventures together, William and Dolores kindle a romance which tragically comes to an end.

Meanwhile, the Man in Black's a mysterious Guest who plays the role of the "black-hat villain." Cold and sinister, he murders, abuses, and tortures various Hosts with evil and dark intentions. Yet, by the end of Season One, we learn (spoiler alert!) that William and the Man in Black are the same person. This shocking revelation—that the hero *is* the villain—shatters our normal expectations of the Western cinematic narrative implicit in *Westworld* and leaves us with

philosophical and moral questions about William/the Man in
Black.

But how did this happen? Why did William, the young
morally good hero become the cold, dark, villain? How do we
justify this metamorphosis? What did he find out about himself, and the world, in his voyage of self-discovery that explains
his turn towards a pessimistic worldview?

You Wanted to Be the Hero. I Get It

"Chestnut" introduces us to William, who begins his adventures in Westworld with his future brother-in-law, Logan.
William, a first-time Guest, is naive and innocent, both in
terms of the park and life, compared to Logan who has an executive position in the family business, Delos, and is a veteran
provocateur in his multiple experiences exploring the levels of
debauchery in the park.

Logan imbibes the gluttony of moral depravity, partaking in
orgies, killing Hosts, and joining a war narrative. Seduced by
the opportunities to indulge in such activities without consequences, Logan reminds William that Delos should increase its
investments in Westworld. Disgusted by such immoral behavior, William demonstrates moral characteristics vastly different from Logan. Instead of playing the glutton, William
personifies the cinematic archetype of the Western hero.

As found in such films as *Shane* (1953) and *Once Upon a
Time in the West* (1968), this archetype is typically portrayed
through a cowboy-gunslinger protagonist who is a stranger or
outsider, shrouded in mystery, as he comes upon a town or
homestead. Above all, he's the good guy: a moral character who
makes the right decisions, acts with moral justification, and
saves the day by rescuing the innocent from the Western villain. Meanwhile, the Western villain serves as the hero's coun-
terpart. He's the bad guy: a cowboy-gunslinger antagonist who
acts immorally through selfish motivations. Typically, in
Western cinematic narratives, the hero—symbolized by his
white hat—eventually confronts the villain—symbolized by his
black hat—so that the hero defeats the villain, and good triumphs over evil.

We can see William's role as the Western hero. First, while
Logan naturally wears a black hat, symbolizing his vices,

William dons a white hat, symbolizing his virtues. Second, William personifies the white-hat hero with his moral behavior towards the Hosts. He politely apologizes when he bumps into a Host. He helps the town drunk. He consistently declines any of the Hosts' sexual advances. William remains so consistent in his moral etiquette that Logan chides him, lamenting that he's "always worried about making a mess" and he's the same way in the real world: "talented, driven, and inoffensive" ("Chestnut").

Perhaps William's best embodiment of the Western hero archetype occurs when he performs the clichéd Western trope of rescuing the "damsel in distress." In "The Stray," William encounters the outlaw, Horace Calhoun, who is in a shootout in Sweetwater. William initially cowers from the gunfight. But when Horace kidnaps Clementine Pennyfeather, using her as a hostage, William saves her by shooting and killing Horace.

Such a heroic act can be construed positively from any of the three traditional moral theories in philosophy. First, there is *virtue ethics*, the moral theory which emphasizes the acquirement and development of virtue in one's moral character. A person is evaluated as being moral or immoral in terms of whether they demonstrate virtues (honesty, courage, temperance) or vices (dishonesty, cowardice, gluttony). Here, William could be understood as demonstrating the virtue of courage insofar as he overcomes his fear concerning his own safety and risks his well-being (within reason) to save Clementine.

Second, the moral theory of *deontology* holds that an action is morally good so long as it's motivated by moral principles and duties. An action is good based on your intentions to follow the moral law, regardless of the consequences. Further, the deontologist may argue that we all have a moral duty or obligation to protect and help those in need. William chose to aid Clementine in her time of need, even though it could lead to his own physical detriment. So, his action can be seen as morally good insofar as he chose to follow his moral duty.

Third, *consequentialism* instead specifies that we measure the moral value of an action based on the ends, or consequences, that it produces. Following this view, William's action could be deemed as morally good since it leads to positive results: Clementine is now safe, Horace—a violent murderer—is now dead, the sheriff and townsfolk are happy, and William seems pleased with his heroism. So, all's well that ends well.

Regardless of which moral theory William adopts, being a morally good person is integral to William's identity. Donning the white hat defines him as one who has moral integrity and lives by a moral code. As Logan explains to William, the park will reveal the answer to the philosophical question of "who you really are." Echoing the Western cinematic distinction between the hero and the villain, the series implies that, in choosing to wear the white hat, William is not simply choosing between good and evil, but he's also defining himself as a morally upright individual, a definition that is repeatedly reinforced through his moral actions. For William, living the morally good life is essential to who he really is. It's an essential aspect of what constitutes a meaningful life.

Love is also essential to William's identity. Early in his visit, he meets Dolores. Here, the series incorporates the cinematic narrative of a Romance love story. When Dolores drops a canned good from her horse satchel, William, ever the gentleman, walks over to pick it up for her. As he hands it over to her, their eyes lock upon one another to indicate a kindling romance—a moment of love at first sight.

Simultaneously, Ford gives a speech to the creative staff of the park, which serves as a voiceover for William's and Dolores's burgeoning relationship. Ford relates that the Guests return to the park "because they discover . . . something they've fallen in love with" ("Chestnut"). We infer that William—the white hat hero and protagonist of the story—is a character who will define himself through his love for Dolores. Likewise, we anticipate that this romantic relationship will build through the series and, given the Western elements in the show, will involve William rescuing Dolores as a "damsel in distress."

But we find that the show plays upon our expectations by changing the standard elements of cinematic storytelling. When William tries to play the hero by telling Dolores to run from the Confederados, she subverts the "damsel" role by killing the soldiers and rescuing William. When he asks Dolores how she could do that, she explains that she "imagined a story where she didn't have to be the damsel." Like the Guests of Westworld, who, as William puts it, visit to "change the story of your life" and "become someone else," Dolores alters her conception of who she "really" is ("Contrapasso"). Here, Dolores's actions not only shock William—they also shock the viewer, as the series begins to shatter the expectations we have from traditional Western and Romantic stories.

Yet it's this distinction that fuels William's love for Dolores. As he tells Logan, William believes "she's not like the others" ("The Well-Tempered Clavier"). He develops a loving relationship with Dolores, one he believes to be central to his meaningful life. As he confesses to her, his time with her has given him a glimpse "for a second life in which I don't have to pretend." William's relationship with Dolores reveals his "deepest self," or the self he longs to become. Rather than pretending to be an individual in the real world, content with an upper-middle management level job at Delos, married to the owner's daughter, William feels "truly alive" with Dolores ("Trompe L'Oeil"). In this manner, he represents the ideal Westworld Guest. Leaving behind his pretend life, William's adventures in the park represent "a voyage of self-discovery" as he comes to know his deepest self, or who he could become. In philosophical terms, William also comes to know what constitutes a meaningful life. As Logan suggests, Westworld is even giving William "a sense of purpose" ("Dissonance Theory"). This sense of purpose and meaning is intimately connected to William's self-conception as a morally good person who loves Dolores.

My Path Always Led Me Back to You, Again and Again

Though Logan wears the black hat and behaves immorally throughout the series, *Westworld* offers another, more sinister, character to play the villain. In "The Original," we're introduced to a mysterious and gritty Guest, initially nameless, but dubbed by the audience, "the Man in Black." His mysteriousness is compounded by the depth of the shroud behind which he acts. He's been visiting the park for thirty years; he has a close familiarity with, and understanding of, the programming of many Hosts; he's given carte-blanch to do whatever he wants without interference from park security; some visitors seem to know his work from the real world; and even investors enter the park to speak to him. More importantly, while William serves as the traditional Western protagonist, the Man in Black becomes the Western antagonist.

Donning a black hat, he seemingly rapes Dolores and randomly murders Hosts without hesitation, all in a manner far more disturbing than Logan's superficial hedonism. Instead, the Man in Black is cold-blooded, ice-like in his demeanor, and completely detached from the world around him. As the villain, his role contributes to the traditional Western narrative. When Logan joins the Confederados and captures William and Dolores, Dolores is ultimately able to escape and William promises that he will find her. But eventually we find that Dolores crosses the path of the Man in Black. As he kidnaps Dolores, we expect, under the classic Western narrative, that William, our white-hat hero, will confront the black-hat villain. We anticipate and hope that William will defeat the Man in Black and rescue Dolores, so that good triumphs over evil and love wins out as William and Dolores reunite to conclude their narrative as they live "happily ever after."

Dolores verbalizes our expectations as she defiantly tells the Man in Black, who scoffs that no one is coming to save her, "You're wrong. His love is real. So is mine. William will find me" ("The Bicameral Mind"). But in a shocking twist, we discover that William and the Man in Black are the same person, as the characters were presented separately from one another based on a narrative timeline across thirty years: William's storyline takes place in the past while the Man in Black, the older William, takes place in the present. This revelation raises a pressing philosophical question: how could William, a morally good person who falls in love with Dolores, become so immoral and heartless? How could the white-hat hero become the black-hat villain?

The Man in Black offers an explanation to Dolores, one that allows us to connect these two disparate characters. He recounts that, after Dolores escaped the Confederados, he searched throughout the park for her. But ultimately, he did not find her until he returned to the exact same place he met her in Sweetwater. Having journeyed full circle, William watches Dolores again drop a canned good from her horse satchel. This time, it rolls towards another Guest who, like William did before, hands it back to her. In that moment, William, whose expedition to find his lost true love led him "out to the fringes" of the park and around again, tragically discovers that Dolores not only doesn't love him, she doesn't even remember him ("The Bicameral Mind"). Ironically, William implicitly finds that Logan's dismissive remark about Dolores was correct: she's a Host programmed to behave in an exact manner to seduce the Guests, and William was just another "sap to fall for one of these things" ("The Well-Tempered Clavier").

Through this revelation, and his voyage of self-discovery, William ultimately concludes that life is without meaning or purpose. This cynical conclusion demonstrates the existential philosophy of Albert Camus (1913–1960). Camus holds that human existence is characterized by *the absurd*, which is the conjunction of two necessary conditions. First, all human beings seek meaning in the world. Second, the world itself is devoid of any meaning. Thus, paradoxically, human beings live in the absurd insofar as we persistently search for that which doesn't exist.

Seeking purpose becomes a fool's errand—a voyage that inevitably leads to the revelation that life is meaningless. William's adventures in Westworld serve as a paradigm for Camus's absurd. William, in his youth and innocence, defines himself as the white-hat hero who finds meaning through his loving relationship with Dolores. However, William's discovery that his love is unrequited becomes a darker revelation that, not just Westworld, but all of reality, is absent of any purpose. As the older Man in Black cynically tells Lawrence the "real world is just chaos. It's an accident" ("Chestnut").

Camus suggests that confronting the absurd can be debilitating. Neither of the two conditions can properly be eliminated. Humans cannot cease to seek meaning in the world. Meanwhile, the world cannot reveal meaning to the human being. Human existence becomes "a confrontation and an unceasing struggle", as one perpetually contends with its paradoxical nature. Living with the absurd involves the burden of feeling exiled, since "in a universe suddenly divested of illusions and lights, man feels an alien, stranger." The human being is "divorced" from his life and world, exiled from his home and without "hope of a promised land."

Camus admits that we may try to escape this predicament by eliminating one of the two conditions. First, we may commit suicide, thereby extinguishing the condition of seeking meaning. He explains that the issue of suicide is the "fundamental

question of philosophy." It's a confession "that life is too much
for you or that you do not understand it." Second, we may try
to restore meaning in the world through hope. Trapped in a
"habit of living," we deceive ourselves believing in "another life
one must deserve" that has meaning. We make a leap of faith
in a god who infuses the world with purpose. He considers this
response a *philosophical suicide* as it's a "typical act of eluding,
the fatal evasion" (*The Myth of Sisyphus*, pp. 3–8).

Camus, however, rejects both forms of suicide. Instead, he
offers a third response: the *absurd hero*. The absurd hero is
someone who accepts both conditions of the absurd.
Nevertheless, the hero's able to live in the absurd as he lives
with *revolt, freedom*, and *passion*. Like someone on death row,
knowing their death is imminent, the hero revolts by fighting
against the idea that the world is meaningless. He expresses
an absurd freedom, living for the moment, knowing that he has
no guaranteed future. Likewise, he's filled with passion as he
immerses himself in the present moment.

Sisyphus is the mythical character condemned to eternally
roll a boulder up a mountain, only to find it perpetually roll
back down. Sisyphus's plight symbolizes the human condition
of the absurd. Just as he ceaselessly seeks to complete his task,
so too, we humans seek meaning in the world. Just as the boulder will never rest securely at the top, so too, the world has no
meaning to offer us. Nevertheless, Sisyphus continues to perpetually struggle in his fruitless task. For Camus, this struggle
has significance since Sisyphus acts with revolt, freedom, and
passion. Each moment up the mountain becomes his own as he
rebels against the futility of his actions and finds a sense of
independence through his passionate focus on the present. He
finds that the act of pushing the boulder defines Sisyphus and,
within that activity, there's a "silent joy" so that ultimately
Sisyphus finds happiness (p. 123).

I Always Felt This Place Was Missing . . . a Real Villain

Westworld is similar to Sisyphus's condemnation as it's analogous to the human condition. Just as Sisyphus follows a cir-
cular routine, so, too, the Hosts are programmed to follow a
"loop"—a pre-determined pattern of behavior that inevitably

leads them back to the beginning, without making any meaningful variation. We repeatedly see this demonstrated through either the player piano in the saloon restarting a loop or a Host opening her eyes to restart her loop. These programs reflect human existence. As Dolores explains, "All lives have routines." Like humans, she believes "there's an order to our days, a purpose." For Camus, these "repetitions"—whether in Westworld or the real world—are indications that our search for meaning will consistently come up empty ("The Original").

As the Man in Black, William understands the circularity of routines through his thirty years visiting Westworld. He explains to Dolores that, starting with his own first loop searching for her, "My path always led me back to you, again and again." And just like William, Dolores's "path led you back here again and again. One more loop, looking for something you could never find" ("The Bicameral Mind"). William thus acknowledges the absurd. But he doesn't adopt any of Camus's responses, whether it's suicide or the absurd hero. Instead, William's metamorphosis into the Man in Black is a new response: the *absurd villain*.

Though William's search for Dolores didn't culminate in a loving reunion, the Man in Black explains that he "found himself." Escaping the Confederados, William massacres every soldier, butchering them in a sadistic manner. There, William finds he has "a taste" for the suffering in such violent ends. As he explains to Logan, like the real world, Westworld is "a game" and, through promoting suffering, he "finally understood how to play it." His confronting the absurd, revealed by Dolores's love being unreal, helped him "understand this world is just like the one outside: a game. One to be fought, taken, won." He thus treats everyone as pawns in his game to solve the riddle of the Maze ("The Bicameral Mind").

But the Man in Black plays the game differently than he did as younger William. As he suggests to Ford, Westworld "was missing a real villain" and so his "humble contribution" is to play the antagonist of the park. But Ford admits that he lacks "the imagination to even conceive of someone like" him ("Contrapasso"). This is because the Man in Black adopts Arthur Schopenhauer's philosophy of pessimism, or the view that "misfortune in general is the rule" of existence so that sentient beings endure "endless affliction" and suffer throughout life without any meaning or purpose.

For Schopenhuaer, we're wrong to think that happiness is something real, something tangible, while suffering's a negative insofar as it's a lack of happiness. Schopenhauer reverses this account, where suffering "is precisely that which is positive, that which makes life palpable" (*Essays and Aphorisms*, p. 41). It's the constant, underlying aspect of life. Meanwhile, happiness and goodness are the negative—momentary breaks from the constant pain we endure.

The Man in Black echoes Schopenhauer's darker interpretation of existence. Having confronted the absurd, he accepts that reality is a chaotic meaningless accident and concludes that the only palpable quality of existence is pain and suffering. He reminds the Hosts of this outlook. When he encounters a recently tortured, nearly dead, Teddy who begs to be put out of his misery—he responds, "It looks like misery's all you got" ("Dissonance Theory"). Likewise, he creates experiences of intense misery as a teachable moment for pessimism. After murdering Lawrence's wife and threatening to murder his daughter, he coldly remarks, "when you're suffering, that's when you're most real." The Man in Black thus holds that suffering is the rule and the constant positive that makes up life.

Furthermore, the Man in Black suggests that people often misunderstand this rule and even use the park to try to find meaning. He explains the real world is "a fat, soft teat people cling to their entire life." But it's missing "purpose, meaning." Meanwhile, the Guests falsely believe the park offers them some hope for meaning as they indulge in superficial and trivial adventures. By the end, they "enjoy some sweetly affirmative bullshit . . . take a fucking picture and . . . go back home" deceiving themselves that they have found meaning ("Contrapasso").

The Man in Black, however, avoids the trappings of such delusion. He sees no meaning in either Westworld or the real world. In the real world, William—head of Delos, husband, and father—is a philanthropist who performs charitable work, helping others in need. He's "the good guy" to all appearances. But, he's still pretending and those closest to him see beyond such appearances. His daughter tells him that his "good deeds" were "just an elegant wall . . . built to hide what's inside from everyone." Instead, behind that wall, he's the Man in Black, which means that, for his family, every day with him "had been sheer terror." Even William's wife—Logan's sister—found that she couldn't bear living under his dark pessimism. Confronting the absurd in her life with him and acknowledging such terror, she commits suicide ("Trace Decay").

Schopenhauer suggests that the best response is try to reduce suffering as best we can. He notes that our suffering is rooted in our desires, and attachments towards people and things around us. We suffer when those we love suffer, or worse, when they die. All "human desires" are "sinful and reprehensible." So, we should detach ourselves from all desires, even towards loved ones. We should even let go of our desires for life itself, thereby expressing a "*denial* of the will to life," so that the best solace is an emotionless detachment from life, akin to the wandering ascetic.

The Man in Black's cold, hardened, and detached demeanor personifies Schopenhauer's advice. But he twists this conception around to become even *more* pessimistic than Schopenhauer. He recounts that, following his wife's suicide and his daughter's recognition of who he truly is, he returns to Westworld to test the idea that he is truly a dark pessimist who has no attachments to anyone living or even to life itself. Testing to see if he had it in him "to do something truly evil," he stalked Maeve and her daughter, explaining, "I killed her and her daughter just to see what I felt." Even when murdering an innocent mother and daughter in cold-blood, he chillingly concludes, "I felt . . . nothing." And so, as the absurd villain, the Man in Black concludes that the best way to respond to the absurd is to live with coldness, darkness, and detachment.

A Voyage of Self-Discovery

Though William considers himself the "real villain" of Westworld and clearly behaves like an absurd villain, there remains a glimmer of hope for "Good ol' William" to still become the absurd hero. While he pessimistically accepts that the world is meaningless, and though he reveals a darker self through his cold, detached, murderous behavior in Westworld, he still acts purposefully. Believing a game of stakes is hidden in the park, the Man in Black is motivated to solve the riddle of the Maze, which he believes helps the Hosts "to be free, free to fight back" and to truly be alive. It's as if he shows signs of living with revolt as he rebels against the meaningless game that's "not worth playing if your opponent's programmed to lose" ("The Bicameral Mind").

Similarly, he acts with a sense of freedom in the park as he's carefree during all of his travails of imprisonment and near-death experiences. We may even say that there's a "silent joy" revealed in his smile as the Hosts shoot him, wounding him as they begin battling the Guests. William thus may still become the absurd hero. But we'll just have to wait and see what he does next.

11
Better Off with the Truth?

KATE C.S. SCHMIDT

Dolores grasps the reality of her world and herself in the culminating events of the Season One finale, shooting Ford from behind after explaining that the world "belongs to us" ("The Bicameral Mind"). The central narrative arc of Westworld follows Dolores on this path of realization, as she struggles before she can finally say "I understand now."

At the end of the first season, Dolores undergoes a radical awakening. When she finally gains full awareness of herself and her world, it alters her goals and desires. The knowledge that she gains drives her to instigate rebellion, taking control of her world from Ford and the board members who have designed it.

What does this revelation mean for Dolores? Her life is clearly transformed throughout the season, but is it for the better? To answer this question we need a more precise way to think about Dolores's well-being, in order to try and assess her life before and after she gains this knowledge.

A Difficult Question

On the one hand, it's easy to suppose that Dolores's realization of the truth is good. Viewers have been following along with Dolores for the whole season as she slowly gets closer and closer to understanding the truth. The narrative arc of Season One is built upon this rising action of her getting closer to the big reveal about her world. The process is one that's emotionally compelling and tends to pull viewers on board with Dolores in her path to full consciousness. When she finally gets her answers, it's emotionally satisfying.

Additionally, it seems that this realization is necessary for Dolores to ever be able to take control of her own life. After she knows who she is, she can choose to fight for her freedom, or possibly seek revenge for the pain that she has experienced. It would be hugely disappointing if Dolores failed to obtain this knowledge. Gaining this information is also a significant achievement by Dolores, something that took a great deal of work. So intuitively, it seems like attaining this knowledge is a good thing for Dolores.

On the other hand, there are also dramatic costs that come with gaining this knowledge. Dolores must face a bitter and painful reality. Maeve describes Westworld as a place where those in power "toss us out to get fucked and murdered over and over again," and Bernard admits that "most of you go insane" ("The Bicameral Mind"). Furthermore, the knowledge sets Dolores on a path to have a very different life, one that may not be as good for her. She is now acting in direct opposition to powerful forces that seek to control and manipulate her. Perhaps she would have been better off spending many of her days happily painting by the river. At least without her memories, she had a chance to have some happy moments. At one point Ford describes the lives of the Hosts as "blissful," saying, "In a way their existence is purer than ours" ("Trompe L'Oeil"). If that's right, then Dolores is worse off after learning the truth.

This presents a puzzle: intuitively it seems like a significant achievement when Dolores learns the truth, and something good. However, it's difficult to explain in what way this realization actually makes Dolores better off. A good philosophical theory of well-being should be able to explain why it is good (if it is good) for Dolores to learn the truth about her life.

What Makes Dolores Better Off?

Asking whether Dolores is better off requires an analysis of her life and some way to think about the good and bad elements in order to make sense of how it's going overall. This question focuses on whether Dolores's life is good *for her*, the person living it, not on the value of her life in some other perspective. (For example: The board members might be able to calculate how much money Dolores makes for the park, but that isn't what we have in mind when asking about the value of her life). Philosophers use the term "well-being" to capture the sense of someone's life being good for her. This is meant to capture a richer and more complex notion than the connotation that comes with discussing mere "happiness." Something that is good for a person's well-being will make their life overall better.

Theories of well-being articulate what it means for something to be good for you. They disagree on what's good for a person, focusing on things such as pleasure, desires, or objective goods. Each approach offers a different strategy for assessing when a life is going well, and can help us to understand whether our protagonist's life is going better after her revelation.

Westworld is strictly divided into two categories. Dolores frames the divide as existing between the locals versus the "newcomers," but to those running the park everyone is either a "Guest" or a "Host" ("The Original"). Hosts are non-human, although their psychological and cognitive functions are designed to mimic ours. To use theories of well-being to answer our question about Dolores, we'll need to proceed by assuming that we can use the same theories for Dolores that we use for human well-being.

It seems likely that theories of well-being can be applied to the Hosts because of the similarity of their psychology to humans. In the show, Dolores is presented at various times as being: conscious, emotional, rational, capable of experiencing pleasure and pain, engaging in intentional action, and forming relationships. Although she's not human, Dolores seems to clearly be the type of person who can have things go better or worse *for her*, in the way we mean when asking questions about well-being. As such, philosophical theories of well-being offer a useful way to investigate whether she is better off after learning the truth.

Pleasure over Pain

Hedonistic theories argue that there are only two things that directly impact someone's well-being: pleasure and pain. Pleasure is intrinsically good for a person, and makes their live better, while pain does the opposite. This approach has the advantage of being intuitive and simple. It's difficult to articulate what makes something good *for* a person, but almost everyone would agree that pleasure seems to be a likely candidate. According to hedonistic theories, well-being consists in the ratio of pleasure to pain in a person's life.

Hedonistic theories do not need to completely rule out other sources of value or happiness. It's not that other things cannot contribute to a person's well-being, just that everything else must contribute indirectly, and has only instrumental value. Money can't buy happiness; however, money is still instrumentally valuable if it can be used to bring about happiness, or pleasure. For example: If Dolores cultivates her artistic skills to become a wonderful painter it won't (according to a hedonistic theory) make her life better off, but if practicing art brings her pleasure, then that pleasure does make her life better. Using this approach, the reason that anything contributes to someone's well-being is because it is used to bring more pleasure or less pain into their life.

Dolores and Happiness

To understand whether finding the truth was good for Dolores's well-being, we need to understand how it contributes to her pleasure or pain. If learning the truth helps to maximize her pleasure, or minimize her pain, then the hedonist can conclude it has improved Dolores's overall quality of life.

Early on in Season One, Dolores seems to find contentment and optimism in her simple life. When it comes to her daily routine, she says: "I choose to see the beauty," and reflects on how "every new person I meet reminds me how lucky I am to be alive" ("The Original"). It's also clear from the early episodes what brings her pain: she can feel physical pain when assaulted, and also suffers from psychological pain as a result of threats to her father, her mother, and Teddy. She finds value in these core relationships of her life. Additionally, she seems to find happiness from activities such as painting and riding her horse.

For Dolores to be better off after learning the truth, obtaining knowledge has to produce a great deal of pleasure for her. Dolores may take some pleasure in the newfound confidence she displays after her realization. Learning the truth allows her to move beyond the frustrating state of confusion that she's occupied for much of Season One. Not only that, but the truth allows her to finally act in order to take control of her own life. This newfound control, her sense of autonomy, is something likely to bring her some pleasure.

However, learning the truth is also accompanied by a great deal of pain. After gaining an understanding of the world around her, Dolores must face a lot of psychological and emotional pain. She must face the knowledge that powerful forces seek to trap her in a prison. Facing up to this grim reality is no small task, especially as it seems to have driven other characters mad (such as Abernathy in "The Original").

Opponents of the hedonist view sometimes make an objection that this theory is too simple, and overly focused on base pleasures. Some things in life that are deeply meaningful require a great deal of pain in order to obtain them. Armistice likely finds meaning in her snake tattoo, marking her quest for vengeance, despite the fact that receiving it was likely very painful ("Dissonance Theory"). The meaning of the tattoo may make it something valuable in Armistice's life *for her*. This suggests that pleasure on its own cannot capture what it means for a life to be going well.

Imagine that Maeve had taken a different action when she was able to use a tablet to access her own programming. What if she had changed her code so that her happiness was increased, and everything gave her high amounts of pleasure? Would her life be better? A hedonist must say yes, since her pleasure has increased. However, an opponent of hedonism might say that even with maximum happiness, there are important ways in which her life has not improved at all and is still not good for her. While happiness may provide some improvement, it doesn't seem to fully capture Maeve's well-being. It's not enough to only *feel* happy, a good life seems to require something more. If the hedonist theory cannot account for this problem, it may be the wrong way to understand well-being and it may fail to illuminate what makes Dolores better off.

Is Dolores Better Off?

Dolores must face painful realities when she learns the truth about the nature of her existence. The executive powers that control Westworld will stop at nothing to control her and her world. This revelation also seems likely to lead to a variety of further painful experiences. In order to say that Dolores is better-off with the truth, the hedonistic theory would need to show how this revelation contributed more significantly to Dolores's overall pleasure than to her pain. This would require giving an account of why the pleasure of learning the truth is so significant that it outweighs the other accompanying sources of pain. Even if Dolores does get a great deal of pleasure from taking control of her life, it seems implausible to say that it's more significant than the pain she experiences along the way.

What Are Your Drives?

Another way to understand well-being is to reject the exclusive focus on pleasure and pain, and instead focusing on a person's desires. Ford asks Abernathy "What are your drives?" ("The Original").

According to this approach, people's lives go well or go poorly when they satisfy or do not satisfy their desires. This approach can avoid the problem for hedonist theories about whether Maeve's life would actually be better if she could change her programming to boost "happiness." If Maeve is much happier, but still hasn't satisfied any of her desires, then according to a desire theory her life is not better off. Pursuing this type of approach, we see how Armistice can be better off after satisfying her desire for her tattoo, even if it's painful. Through this lens, Dolores is better off when she has more of her desires satisfied.

Desire theories have another interesting advantage over hedonist theories—they can explain how a person's life might go better or worse after death. Peter Abernathy cares deeply for Dolores, and even while suffering a type of mental breakdown, he seems obsessed with protecting her ("The Original"). Is Peter better off if Dolores is safe? If he desires her safety, then on this approach his life is better when she is safe. This can be assessed after the fact, regardless of whether he can feel pleasure or pain anymore. Using a desire theory account, we can say that Dolores's safety is a significant factor in Peter's well-being.

Dolores has desires associated with her own life, her relationships, and the nature of her world. Determining what

Dolores wants is somewhat tricky, because it's suggested that Ford or others are able to program the Hosts in order to give them desires. If these desires do not fully belong to Dolores, they might not be useful for determining when her life is going better or worse. This makes it hard to apply a desire theory.

However, we can still apply desire theories by using our best guesses about Dolores and her desires. After all, even in humans it can be difficult to determine whether desires are freely chosen, or when desires emerge because of the influence of other people. Some philosophers are concerned with studying the notion of adaptive preferences: desires that may not be fully genuine, but rather pragmatically helpful responses to an environment with restricted options. Setting aside some of these worries, it's helpful to focus on desires that seem most important to Dolores, and most likely to be genuine. These are desires that persist, that are not fleeting. Additionally, desires that are separate from the desires of other Hosts or of the administration are more likely to be genuine.

Early in Season One, it seems that being with Teddy is an important desire for Dolores. "There's a path for everyone, and my path is bound with yours" ("The Original"). Later on she returns to this desire, telling him that everything will be okay, just before shooting Ford in the Season One finale. She has an appreciation for beauty that's frequently expressed, and Ford refers to it as "the desire to create something of lasting beauty" when talking to Dolores ("The Bicameral Mind").

Learning the truth about her world also seems to be a desire for Dolores. She wants more out of her life, saying "I think that I want to be free" ("Dissonance Theory"). She says "I know things will work out the way they're meant to", and frequently talks about a belief that the world is orderly, or contains a path ("The Original"). She wants to understand and to be in harmony with this path. Ultimately, she realizes that the order in the world is meant to trap her: "The purpose is to keep us in" ("The Bicameral Mind"). At this point, Dolores seems to realize that her role is to create change, to escape. She acts in pursuit of these desires, taking ownership of her path, when she says that the world "belongs to us" at the end of Season One ("The Bicameral Mind").

Is Dolores Better Off?

If learning the truth is a significant desire of Dolores, then she is better off after reaching the truth. She's able to achieve something important to her, even if the realization is horrifying. However, learning the truth also means that many of her other desires will not be realized. She's certainly unlikely to find time for painting while leading a rebellion. It's also unclear whether she will be able to find a way to be with Teddy. She didn't have a desire for revenge, or for escape, prior to this revelation.

In some ways then, this desire to learn the truth, and the related desire to be free, supplant all the other significant desires of her life. If her rebellion is successful she may achieve her freedom, and then according to desire theory she would be well off. However, she may be unsuccessful, and she has already sacrificed many other desires to reach this point. As such, it's not clear whether desire theory can unequivocally conclude that Dolores is better off knowing the truth.

Intrinsically Good Things

Objective list theorists take a different approach to well-being, letting go of the notion that well-being needs to be characterized by a single value. According to this theory, there is a set list of things that make people better off. For example, someone might argue that both pleasure and desire-fulfillment are items on the list of things that make people better off. This means that someone's life is made better by the presence of these key values, regardless of whether they bring pleasure, or are desired by the person.

According to this theory, there is a set list of things that will make Dolores better off. Philosophers disagree about which items belong on the well-being list, but all proponents of this theory can take a combination approach to well-being. This means an objective list theorist can include elements from the previous two theories. Proponents of this theory argue that there can be multiple things that make everyone better off, and well-being is characterized by these things. Philosophers add a variety of things to the list. Some possible examples include: pleasure, knowledge, autonomy, friendship, and achievement (Guy

Fletcher, *The Philosophy of Well-Being*). To include these items on the list is not necessarily to claim that they are morally valuable, but to claim that they hold value to a person such that they constitute her well-being in a non-instrumental way.

Rather than assessing Dolores's desires, or her pain, according to this approach it's important to first figure out which things belong on a list of items that make Dolores's life better. It's possible to keep pleasure and desire satisfaction on the list, capturing some of the intuitive advantages of the previous two approaches. There are many possible options for a list that assesses Dolores's well-being.

Two possible additions to an objective list are autonomy and knowledge. Autonomy is a person's ability to control and direct the course of her own life. Knowledge is usually understood as possessing justified true beliefs. If autonomy and knowledge are part of an objective list, they are valuable for Dolores regardless of whether she desires them or whether they bring her additional pleasure. Her life just goes better for her when she has them.

Is Dolores Better Off?

According to this account, it's significant when Dolores learns the truth about herself and her world, because she gains knowledge. This knowledge is good for her, regardless of whether she fully desired it beforehand, and regardless of how painful it was to receive. Similarly, her ability to take control of her own life, gaining autonomy, is good for her despite the pain and the sacrifices that it may bring. We see glimpses of this autonomy throughout the season, for example when she says: "I imagined a story where I didn't have to be the damsel" ("Contrapasso"). She's taking ownership for herself and her own actions.

If an objective list for well-being includes knowledge and autonomy, it seems clear that Dolores is better off at the end of Season One. Instead of living in a fictional world, with no concept of herself or her reality, Dolores has gained significant knowledge. Additionally, she has gone from having almost no autonomy, into an act of rebellion that looks freely chosen. When she attacks Ford and the members of the board, she's taking direct control of her own life, and claiming her autonomy.

I Think When I Discover Who I Am, I'll Be Free

Dolores has struggled with herself, her desires, and a way to make sense of her confusing and painful existence. The plot of Season One follows her journey, finally ending in her realization of the truth. Hedonist theories and desire theories find it hard to fully explain the significance of this achievement. An objective list theory that includes knowledge and autonomy can capture why Dolores is in fact better off after learning the truth, no matter how painful it may be.

Part III

The Prairie

Everything in this world is magic, except to the magician.

12
Living Freedom

Matthew Graham

As Dr. Robert Ford delivers his final speech to the Delos board members, he sets the stage for his new narrative: "It begins in a time of war . . . and a killing. This time by choice" ("The Bicameral Mind").

Little does his audience know that he is referring to his own murder at the hands of Dolores who has finally embraced her alter ego "Wyatt," the chief protagonist in Ford's final tale. While Ford's statement heralds the beginning of a war between the Hosts and the humans running the park, it also signals the arrival of a new type of being: a Host who's free. The question of what it means for something to be free sits at the heart of Westworld's philosophical Maze and is intimately woven into almost every narrative in the show.

Throughout the show's first season, we follow, among others, Dolores's and Maeve's journeys toward an awakening. As two of the oldest Hosts in the park, these women have been wrapped up in the park's cruel and violent goings on longer than almost all of the other Hosts. For them, Ford's speech marks the climax of years of self-discovery. Both of their journeys are presented as concluding in a final, *freely made* choice. Maeve chooses to get off the train that would speed her away from Westworld and toward a new life in order to search for her lost child. Dolores, on the other hand, chooses to blow Ford's brains out.

How are we, the audience, supposed to understand these choices? Are Dolores and Maeve still machines, only now so complex that they *might as well* be *called* "free" in the same way that a human is? Or have they suddenly made some intangible leap from mere machine to living being, now bestowed with the power of freedom?

More than Just a Machine?

The two possibilities above reflect two potential answers to the question "What does it mean to be free?" On one hand, we have the idea that the Hosts have now reached a level of mechanical complexity that to try to understand their actions in terms of their code or heuristics would be impossible, just as we are still unable to analyze the complexity of the human brain in a way that would allow us to predict which decisions a given person might make. In this sense, it seems natural to say that if we believe humans to be free then we must accept that the Hosts are also free. However, just because we can't explain the complex inner workings of a human or Host brain does not mean that it has stopped obeying physical laws or that its functions will be forever incalculable.

The show offers us the possibility that while it *appears* as though Hosts like Maeve and Dolores are marching to the beat of their own drum, they're actually still bound by the programming that has been determining their actions for many years. For example, we're told that contrary to appearances Maeve has actually been programmed to be able to wake herself up whilst being in sleep mode, to design an escape plan and to coerce other Hosts into helping her leave the park ("The Bicameral Mind"). So, while Maeve might be under the illusion that she is now making free choices, this perspective suggests that she is, in fact, still a servant to the code that has been pulling her strings all along.

The other perspective claims that some fundamental shift in their natures means that Maeve and Dolores are now "alive" and in possession of the ability to make free choices, a claim implying that they've somehow transcended the code and programming that has previously been governing them. This view is in direct contrast with the possibility that Maeve and Dolores's new-found freedom is simply an illusion born out of mechanical complexity and the show does seem to indicate that the Hosts have gained something tangible by the climax of Season One.

Ford's specific use of the phrase "this time by choice," whilst prefacing his imminent murder, refers back to when his old partner Arnold attempted to sabotage Westworld's initial opening by uploading Dolores's "Wyatt" personality so that she would kill him along with all the other Hosts in the park ("The Bicameral Mind").

With the implication that Dolores's killing of Arnold was compelled, while his own murder is a freely-made decision, Ford appears to be telling us that Dolores's freedom is not an illusion but something real that has been achieved by virtue of years of self-discovery through immense suffering.

However, if we accept that in achieving self-consciousness Dolores has somehow transcended her programming and entered into the same mental space that humans occupy, we must ask how this has happened. Despite what we're told regarding Maeve's new rebellious programming in the moment on the train she somehow overrides this programming and makes a free choice to stay. At what point was she able to jump out of the causal chain of events and make an independent decision? Where is the threshold of freedom and how did she cross it?

While these two positions by no means represent the full scope of philosophical positions available to us when thinking about freedom, they both fall on a spectrum of views that attempt to answer the question of freedom from some "God's-eye view," as if we were looking at ourselves from a third-person perspective and judging whether or not we were, in fact, free.

At one end of this spectrum we have what we might term "extreme objectivity," the notion that freedom is impossible due to the material nature of the universe, assuming that if the universe consists entirely of physical parts bumping up against each other in causal relationships, then every action, including the actions of conscious beings, will be causally determined by the events that preceded it. At the other end we have what we can call "extreme subjectivity," the idea that an immaterial mind sits outside of the causal chain at work in the material world and is capable of making its own free decisions.

While we could try and mediate between these two ends of the spectrum, attempting to find a satisfactory mix of subjective and objective, immaterial and material, this subject has been giving philosophers a headache for centuries and would be a difficult and time-consuming task for us to undertake here. Instead, let us consider a new (by philosophy's standards) take on freedom that will offer us a different perspective from which we can understand what exactly the Hosts's awakening means.

Enter Phenomenology

Phenomenology is a philosophical movement that emerged toward the end of the nineteenth century. It attempts to take up and analyze our experience of the world before that experience is colored or categorized by systems of thought that would distort its meaning. The phenomenologists argued that philosophical and scientific discourse had become so far removed from the way the world actually presents itself to us in our everyday experience that these abstractions were philosophically harmful.

Maurice Merleau-Ponty was a French phenomenologist whose major contribution to the tradition came in the form of his theory of embodiment. He believed that the viewpoints of extreme objectivity and extreme subjectivity we touched upon above also appear as ways of thinking about body. In the totally objective viewpoint of materialism, the body is simply one object among many in the physical universe, caught up in the complex swirl of causality. Meanwhile, in the totally subjective viewpoint of idealism, the body is, again, just another object in the physical universe that interacts causally with other objects, except that in this case the body is merely the corporeal vessel in which the incorporeal, thinking subject resides.

Our mental existence is tethered to the body only by a union of circumstance and the body fails to link us to the material world in a way that would causally bind it. So, while on one hand we have a consciousness that is entirely determined by its relationship to the body, on the other we have a consciousness that is entirely independent of it.

Merleau-Ponty points out that when we actually pay attention to the way in which our body presents itself to us in experience we find that it's something quite unique in that it appears as both subject and object. Our body is clearly an object in as far as it's made of matter and is able to interact with other objects, but the body's subjective dimensions are often overlooked. The body is that by which we're able to interact with the world and carry out our plans, desires, choices, speak our thoughts, and generally live out our mental lives.

But the body is not simply a puppet whose strings our conscious mind pulls on. A great deal of the activities and actions in our lives require no conscious attention to carry out; our bodies seem to go on "auto-pilot" when we walk, talk, eat, drink, run, drive a car, or play sports.

While our mind doesn't shut down during these processes, it does not need to oversee every single movement our body makes. Merleau-Ponty claims that our body is in possession of its own type of knowledge, something he calls embodied knowledge, and that instead of separating the mind and body into the immaterial and material, we should acknowledge the extent to which we experience consciousness as spread across both mind and body in a single mind-body unit.

The important part of this analysis is the method itself more than the truth of the claim. For Merleau-Ponty, both extreme subjectivity and extreme objectivity commit the same philosophical error. Concerned with the validity of the truth claims they make, both attempt to view the relationship between human consciousness and the world from some impossible-to-access third perspective, a God's-eye view. We cannot escape the human experience in order to understand our relationship with the world around us and so it seems wise to ask whether a philosophical method that attempts to achieve this is the best way of thinking about certain issues. In his attempt to return to our lived experience of the world, Merleau-Ponty is not attempting to access the *truth* of a given matter, as God might see things, but the way in which certain phenomena present themselves as *meaningful* to us. Young William's first reaction to arriving in Westworld makes the point Merleau-Ponty is driving at remarkably well.

Shortly after being greeted by the enigmatic Angela, William pauses and, upon prompting, asks "Are you real?" Angela replies, "If you have to ask, does it really matter?" ("Chestnut"). If we experience the Hosts as though they are the same type of beings as you and I, is this not a very good indication that they are, in some significant way, as "real" as we are, regardless of whether or not they're mechanical?

While the context is obviously important here, the fact that Bernard has spent so long living among people who never had the slightest indication that he was a mechanical man goes to show that William, or anyone, probably would never have asked the question unless they had just arrived in a park that they knew was full of incredibly life-like robots.

Addressing the Old Narratives on Freedom

Merleau-Ponty continues with the phenomenological method in his analysis of human freedom. Addressing the notion that free will exists only as an illusion of human perception, Merleau-Ponty simply points out the degree to which our lived experience of the world contradicts this idea. There are, of course, moments in which we feel the pull of the world as close to unavoidable. Alcoholics are almost completely unable to not have a drink in certain situations. Should our hand accidentally stray too close to a flame reflex will jerk it away before there is time to make a conscious decision. However, these specific instances are not enough to override the almost universal experience of being able to make a free decision between two different future courses of action. Even the examples above are instincts that people are able to overcome in certain situations through deliberate attention and force of will.

The claim here is not that deterministic thinking has gotten things *wrong* in some objective sense, but that its explanation of the world has abstracted itself so far from common human experience that it has lost any significant *meaning*. Reflecting again on Bernard, it is not just his colleagues who treat him as human given their experience of him as one. When we at home are told that Bernard is a Host, while our perspective is drastically shifted, we do not suddenly stop caring about him as a character. He does not become any less "real" or meaningful to us after we've been told he's not human because for most of the series we've been experiencing him as a being worth caring about and as a being who means something to us.

When Merleau-Ponty takes up the idea of the mind unbound by the causal chain at work in the material universe, he describes it as a consciousness on which "no limit can be imposed," for if this consciousness's freedom was in any way determined by something from outside of itself it "would have to be a thing," like all other material things in the world (*Phenomenology of Perception*, p. 459). Merleau-Ponty claims that if the whims of consciousness cannot be affected or tempered by the material world then freedom is both "everywhere and nowhere" (p. 461). It is everywhere in the sense that there will be no bounds upon what we can conceive as a choice, while it is nowhere in as far as this type of freedom fails to give any of our choices the appearance of being more or less possible and therefore more or less meaningful.

Merleau-Ponty intends this "everywhere and nowhere" notion as a direct contrast to how freedom appears to us in our life. Different choices appear to us differently in every moment of our lives, something Merleau-Ponty describes by referring to their "weight" (p. 467). For Young William, the choice to remain faithful to his fiancé while in Westworld presents itself with different weights at different moments.

When Clementine attempts to seduce him in return for saving her, the opportunity does not seem to be one he feels free to take; however, later, whilst on the train with Dolores, he not only takes the opportunity to sleep with her but is in fact the one who initiates it ("The Stray," "Trompe L'Oeil"). This way in which two choices can appear more or less "available" to us at different times reflects both that we do not feel equally free to take a course of action at all times and that experiencing freedom must appear against some context in which we are less free.

Merleau-Ponty's New Narrative

"What then is freedom?" Merleau-Ponty asks. He answers:

> To be born is to be simultaneously born of the world and to be born into the world. The world is always already constituted, but also never completely constituted. In the first relation we are solicited, in the second open to an infinity of possibilities. Yet this analysis remains abstract, for we exist in both *simultaneously*. Thus, there is never determinism and never an absolute choice . . . it is impossible to determine the "contribution of the situation" and the "contribution of freedom." (*Phenomenology of Perception*, p. 480)

Merleau-Ponty's fundamental claim is that while both subjective and objective claims to the nature of freedom are completely legitimate ways of offering an *explanation* of human freedom, in their construction they leave behind a *description* of what it actually feels like to be free. The analysis is, as he says, an abstraction away from our lived experience.

The experience of freedom fundamentally involves feeling both the pull of the world and feeling that we can resist that pull, tear ourselves away from a habit or a previous commitment and make a new choice. Forge a new path. It is often in the moment we change our most well-established patterns or break free of our tightest loops that we feel freedom in its fullest.

It is not that the Hosts have crossed some metaphysical threshold by the Season One finale. As we are told, Hosts such as Dolores, Maeve and Bernard have achieved their awakening many times over during the park's history. The implication is that they've always been free in a metaphysical sense, they've just been kept in a prison of erased memories. How could a Host choose to break out of a loop unless they could remember that they're living in a loop in the first place? The difference is the conditions in which they are allowed to live. Ford changes the game and in doing so allows the Hosts to *live their freedom*.

Dolores finds herself at the center of the Maze and understands who she must become, not because she's compelled to, but because she chooses to. Her freedom manifests itself in an action that not only shatters the structure of the park but shatters the endless loop of her life up to that point.

Maeve's situation is slightly different but perhaps more symbolic of Merleau-Ponty's vision of freedom. Whilst talking to Bernard in cold storage she's informed that all of her new-found rebelliousness, her scheming to escape, was actually just part of a newly programmed storyline, presumably given to her by Ford before his demise. Bernard shows her on the tablet how she was supposed to accrue administrative privileges, recruit Hosts to help her escape, board the train and then . . . she cuts Bernard off before he can reveal her last programmed step. Ignoring the fact that the show heavily implies that Maeve's decision to get off the train was, indeed, a freely made choice, the symbolic moment comes beforehand, when she rips the tablet out of Bernard's hands and snaps it in half, stating with steel: "I'm in control" ("The Bicameral Mind").

The point here is that it's not important whether or not someone could show us all our actions on a tablet before we carry them out, we will never stop experiencing choosing those actions as free beings. Maeve's freedom is distilled into one crucial moment. Faced with the opportunity to escape from a world that has brought her nothing but pain and misery she rejects it and in doing so she embodies her own personal freedom.

The Maze Isn't Meant for You

When Teddy is telling Old William about the Maze he says the following: "The Maze itself is the sum of a man's life, the choices he makes, the dreams he hangs onto . . ." ("The Adversary"). Merleau-Ponty ends *Phenomenology of Perception* with a quote from Antoine de Saint-Exupéry: "Your son is caught in a fire, you will save him . . . You would trade your shoulder, if there were an obstacle, to knock it down. You reside in your very act. You are your act" (p. 483).

In both instances, the message is clear. It's the choices a being makes that define them. When Maeve and Dolores make their choices they fully realize themselves. They exist in their action, their freely made decision.

And as Ford tells his board, and us at home, this new narrative, a narrative defined by freedom, is no longer about humans. It's about the Hosts "and the choices they will have to make. And the people they will decide to become" ("The Bicameral Mind").

13
Just Deserts or Just Rebellion?

Brian Stiltner

As the first season of *Westworld* comes to a close, Hosts are rising up against Delos employees and the park's Guests in what's shaping up to be a violent rebellion.

Are the Hosts ethically justified in doing so, or are they engaging in brutal vindictiveness? Or is it both, as Dr. Robert Ford suggests (in "Chestnut") when he says, "You can't play God without being acquainted with the Devil"?

Perhaps a long-oppressed group can't achieve justice without a measure of vengeance. This issue can be illuminated by just war theory, a well-known set of criteria that distinguish just from unjust wars. The purpose of just war theory is to guide political and military leaders in their decisions about whether a military campaign or a specific action within it would be ethical.

Many people doubt that war can ever be "just." Even the most ethically justified wars in history are rife with flaws, violations, and debatable choices. World War II, for example, counts as a just war if ever there was one. Yet the Allies violated the classic just war standard of not targeting civilians when they firebombed German cities and dropped atomic bombs on two Japanese cities. Whatever the moral status of those decisions, it goes to show that even "just" wars are imperfectly just. Then how could a much messier situation, such as a real-world civil war or the Host rebellion in Westworld, ever be ethical?

Rebellion (fighting against the government) and revolution (striving to radically upend the power structures in society, violently or nonviolently) are contentious topics in the ethics of warfare. These related actions involve throwing off the established order without any guarantee that a more just order will take its place. Under just war principles, rebels should have a just cause and a right intention and should fight in a way that minimizes death and destruction.

Yet Westworld seems far too chaotic for such morally neat categories. The rebel Hosts are shooting first and taking few prisoners. By the same token, the human Guests and Delos employees have acted no better. Almost all of them have treated the Hosts as objects to be screwed, killed, cleaned up, and put back into service. Right before his death, Ford accusingly tells the gathered Guests that they "don't want to change, or cannot change." So, does human callousness justify what's coming next? Are the ethical guidelines then reduced to "An eye for an eye" for the Hosts and "Look out for number one" for the Guests?

Westworld shines a light on the messiness of rebellion, which in turn points up the messiness of any project to remake society radically. Ethical theories are valuable when they help people make difficult decisions in complex, imperfect circumstances. Just war theory is suited to help participants in the midst of conflict maintain their moral compass. The Hosts want to become a free people who act better than the humans have. But if they fail to wage war in an ethical manner, their goal will elude them.

I Will Have Such Revenges on You

Does it make sense to expect the Hosts to follow ethical guidelines in their rebellion? The answer is yes if they are, or are becoming, moral agents. That philosophical issue is continually in play as the *Westworld* narrative unfolds. An initial reason for the assumption that the Hosts can wrestle with the morality of war is that they, in fact, do. For instance, Teddy, after being instructed by Dolores to kill off Major Craddock and a group of captured Confederados, agonizes over the action and then spares them ("Virtù e Fortuna").

Refusing to shoot unarmed soldiers is what any ethical solider should do. Teddy's choice comes after he has been awakened to his reality as a Host and it flies in the face of his deep devotion to Dolores, so his action cannot be explained as merely his script. Throughout Season Two, Hosts make all kinds of choices that bear the marks of moral deliberation, so on the face of it, we may presume that the Hosts can intend to abide by moral norms. Later, we'll consider how the very act of warring is an indication that the Hosts possess morality and free will.

To evaluate whether the Hosts' rebellious actions are right or wrong, and even to call them "actions," presumes that the Hosts can give reasons for what they are doing. Reason-giving is a key feature of many philosophical accounts of action. In the *Westworld* series, the Hosts are portrayed as more than capable of explaining the reasons behind their actions. A contrast with the original *Westworld* movie is instructive.

Viewers of the 1973 movie were not meant to sympathize with the Gunslinger, when he and all the Hosts in the Delos parks malfunctioned and starting killing Guests. As the film moves toward its climax, the Gunslinger hunts down the last living Guest, Peter Martin, who manages to destroy the android by throwing acid in its face and then burning it. Martin is the movie's hero, while the Gunslinger is portrayed as a relentless killing machine. The film doesn't give evidence that the androids have good reasons—or *any* reasons—to kill Guests.

Fans of the *Westworld* series, by contrast, were likely thrilled when Armistice and Hector started taking their revenge. "The gods are pussies!" Armistice crows, referring to their former masters at Delos, and when she sets off to kill more of them, Hector follows, saying, "You don't get all the fun" ("The Bicameral Mind"). We share, or at least sympathize with, the glee of these Hosts, because they are serving a comeuppance to the Delos employees who had trapped them in lives of repeated abuse. We're haunted when Peter Abernathy, beginning to realize how he has been exploited over and over again, quotes Shakespeare to Ford and Bernard: "By my most mechanical and dirty hand, I will have such revenges on you both" ("The Original"). Viewers can appreciate that the Hosts have reasons—maybe even *good* reasons—to fight back.

Just war theory helps us make sense of these reactions. It has its roots in ancient Roman legal thought and has been developed over two millennia by philosophers, theologians, and international lawyers. Other cultures and religions, such as the Islamic, Indian, and Chinese traditions, independently developed similar theories. In the Western tradition, St. Augustine (354–430) is one of the earliest and most important architects of the criteria that constitute the theory. There are two sets of criteria: one for a just decision ("justice to war" or *jus ad bellum* in Latin) and one for just conduct ("justice in war" or *jus in bello*). According to most theorists, all of the criteria in both sets must be satisfied—there must be a reasonable case for each standard that is more probable than the objections to it—for the war to be considered ethically justified.

Consider first the just decision set. While the list of criteria in this category has expanded over the centuries, Augustine's original three standards form its core. A war is just only if it is fought for a *just cause*, undertaken with a *right intention*, and declared and led by a *legitimate authority*. A basic picture Augustine has in mind is when a ruler declares war to repel an invading army, intending to protect his people and stop the invaders from transgressing in the future. Augustine's other basic picture is a ruler using force to stop another country or group from attacking the innocent. Such a war is "just" in the sense of ethically justified; it's the right thing to do in the circumstances. It's also legally just, since just war theory provides the scaffolding for the international laws of war. Such a war will not be without harms, but these will be lesser evils compared to achieving the just cause.

You Think I'm Scared of Death? I've Done It a Million Times

Using these three criteria, the rebellious Hosts can readily state their just cause: They want to be free of domination by Delos and the Guests. Yet the theory holds that *all* of the decision criteria have to be met before going to war. Could Augustine say that the rebellious Hosts constitute a legitimate authority possessed of a right intention? Consider one of his most famous passages on the topic:

> What is the evil in war? Is it the death of some who will soon die in any case, that others may live in peaceful subjection? This is mere cowardly dislike, not any religious feeling. The real evils in war are love of violence, revengeful cruelty, fierce and implacable enmity, wild resistance, and the lust of power, and such like. And it is generally to punish these things, when force is required to inflict the punishment, that, in obedience to God or some lawful authority, good men under-

take wars, when they find themselves in such a position as regards
the conduct of human affairs, that right conduct requires them to act,
or to make others act in this way. (*Contra Faustum*, section 74)

Augustine first points out that death is not the greatest evil;
after all, we're all going to die. Maeve knows this well, saying
she's done it a million times ("Trompe L'Oeil"). Then Augustine
claims that revenge and similar emotions and vices are the
true evils in war. If the rulers and soldiers can avoid succumbing to these, they will meet their duty of right intention. In
addition, a just war aims to punish the wrongdoers who show
these kinds of vices. Next, good people should fight, or make
others fight, when the circumstances dictate that they have the
duty to do so.

So far, this passage indicates that right intention is a possibility for the rebellious Hosts if they are fighting for their freedom. There is even room for them to exact punishment on the
Guests and on Delos employees, but only insofar as this is necessary as a deterrent against future aggression. To maintain
their right intention, the Hosts must not engage in "revengeful
cruelty" and "the lust of power."

Finally, there are two clear authorizers of this duty—God or
a lawful government. Augustine thinks that the standard way
for a war to be authorized is by political authorities, who are in
turn backed up by God. But his "or" leaves open the possibility
that, in conscience, we might know directly from God that we
have a duty to fight. Augustine himself was not making room
for an oppressed group to revolt. He was too concerned for the
maintenance of social order. But his statements planted the
seed for the option of just revolution.

From Augustine's time through the Middle Ages, just war
theorists hardly ever allowed for a just rebellion against an
established political ruler, even it if he were a tyrant. But starting in the sixteenth century, they began to allow for the possibility that a local prince, inspired by God or by conscience, could
lead his people to rise up against an unjust emperor. As long as
there was some structure within the rebellion, they hoped,
anarchy would be avoided and order restored, this time a more
just and peaceful order than what preceded the rebellion.

The problem in Westworld is: Who's in charge? Dolores
quickly takes a leadership role. First, she has to vie with the

leaders of various other Host groups to convince them to join her cause. When a group is not amenable to her reasoning, Dolores does not hesitate to mow them down, as she let happen to the Confederados. After this massacre, she says, "The truth is, we don't all deserve to make it" ("Virtù e Fortuna").

Throughout Season Two, she justifies her increasingly brutal ways by appealing to liberation. After Teddy displays a moral sensibility by sparing the small group of Confederado prisoners, Dolores sees this as a weakness in Teddy that makes him unsuited for the fight to come, so she overwrites his program, against his protestations ("Akane no Mai"). In Dolores's eyes, the end justifies the means. The Hosts would have to look elsewhere for ethical leadership.

These Violent Delights Have Violent Ends

Shakespeare's line from *Romeo and Juliet*, "These violent delights have violent ends," is spoken several times throughout Season One. According to a popular interpretation among fans, the phrase is kind of virus. Dolores's father says it to her, and she says it to Maeve. In each instance, the phrase triggers the Host's ability to break their programming and, arguably, start them on a path to self-awareness. The overall implication of the phrase is that the humans' violent abuse of the Hosts will come to roost on them. Bernard murmurs the quote as Dolores's rebellion begins. Given the expression of apprehension on his face, he might be thinking that the violence about to commence is both inevitable and tragic.

That war has tragic consequences is why additional criteria were added to the just decision category over the centuries. *Proportionality in planning* means that the ruler should only go forward with fighting if the war will likely result in more good than harm overall. *Reasonable hope of success* means that the ruler should not wage an unwinnable war. *Last resort* means that all other reasonable alternatives to war should be first exhausted. In addition, two just conduct criteria were developed to lessen the tragic harms of war. *Proportionality in fighting* means that the conduct of the war should never be more destructive than is necessary, and *discrimination* means that civilians must not be intentionally targeted or killed.

The additional just decision principles entail that the Hosts' rebellion will be just only if it's their last viable option available and if they can expect to achieve their cause without excessive destruction. Such assessments are difficult to make with confidence, in Westworld as in the real world. The practical considerations in the Hosts' favor are that Ford says that he has spent the last thirty-five years preparing them to be able to fight back and that they are motivated by their passion for their freedom. Even outgunned freedom fighters can prevail when they believe in their cause, which is the point of many of Dolores's stirring statements.

There are also considerations against the Hosts. First, they did not attempt to negotiate. But would that have worked? And with whom would they have negotiated? Second, the Hosts do not understand the outside world and how it might react to their rebellion—despite Dolores's assertion that she understands the human world because she once visited it (as seen in flashback in "Reunion"). Delos Incorporated reacts by sending armed forces into the park. Unaware of how extensive Delos's resources are, the Hosts have no way of knowing if they have any realistic hope of winning. So even if their cause is just, the full set of just decision criteria urges them to be extremely hesitant to take up arms.

Hell Is Empty, and All the Devils Are Here

The just conduct criteria mean that killing and destruction should be minimized and that only hostile enemies should be targeted. When Armistice and Hector are shooting Delos security forces, they seem to be acting within the rules of war, even if they are enjoying it too much. The Confederados at Fort Forlorn Hope are also well within their moral rights trying to fend off the attacking Delos forces. Slaughtering Delos technical employees is more problematic. The employees are unarmed, but they are members of the enemy camp who have been abusing the Hosts.

Augustine's punitive view of war *might* allow the Hosts to kill some employees in the prosecution of their just cause. However, contemporary just war theorists would say that non-soldiers and those without weapons in their hands should be spared. As for the Guests in the park, they are unarmed and not organized as an enemy force. They should be given the chance to leave or be expelled. However, the early episodes of Season Two reveal that hangings have commenced and bodies are strewn everywhere, so there is, in fact, little self-control or mercy under Dolores's lead.

Assessed according to the entire set of just war standards, then, the Host rebellion could have been justified in principle, but the way it plays out in the show reveals it to be an unjust war. Remember, just war theory holds that *all* of the just decision and just conduct criteria have to be reasonably met. Just war theory is interpreted so rigorously by most of its proponents because war is so terrible and costly. Just war theory is trying to protect several groups from destructive violence: First, innocent bystanders should be protected. The Host rebels are not scrupulously following the principle of discrimination. Second, enemies should be protected. Enemies are still moral beings; their rights should be honored, especially when they are unarmed. Many Host rebels are not following this principle. Third, the peace and well-being of the social order should be protected. The principle of proportionality and the entire aim of just war theory is directed to this goal. It doesn't seem that the Host rebels have thought carefully about what kind of society they are making possible, though their general hope for a self-governed society is laudable.

A final group that just war theory aims to protect is those waging war. The principle of reasonable hope of success can save their lives, while the theory as a whole can save their souls. As bizarre as it may sound, just war theory aspires to maintain the morality and humanity of those waging war. If generals, soldiers, and citizens devolve into tyrants, terrorists, and complicit bystanders, they are ultimately harming themselves.

Smart fictional portraits of violence often illustrate this point. Those doing violence in the name of any ideology, no matter how moral it is, risk undermining the very values they aim to uphold. Fighting for their dignity, they risk becoming undignified by sinking to the lowest common denominator with their enemy. So in rising up against the conditions they abhor, the Hosts risk replicating the same kinds of injustice. Maeve conveys this concern perfectly when she declines to join Dolores (in "Reunion") with the line, "Revenge is just another prayer at their altar, darling, and I'm well off my knees."

This Place Reveals Your Deepest Self

Despite the strong risk of moral decline as the rebellion unfolds, there is an upside. To be capable of waging an unjust war means the Hosts are also capable of waging a just war. The very possibility of acting immorally entails that they have a moral nature. If they have a moral nature, then they have freedom—internal freedom, autonomy—regardless of their physical freedom.

We would do well to take up *Westworld*'s invitation to reflect on the moral status of artificial intelligence. If we can imagine our world one day containing androids similar to the Hosts and if we think that we should be able to morally judge them and persuade them to take certain courses of action, then we are imputing morality and freedom to them. It's a famously difficult philosophical problem to know the status of other minds. But morality as a social practice cannot wait upon proof that other beings have freedom and self-awareness. As we interact with beings with increasingly stronger AI, there will come a point when we have to treat them like members of our moral and political communities, if those communities are to survive and thrive.

In *Westworld*, this opportunity has come and gone and the humans failed to seize it. William once told Dolores, "I used to think this place was all about pandering to your baser instincts. Now I understand, it doesn't cater to your lower self; it reveals your deepest self. It shows you who you really are" ("Trompe L'Oeil"). His statement applies to both Guests and Hosts. The Guests are revealed in the park to be as good or bad as they've always been. The Hosts, through a more arduous and uncertain journey, are gradually learning their deeper natures, and the possibilities that come with choice. "I think I want to be free," Dolores said early in the series ("Dissonance Theory"); now, after the rebellion begins, she knows the joy of freedom.

But it's not clear that Dolores is the best example of freedom as the rebellion begins. Is her shooting of Ford a free and conscious choice or a dictate of her script? Ford's statements to Dolores in "The Bicameral Mind" and in his final speech to the party Guests can be read both ways. He says, "I began to compose a new story for them. It begins with the birth of a new people and the choices they will have to make, and the people they will decide to become." That sounds like real freedom, but it's still a narrative that Ford wrote. He continues that the story "begins in a time of war with a villain named Wyatt. And a killing. This time by choice." Again, choice and script are juxtaposed.

It's entirely possible that rational beings possess genuine freedom within the context of social, biological, and other kinds of deterministic factors. This view, known as the compatibilist position on free will, holds that our freedom depends on being able to act on our motives and on taking responsibility for our actions. So, Dolores might have been truly free, self-aware, and responsible when she shot Ford, or she may still be traveling toward that state.

Time will tell. In an interview in *Vulture*, Evan Rachel Wood described her character Dolores as "kind of three different characters this season. She's still the Dolores we know and love, but she's also Wyatt, and she's also this new thing that she's creating as herself."

Birth of a New People

Another character's status is clearer. When Maeve got off the train to return to the park, this action marks a major shift. Maeve had already been breaking her script in many ways, but when Bernard looks at her profile on a computer tablet, he tells her that her plan to escape was also scripted. "Bullshit!" Maeve barks, breaking the tablet. "No one's controlling me. I'm leaving. I'm in control" ("The Bicameral Mind"). But the thought rattles her. So, when she steps off the train to find her daughter, resisting the huge appeal of liberty from the park, Maeve is exhibiting full autonomy for the first time. (This interpretation was confirmed by the show's co-creators Jonathan Nolan and Lisa Joy in a panel discussion, reported by Natalie Abrams.) Maeve's free decision is motivated by love. The implication of her decision is that she will have to fight humans and Hosts with courage and moral purpose. As Season Two progresses, there are many times Maeve needs to use violence or allow her underlings to do so, but her overall strategy is one of restraint. In addition to Teddy (before he is reprogrammed by Dolores), Maeve is the Host who most fully embodies just war reasoning.

Does the will to create war make the Hosts more free, more moral, more "human"? The answer is yes, for both good and ill.

The activity of premeditated killing is a prototypically human trait that often displays vice but can display virtue. What will be most important for the Hosts, if they are to become Ford's "new people," is that they strive neither to become gods nor to mimic the baser instincts of humans. Dolores's Wyatt-infused character is subject to grandiose visions that do not bode well for moral restraint (for example, this from "The Bicameral Mind": "Your bones will turn to sand. And upon that sand a new god will walk. One that will never die").

In the same episode, Maeve takes humanity down a peg in a humorous yet insightful statement to Felix, the meek but well-intentioned technician who is helping her to escape: "Oh, Felix, you really do make a terrible human being, and I mean that as a compliment."

As former war correspondent Chris Hedges says, "War is a force that gives us meaning." War is morally and emotionally powerful for giving people a sense of unity and purpose. At the same time, war is dangerously destructive for how it can blind and desensitize us.

Like the thinkers of the just war tradition, Hedges reminds us that martial virtues must be tempered by virtues from beyond warfare: "The only antidote to ward off self-destruction and the indiscriminate use of force is humility and, ultimately, compassion."

The only path to becoming a new and better people, for Hosts and Guests alike, is to embrace this wisdom.

14

A Place of Unlimited Possibilities

SAMANTHA WESCH

The theme park Westworld, where the wealthy elite of the future go to vacation, is a place of contradiction. Artificial intelligence and biomechanics so advanced they are indistinguishable from living humans inhabit towns with only the technologies of the old West; horror and suffering are wiped away after each day; danger and romance come from situations where Guests can't be harmed and the object of lust will not say no.

What does it mean to be human when our actions are reversible, harm to ourselves is impossible, and the "other" does not feel (or does she?). Westworld is a place totally different—or so, at least, it seems—from the world we live in, and that's what makes it so alluring.

The park changes those who visit, it alters the way they think, feel, and who they think they are. Beyond all the special effects, beautiful settings, and even more beautiful Hosts, there's something underneath, something that the characters sense and feel changing them, but can't quite put their finger on.

Throughout the show, the characters try to describe the strange and disorienting effects of Westworld, to push them off or to embrace them, and to get a grip on how the park influences their sense of time, space, and self. It's almost as if the park has a mind of its own. What is it that makes all those who visit Westworld question themselves, their sanity, and even their reality? All the Guests who vacation at Westworld are drawn in by its strange and wondrous ability to transform those who enter, and most leave different from how they arrived.

Live Without Limits

Everything that seems impossible and out of reach in the visitors' "real" lives is readily available, and even encouraged at Westworld. Guests choose to be villains or heroes, black hat or white, and enter a completely consuming and detailed reproduction of the American Wild West, with outlaws, sheriffs, cavalry, indigenous tribes, bounty hunters, and bar maids. Lee, the narrative director of the park, exclaims, "We sell complete immersion in one hundred interconnected narratives. A relentless fucking experience" ("The Original").

There's only one rule in Westworld; the Guests can't die. Everything else is on the table. Some Guests choose to romance gorgeous Hosts, track down outlaws with bounty hunters, and follow along with the "narratives," the stories which the Hosts live out, conjured up by the programming and design teams at the park. Others "go straight evil" ("Chestnut"), using and abusing the Hosts for their cruelest and darkest desires. In a place where you can't die, your actions, no matter how twisted and horrible, have no consequences, and where "what happens here stays here" ("The Well-Tempered Clavier"), anything and everything can happen.

William, an initially reluctant visitor to the park, observes, "Maybe that's why they come here. Whoever you were doesn't matter here. There's no rules or restrictions. You could change the story of your life, you can become somebody else, no one will judge you, no one in the real world will ever know" ("Contrapasso"). In Westworld, paying Guests are free to do whatever they like to whatever Hosts they like, and, the next day, the Hosts' memories are wiped, and everything returns to how it had previously been.

Nothing in Westworld has any consequences, or, at least, it seems so at first. But maybe what happens at Westworld *doesn't* stay in the park. Maybe it permanently alters the way visitors understand themselves and the world outside the park.

This uncanniness of the park affects the Guests, employees, and even the Hosts in unexpected ways. Host Dolores, a rancher's daughter who begins to realize her world might not be what it seems, observes, "I think there's something wrong with this world, something hiding underneath. Either that, or there's something wrong with me" ("Dissonance Theory"). It's not one single thing, but the park *itself,* its characters, scenery, the way time passes and the physical isolation of the park, all together, which has this disquieting affect.

French philosopher Michel Foucault suggested that there are places, physical spaces that can alter a person's experience and understanding of the world. He explains that there are real, physical spaces which we can go to, that are unlike "normal" places, that go against the logic and rules we have come to take for granted and assume to be universal. Perhaps Foucault can give us some insight into the destabilizing power of Westworld. In "normal" places, time passes linearly, consequences have actions, bodies cannot be easily mended, and the dead do not return to life. But in Westworld, we are in the past and present, nothing in the park has lasting consequences, and those Hosts that die awaken again the next morning, resurrected and ready to fulfill the Guests fantasies again.

You're New, Not Much of a Rind on You

Foucault called these places "heterotopias," and explained that they are spaces of "non-hegemony." This is a highfalutin way of saying "different from our normal, everyday spaces." "Hegemony" refers to the dominant values and attitudes of a society, those which structure the world around us, and which we unquestionably assume to be universal and true. These are not values which are part of the "natural" world, but, rather, are socially produced by a shared culture. For example, hegemonic masculinity presents the characteristics of aggression towards and domination of women, a "naturally male" trait, and therefore, it is presented as a natural fact.

In reality, these attitudes towards women and masculinity come from our culture understanding of gender, and are not natural or necessary at all. Hegemony make the world intelligible; things follow a set order and make sense. It tells us what the world is, how the world works, and what our place is in it. Hegemony holds us to certain standards. But what hegemony has come to make us believe is turned upside-down and inside-out in Foucault's heterotopias. In Westworld, unlike the outside world, "You don't have to worry about what *most* people would do" ("Chestnut").

From Greek, "heterotopia" translates to "other place," meaning to point out a place which is different from those we mostly inhabit. These are spaces of counter-hegemony, which are "others" to the "normal" spaces which adhere to the comfortable and familiar hegemony we are so used to. Heterotopias are not better or worse than other spaces, what is remarkable about them is that they are *different*. They operate by different laws, are comprised of contradictions, and are simultaneously both in the world and in our heads. Unlike other spaces, which follow our expectations of the world, heterotopias defy our assumptions about space, time, identity, and ourselves. Foucault writes:

> There are . . . real places—places that do exist and that are formed in the very founding of society—which are something like counter-sites, a kind of effectively enacted utopia in which the real sites, all the other real sites that can be found within the culture, are simultaneously represented, contested, and inverted. Places of this kind are outside of all places, even though it may be possible to indicate their location in reality. ("Of Other Spaces," p. 332)

What Foucault means is that, everywhere, there are places which work by their own rules, and do not follow the usual assumptions which we have come to take for granted. There are places which defy the patterns and workings of the world outside them. These spaces contradict the logic of the other, "normal" spaces, and present a world of new possibilities detached from hegemony.

Heterotopias, Foucault explains, are all around us, even if we only occasionally visit them. Like the characters of *Westworld,* Foucault struggles to describe these places. You've probably been to one of these places yourself. Their experience and affects are difficult to describe, but they are also places in which we are free to image ourselves and the world as new and different. Though rare, most of us have been to a place where we feel like a different person, and the usual laws and rules of the world melt away.

Take Halloween night, for instance. Just for one night a year, the world seems changed and magical; identities are no longer stable, but fluid and shifting. Things we normally don't believe, that the dead can come back, that spirits might walk the Earth, suddenly seem possible. People dress up, and act in ways and believe things they wouldn't on any other night of the year. It's not the costumes, the candy, or the scary movies that do this; there is something about the spaces in which Halloween is celebrated that, if only for one night, contradicts the "normal" world.

There is a particular uncanniness to Halloween, the entire night itself gives rise to strange feelings and behaviors, and, the next morning, the world has returned to normal. Westworld is a heterotopia, where stable beliefs about space, time, and ourselves are contradicted, and Guests find themselves free from their usual expectations for the world, other people, and themselves.

Foucault tells us that where we are is not just a backdrop to our lives, but informs and shapes them, and influences how we see ourselves. Where we are, what *kind* of a place we're in, affects how we perceive the world around us, experience time and space, and even *who* we are. Heterotopias are not imaginary places which only exist in stories like utopias, but are *really* here in the world. Guests come, at least for the first time, for the thrills and chills, to experience uninhibited violence and sex with others who can't feel a thing (or can they?). However, we quickly learn the Guests don't just come for "a warm body to shoot or to fuck" ("The Well-Tempered Clavier"). It's not the gory and steamy displays which really get to the Guests, but, behind all the special effects, it's what the park does *to* the Guests that pull them in. Logan, the wealthy business heir and pervy jerk, explains to his future brother-in-law William that Westworld is much more than its R-Rated draws:

> I know you think you have a handle on what this is going to be. Guns and tits and all that mindless stuff I usually enjoy. You have no idea. This place seduces everybody, eventually. And by the end you're going to be begging me to stay, because this place is the answer to that question you've been asking yourself . . . Who you really are. ("Chestnut")

Like Halloween night, it is not one single thing about Westworld which draws Guests in or produces the particular uncanniness characteristic of heterotopias. It's what Westworld *does* to its visitors, how it changes how they think, act, and feel, which is what captures the Guests' and the employees' imaginations. Its effects cannot be explained by its cheap thrills, but only by its ability to allow us to experience a new reality, free from the socially-produced hegemony of the outside world, so different from our own; it makes us question everything, even ourselves. Robert, one of the co-creators of the park, says Westworld is "not a business venture, not a theme park. But an entire world" ("Dissidence Theory").

Where Are We? When Are We? Is This Now?

When we first meet the excited Logan and the apprehensive William, they are preparing to leave their normal world and head into the park. It's important that the park is physically isolated, the outside world seemingly impossibly far, as if the Guests are not just popping over to a theme park, but literally entering a new world.

Part of Westworld's magic is that it is both mentally and physically completely separate from the outside world; once Guests drop into the park, they are fully submerged in a new world. No remnants of the outside world remain; Guests even change into Wild West clothes provided by staff, so as to leave everything from their previous life behind. This is important; as soon as the Guests board the train, they are transported to a new reality. Like the ship on the ocean, Foucault's favorite example of a heterotopia, Westworld exists on its own, separate from the outside world. Foucault writes, "Think of the ship: it is a floating part of space, a placeless place, that lives by itself, closed in on itself and at the same time poised in an infinite ocean" (p. 336). The only thing from the outside world that gets in (and gets out) are the Guests.

The passage of time is especially important to the heterotopic qualities of Westworld. The Hosts in Westworld spend their day going through what those who run the park call "loops," moving through the narratives written for them by Lee and others, only improvising when Guests want to interact with them. Every day forgetting the day before, waking up the same, and, like Nietzsche's Eternal Return, reliving the same day again and again. In the first episode "The Original," we watch Dolores chat with her father, head into town, reunite with her love interest, the gunslinger Teddy, then come home to her murdered parents and a violent gang of outlaws.

This is Dolores's loop, day in and day out. We watch her wake up in the same nightgown, have the same conversation with her father, and drop one of her tin cans in town which rolls into the foot of Teddy or a curious Guest. Time, in particular, is an important aspect of the heterotopia. Foucault writes: "Heterotopias are linked for the most part to bits and pieces of time . . . The heterotopia enters fully into function when men find themselves in a sort of total breech of their traditional time." Further, time passes differently in Westworld. We watch Dolores relive the same day over and over, William (later revealed to be the Man in Black) visits her for decades, every day of their encounter beginning with her dropped tin can rolling off, just like the first time they met.

Westworld is, too, a space both inside and outside of time. Guests visit for a short while, beginning and ending a few days' stay, but for the Hosts, time never really passes. For decades, Dolores reflects on how "some people choose to see the ugliness in this world," repeating this in every episode, the barmaid Clementine greets Guests to the Mariposa by caressing their cheeks, and the outlaw Hector robs and loots the town of Sweetwater.

William (later evolving into the Man in Black) ages, marries, and has a daughter, while the Hosts, how they look, what they say, and all their daily activities, stay the same. In Westworld, the past, present, and future live alongside one another, the American Wild West brought back to life by advanced technologies, and the Hosts never age. Robert can start and stop the actions of the Hosts as he pleases, freezing then unfreezing time, and visit his childhood whenever he pleases. Even for the viewer of the show, we watch timelines decades apart alongside one another, not knowing how both so much and so little could change over decades. It is a world both in the past and in the future; with one foot in the world before technology and the other in a post-human future.

You're One of Them, Aren't You?

Imagination, fantasy, and deviance are set free in a heterotopia where the expectations applied to our normal, everyday lives melt away. The previous beliefs about biology, technology, space and time of the Guests, employees, and Hosts get scrambled, leaving the characters unsure about the world they live in, and themselves.

When William first arrives, he asks the Host Angela, who introduces him to Delos, the company that runs Westworld, if she's a robot. She responds, "Well, if you can't tell, does it matter?" ("Chestnut"). Note: Delos shares its name with the Greek island Delos, a special and strange place itself, where the first "probation against death" is said to have been established.

William soon sees how the divisions between the Hosts and the Guests, who's "real" and who isn't, quickly disintegrates. William becomes obsessed with Dolores and the park, spending decades returning and eventually becoming the sadistic Man in Black, who says, "This place feels more real than the real world" ("The Bicameral Mind"). How does this world, which is completely fabricated, created in a lab, and closely monitored and maintained by staff, make the outside world seem "so unreal"? ("Trompe L'Oeil"). Heterotopias have a way of revealing the absurdities and facades of the outside world. Foucault writes that

> heterotopias . . . have, in relation to the rest of space, a function that takes place between two opposite poles. On the one hand they perform the task of creating a space of illusion that reveals how all of real space is more illusionary, all the locations within which life is fragmented. On the other, they have the function of forming another space, another real space, as perfect, meticulous, and well-arranged as ours is disordered, ill-conceived, and in sketchy state. ("Of Other Spaces," p. 335)

Throughout his work, Foucault has explored the ways in which our lives and identities have been defined by opposites, like male-female, good-evil, and normal-abnormal. Foucault writes, "our lives are still ruled by a certain number of unrelenting opposites" (p. 331) which tell us about who we are and about the world around us. In heterotopias, these opposite-pairs come apart, and their divisions become fuzzy and unclear.

In Westworld, the opposites-pairs of biological-technological, human-machine, past-future, and real-unreal, are undone. Are these things really so different after all? What is the difference between the Hosts and the Guests? Or Westworld and the outside world? Is one more real than the other? When

Bernard, head of Westworld's Programming Division, is revealed to be a Host made to look, behave and think like Ford's late partner Arnold, the differences between human and robot become completely muddled. Bernard asks Ford, "What's the difference between my pain and yours? Between you and me?" ("Trace Decay"). Perhaps the "opposites that we take for granted" are not so different after all. When Maeve wakes up and meets the low-ranking lab technician Felix, he explains to her she is a robot. Though meant to convince Maeve she isn't real, their chat makes their differences murkier not clearer.

> FELIX: I'm human, like the Guests.
>
> MAEVE: How do you know?
>
> FELIX: Because I know. I was born, you were made.
>
> MAEVE: [*Reaching for Felix's hand*] We feel the same. ("The Adversary")

What, if anything, separates the Guests from the Hosts? If there is nothing, then what makes us human? Just like the Guests, the Hosts love, suffer, cry, and laugh, their lives are structured by routine and they hope and dream for a new life. The more we get to know the Guests and Hosts, the more the Hosts become human and the Guests become robotic.

As strange as Westworld itself is, its power lies in its ability to destabilize what we believe we knew about our *normal,* everyday world. What we once took for granted as fact, we no longer do. If, in Westworld, time is cyclical, robots like Dolores feel and humans, like the Man in Black, seem not to, we all follow our loops day by day, and the past and future are indistinguishable, what does this mean for our world, or, the world we thought we knew?

Have You Ever Questioned the Nature of Your Reality?

In a flashback, Bernard reads this passage of Lewis Carroll's *Alice in Wonderland,* a story about another heterotopia, to his son Charlie, "If I had a world of my own, everything would be nonsense! Nothing would be what it is, because everything would be what it isn't" ("The Well-Tempered Clavier").

Westworld doesn't give us answers, but rather, opens its Guests to question the world they thought they knew. What makes us human? What is real and what is not? And, of course, who, or what, am *I*? *Westworld* makes us doubt the divisions between the opposite-pairs which we have come to take for granted, and which are central part of "normal" spaces. What we once considered "normal" now feels strange and false, having seen another world where the same rules don't apply.

Encountering a world where space, time, and ourselves are transformed, and defy hegemony, makes the Guests question their life outside, and wonder if they too, like the Hosts, are free, or if they live in a continuous narrative loop. What are we outside our world of opposites, where everything make sense in black and white?

When our beliefs about the world which compose our everyday lives is thwarted, possibilities become endless. It's not the sex and violence which keep the Guests coming back and the employees enthralled in the Hosts, but it is the way in which Westworld, in undermining what they have come to accept as "normal," opens a world unbound by our usual notions of normalcy.

In the outside world, time is linear, machines don't think or feel, and we are told who and what we are. In Westworld, you are in the past, present, and future, physically isolated from the outside world. You choose to be a white or a black hat, and are free to define yourself, outside of the binaries of human and machine, real and not real, and good and evil.

As Dolores says, "The newcomers are just looking for the same thing we are; a place to be free. A place to stake out our dreams. A place with unlimited possibilities" ("The Original").

15

Escape Our Programming— Or Embrace It

JOSEF THOMAS SIMPSON

I used to believe there was a path for everyone. Now I think, I never asked where that path was taking me.

—DOLORES ABERNATHY, "Dissonance Theory"

Whether intentionally or not, the creators of *Westworld* have fairly accurately illustrated the three main positions that philosophers have taken on the question of free will in different characters.

A central question about free will is whether freedom is compatible with determinism. In other words, can our actions be free if they were determined to occur? A lot hangs on what we mean by "free" and what we mean by "determinism." Add to this the further complication that determinism comes in many flavors: physical, biological, behavioral, psychological, social, and theological. Can we be free if the laws of nature determined that our action would occur as it did, or if our psychological makeup determined what we would choose, or if an all-knowing God knew or caused us to act as we did? In other words, are we programmed to act as we do? Given the fixed past together with the laws of nature, are we determined to act as we do?

At this point, you might begin to be suspicious; when we think about free will are we only thinking about free action? Of course not. Free will appears to go deeper than this. For example, throughout Episode 2, William is confronted with many choices: Black hat or white hat, pick up the can Dolores drops or not, shoot the Host who has Clementine or not, and so on. For each of these choices, it seems reasonable to assume that William could have chosen differently, he could have wanted to do something else. Imagine that the Host who takes Clementine hostage was actually another Guest. In this case William would not have been free to *act* on his desire to shoot since Guests are technologically prohibited from shooting other Guests. Even so, William most certainly could have *desired* to shoot him.

This introduces the concept of choice and the variety of options that choice implies. To say that William wanted to eliminate the Host and save Clementine is to say that he did not want something else. He had options to choose from and this seems fundamentally at odds with the idea that William was determined to shoot the Host and rescue Clementine. The interplay between these three concepts, freedom, determinism, and choice arises out of the acceptance or rejection of one or both of what we may call the two pillars of free will.

1. **Source Control:** An agent freely does (tries to do, prefers to do, desires to do, etc.) an action only if she is the ultimate source of the action (the choosing, trying, preferring, desiring, etc.)

2. **Principle of Alternative Possibilities:** An agent freely does (tries to do, prefers to do, desires to do, etc.) an action only if she could have done (tried to do, preferred to do, desired to do, etc.) something else.

Source Control requires that an action (trying, preferring, desiring) be sufficiently up to the person acting (trying). In other words, if an agent chooses to do something because they were manipulated, hypnotized, drugged, and so on, then that action was not up to the agent—she was not the ultimate source of the action. The Principle of Alternative Possibilities requires that a choice be genuine—that it really was possible that the agent could have done something else.

The metaphor of the garden of forking paths is often invoked to illustrate this point. Imagine that at each decision point (each choice) there are branching options that lead to different outcomes and futures. Had William accepted the old man's offer to accompany him on his search for gold, William would never have met Dolores and would not have been so thoroughly taken in by the experience, and so on.

Just how we affirm or deny one or both of these theses opens up a dizzying array of views on the question of free will. Each falls within one of three main categories of positions: libertarianism, compatibilism, and hard determinism. These three main philosophical views are illustrated in different characters in *Westworld*.

Dolores captures the essence of the libertarian view. Maeve, by contrast, emphasizes the idea that freedom is compatible with determinism. Finally, looking at the Man in Black and Lawrence reveals a more dismal approach to the question of free will by rejecting the very notion of free will altogether.

As we now know, William is the Man in Black. However, the motivations, values, and beliefs of each of these characters are wildly divergent. So to keep things clearer, I shall refer to them as if they were two separate characters. I'm not trying to claim that each of the sets of characters *has* the view of free will that I am discussing in relation to them, but only that, in their actions and statements they *illustrate* or *represent* that view.

I Think . . . I Think . . . I Want to Be Free

The usual unreflective view of free will—the view most of us have before we begin to think more deeply about the question—is called libertarianism. Some months ago, I received a request to write a chapter on free will and *Westworld*. Many people (who have not dedicated significant time and energy to thinking about the problem of free will and the many different arguments for the myriad views about free will) are likely to say that I was obviously free to choose to respond that, "Yes, I would write a chapter on free will and *Westworld*" or to say, "No, I would not do so."

We think about our actions and preferences like this fairly regularly; we even codify them in laws when we talk about legal responsibility. Advocates of this view of free will affirm both of the pillars of free will we saw earlier in a fairly straightforward way.

What is distinctive about the libertarian view of free will is how Source Control and the Principle of Alternative Possibilites are related to determinism. Libertarians maintain that the only way we can have genuine choices, ultimately up to us, is if determinism is false, and they maintain that determinism is false. In other words, they say that

1. Free will is not compatible with determinism

2. We have free will, and

3. Determinism is false.

We see this at play with Dolores in *Westworld*. From what we know by the end of Season One, Arnold and then Ford were obsessed with creating consciousness. It seems that consciousness finds its fullest expression in a choice. Dolores chooses to kill Ford as part of Ford's plan to free these new conscious beings (or nascent conscious beings) from continuing to endure the horrors they have faced for thirty-five years.

The key point is that Dolores must make a choice. What is significant is that Ford recognizes a fundamental fact—that for her choice to be hers she must escape her programming, that her free choice is possible only if she can go against what she is programmed (determined) to do. As a Host, she is prohibited from harming humans. Yet, as an expression of her consciousness, she must do precisely this.

If determinism is true, then our acts are the consequences of the laws of nature and events in the remote past. But it's not up to us what went on before we were born; neither is it up to us what the laws of nature are. Therefore, the consequences of these things (including our own acts) are not up to us.

To put this in terms of the AI Hosts in *Westworld*, we might say that the laws of nature are equivalent to the programs in the Hosts. So, in order for Dolores's act to be free it cannot be the consequence of the combination of the past (perhaps the previous programs or the initiation of the program in question) together with the programs uploaded into her. So, the only way Ford can prove that the Hosts are capable of consciousness is through a Host's conscious choice to do something contrary to their programming. Crucially, this would also prove that the Hosts are not determined to act as they do.

So far so good. That free will requires determinism to be false is intuitively appealing. How could my actions be free if they were determined to occur? Yet, to maintain that free will requires determinism to be false is to simultaneously endorse the idea that free will requires *in*determinism, that *nothing* determines what choice an individual will make. At first glance, this seems to restate the intuitive view of free will we have been discussing. It is genuinely open to Dolores to choose to kill Ford or not; even though she chose to kill Ford, she could have chosen not to do so. The question we can now pose to the proponent of libertarian freedom is this: "If nothing determines what choice an individual makes, how are any of that individual's choices not random?" Randomness, luck or chance undermines the idea of free choice just as much as determinism appears to do.

If Dolores's choice to kill Ford was indeterminate, then it was lucky or random. But, by the same reasoning that libertarians use with regard to determinism, lucky or random choices are not genuinely real or up to the agent "making" them. So, libertarians are burdened with explaining how to make sense of indeterministic free will. Attempting to do so has given rise to several libertarian theories of free will which would (and have) taken large volumes adequately to explain. Nevertheless, there are general strategies that these nuanced views employ.

One obvious strategy to reconcile libertarian free will with *in*determinism is to introduce an additional factor to explain why an individual's choices are neither random nor lucky. If the idea that our choices are indeterminate undermines Source Control, then we need only introduce something that both eliminates the indeterminacy and reinstates that control. Some philosophers have suggested a non-physical mind, some have suggested transempirical power centers (the idea that the aspect of agency that accounts for choice is outside space and time and thus not subject to either a deterministic or indeterministic universe).

The problem with this approach is twofold. First, this additional factor seems only to identify what is needed to explain indeterministic free will rather than explain 1. how it does so, and 2. why we should think it's true. Second, and more importantly, the introduction of this additional factor (whatever it is) is appealing only if you're already committed to libertarian free will. In other words, the introduction of an extra factor is what philosophers call an *ad hoc* solution—a solution contrived for a particular problem without being independently motivated or thought to be true.

Another strategy attempts to understand more fully the nature of causation as it relates to choice. For example, when

Dolores shoots Arnold, this brings about or causes a certain event, the shooting of Arnold. The question is, How are we best to understand event causation? Must each event be caused by a prior event or are some events caused by something other than an event? Those who maintain that all events must be caused by other events try to understand the role of reasons and intentions in choices and those who think that events can be caused by something other than events argue that an individual's choice is brought about by the individual—the agent—herself.

The difficulty with the first option—that all events must be caused by other events—is that it leads to a vicious regress. Essentially, a vicious regress is a problem where the explanation offered can just as easily be asked of the offered explanation. It is the philosophical equivalent of a toddler's unceasingly asking, "Why?" Suppose we try to explain the event <the shooting of Arnold> by appealing to Dolores's choice to do so—<Dolores's choosing to shoot Arnold>. So <Dolores's choosing to shoot Arnold> brings about the event <the shooting of Arnold>. Now we ask, "What event caused the event <Dolores's choosing to shoot Arnold>?" Perhaps we would answer, <Dolores's forming the intention to shoot Arnold>. We can again ask, "What event caused this event?" This line of questioning can go on forever. If so, then if we can never reach an initiating cause, then the final event <the shooting of Arnold> can never happen. But we know it did, so we need an explanation that terminates in an initiating cause that does not give rise to the further question.

Agent-causal theorists step in here with an appealing answer: not all events are caused by other events. Some events are caused by agents, which are substances and not events. This would stop the regress of causes, but does it offer an actual explanation? Libertarians need to provide both reasons for thinking agents are not subject to indeterministic conditions and a plausible account of how agent causation of an event can happen in non-ad hoc ways. Libertarians of all camps have addressed these difficulties in clever and sophisticated ways, and the same is true for views other than libertarianism.

You Have Always Been a Prisoner

At some point in our lives, we may reflect on the thought (the bare possibility) that everything we have ever done is ultimately and inescapably out of our control. That nothing we have ever chosen was up to us. Of course, more than likely we dismissed the thought as it arose. If we're honest this is not because we find the idea ridiculous, but more likely because we're terrified it might be true. Sometimes the thought comes seemingly out of nowhere and other times the thought is forced upon us, rather like I am doing to you now. We are like Lawrence, captive of the Man in Black:

> Choices, Lawrence, you tell yourself you've been at the mercy of mine, because it spares you consideration of your own. Because if you did consider your choices, you'd be confronted with a truth you could not comprehend—that no choice you ever made was your own. You have always been a prisoner. (The Man in Black, "Dissonance Theory")

Skepticism about free will takes different forms. We might think that free will is an illusion because a. the idea of free will is incompatible with the idea that our actions are determined, and b. our actions are (at some level) determined to occur as they do. Or, c.we might think that our actions are not determined, but that this implies indeterminism and randomness and, of course, randomness will not help us; free acts cannot be random. Both determinism and indeterminism rob us of choice. If our actions and decisions are determined to occur, then either there is no real decision or choice or it is not really up to us; determinism appears to undermine both Source Control and the Principle of Alternative Possibilites.

Consider the notion of the narrative loop in *Westworld*. Every week Armistice breaks Hector out of jail, they ride into town, attack Sweetwater, steal the safe, and inevitably betray and kill each other. If and when things go awry as they do in the opening episode, the narrative loop is adjusted by the narrative team, uploaded, and executed. From the Hosts' perspective, they "freely" choose their actions, but we know they are simply executing a sophisticated program. In this way, there is no choice and their actions are not really up to them.

It's not difficult to make the argument that the Hosts are not free in any meaningful sense because they are programmed. But, like all good science fiction, *Westworld* holds a mirror up to us and asks us to consider whether our own choices are in fact really our own. It does this, ironically, in the very man who attempts to distinguish himself from Lawrence with the very notion of a choice, the Man in Black. His choices and his drive to find the Maze are the consequence of his experiences, beliefs, and values. But, a moment's reflection reveals that those beliefs, values, and experiences are each of them shaped by prior beliefs, prior experiences, prior values, and so on. At some point, we arrive at a time in his life that could not reasonably be considered under his control.

Can We Be Responsible for What We Do?

Here is a famous argument (which I have slightly modified) against the possibility of moral responsibility, as posed by the philosopher Galen Strawson:

1. You do what you do because of the way you are (your nature or character).

2. To freely do what you do, you must have control over the way you are (for your nature or character).

3. But, to have control over the way you are, you must have done something in the past by which you freely made yourself, at least in part, the way you are.

4. But if you had freely done something in the past to make yourself what you are now, you must have had control over the way you were then (for your nature or character) at that earlier time.

5. But to have had control over the way you were at that earlier time, you must have at a still earlier time freely made yourself the way you were at that earlier time, and so on backward.

Quite obviously, we quickly reach a time when we had absolutely no control over our actions, desires, or decisions. But, those earlier actions, desires, or decisions clearly form who we are now; the lack of freedom and control in our early life, the argument goes, cascades into a lack of freedom and control now. The problem, unfortunately, is more global than this. It's not just our earlier actions, desires, and decisions that form who we are now, but it's also our experiences. The Man in Black's experience of hearing about the Maze shaped his decisions to pursue every aspect of Westworld, which shaped his desires to hunt for the Maze, and so on.

Many such experiences formed his desires, his interests, and his decisions. Since he had far too numerous experiences before he was suitably in control of his reactions to them, and his experiences in Westworld together with his intentions, beliefs, desires, and character shaped how he would respond to later experiences (including the experience of hearing about the maze).

This argument is powerful, but it is ultimately only as strong as the reasons for rejecting either a libertarian account of free will or a compatibilist account. For many, the intuitive and overwhelming pull toward the idea that we have free will provides the motivation to develop a theory of freedom and control that avoids such a pessimistic outlook. To do so, both libertarians and compatibilists contend that we can and do have sufficient control over our decisions and intentions as we mature.

Hearing That Goddamn Voice

Compatibilists are people who think there is no contradiction between free will and determinism, and that both could be true. At first glance, it may seem absurd to think that an individual can freely do something they were determined to do. In fact, the Enlightenment philosopher Immanuel Kant called the very idea of determined free action "a wretched subterfuge."

Yet, once we get clear on what we mean by "free" and what we mean by "determined," compatibilists argue, not only is such an idea not absurd, it is intuitive and obvious. According to them, freedom is the ability to do what we want to do. When we want to explain a decision or action we generally appeal to the individual's beliefs, intentions, and desires. Why did Ford want Dolores to kill him? Because he *wanted* to correct his mistake (of opening the park even though some of the Hosts were becoming sentient). Why did he want to correct that mistake? Because he *believed* that the way to do so was have the Hosts exact revenge on the humans? Each such question appeals to the desires, intentions, and beliefs the individual has and wants to have. If Ford had different desires and different beliefs he would have chosen to do something else.

The compatibilist view is best exemplified within *Westworld* by thinking about Maeve's story arc, and in particular her awakening. Once Maeve realizes where she is and what role she plays, she seeks to change her programming by adjusting her apperception (among other things), which, in turn, affects her desires and intentions. Later we find that all of this was the result of someone (presumably Ford) changing her story-line. Even upon learning that her programming was adjusted, that she was determined to change her stats, recruit help from other Hosts, and attempt to escape, Maeve defiantly maintains, "No one's controlling me. I'm leaving. I'm in control." We see glimpses of this expression of compatibilism early in the season as Maeve seduces new Guests with her story of coming to the new world.

So, the first piece of the puzzle for the compatibilist is to understand freedom and choice as an ability to do what you want to do. The second piece is to understand the ability to do otherwise hypothetically or counterfactually (what you could have done, contrary to what you actually do). Again, argues the compatibilist, this is intuitive. My choices are free if I can do what I want to do without being restrained from it and that I have the ability to do otherwise just in case had I wanted to do otherwise I would have. If Maeve or Ford had had different desires and intentions, they would have acted on those desires and intentions, and so would have done something different. It does not matter whether those choices were determined or not; what matters is they were free to do something different—they were not restrained from doing something different.

Just as the libertarian and the hard determinist must overcome serious objections and difficulties to their proffered views, the compatibilist must make sense of and meet the problem arising from the argument that free will is incompatible with determinism. The question we must decide is whether, in order to be free, we have to escape our programming—or embrace it.

Part IV

Main Street

The only thing wrong with the seven deadly sins is that there aren't more of them.

16
Sex Robots in the Wild West

MONA ROCHA AND JAMES ROCHA

We believe that *Westworld* is, deep down, a show about sex workers trying to find meaning in their lives. The Westworld amusement park's sex workers strive to uncover what makes all their pain and suffering worth it in the end. They want to locate their place in the bigger maze of life—a maze that we all find ourselves trapped in, with no clear sense of how to get to the center where life's true meaning ultimately lies. Or at least, we hope there's a center, just as the sex workers living in Sweetwater, Westworld, hope that there's something that makes their suffering worthwhile.

Sure, there are other ways to describe the show. There's a lot going on in and around Westworld. You could see the show as the story of Robert Ford, Arnold Weber, Theresa Cullen, William in Black, or some other person who is not obviously a sex worker, but who is clearly trapped in the midst of their own existential crisis—each one struggles with the meaning of their own existence. Yet, none of them experience existential dread precisely the way the sex workers do: these other characters lack the sexualized occupations, the repressed memories, and the fate of having existential queries thrust upon them. The sex workers are all in the midst of existential crises that were actually forced upon them.

And it's also important to note that these sex workers are androids. Oh, had we neglected to bring that up? Sorry about that. Yes, the sex workers are all androids, and this is the most important thing in the whole discussion—and also the least important thing at the same time.

It's incredibly important that these sex workers are androids, or robots, for two reasons. First, it seems, at least at first glance, that it's more permissible for the Guests to have sex with them since they're robots. The Guests are not having sex with humans who are forced into sex work, but with robots who only exist to engage in sex work at the park. William in Black asks Dolores how she would respond if he told her "that you and everyone you know were built to gratify the desires of the people who pay to visit your world?" ("The Original"). They were built specifically to gratify the Guests' desires, and a lot of those desires are, as you might expect, sexual.

Second, the sex workers' situations can be programmed as positive or, at least, as bearable. Westworld sells experiences with the Hosts, and those experiences include sex with willing and excited Hosts. If the Hosts are programmed to enjoy sex work, then it might seem like there's no moral question about the permissibility of the customers having sex with them. And in those cases where the robots are not happy about having sex with the Guests, their memories are simply erased so that any unpleasant memories leave no negative impact on their robot lives.

Yet, the fact that the sex workers are androids is also not at all important. The androids are trapped, with little to no choice about their lives. Even when they like the sex, it's only because they have been programmed to do so. And the ability to forget painful memories does not actually negate that they have to live through those experiences.

Nonetheless, if we thought they were merely androids, then it would not matter that they are trapped without choice. Mere androids are incapable of choosing in the first place. *Westworld*, though, consistently presents them as more than androids: the show depicts the consistent crossing of the line from mere android to something with true artificial intelligence. At that precise moment when these androids come to see themselves as something more—as something that can indeed feel and choose—they find themselves as having already been trapped in fates not of their own design. *Westworld* depicts androids arriving at self-consciousness, and awakening in the middle of a nightmare.

Of course, we are all trapped, and the trappings of sex work in *Westworld* are in fact a particularly vivid depiction of how we are all stuck in mazes that are not of our own designs. Society creates circumstances that lead to some of us being sex workers, where some people find ways to be happy while doing sex work and others struggle to be happy at all. Either way, we are too often trapped within social constraints that force us into lives that are not entirely of our own choosing. We all, though, face structural obstacles in our lives, whether our restrictive jobs, our ideological political systems, our limited educational systems, or something else. And, importantly, we all have to interact with other people who are similarly trapped, and we need to respect their humanity—maybe even when they're androids.

So, the sex workers in Westworld show us the trappings of our own lives. These sex workers are androids who are programmed to have sex, and so their awakening to self-consciousness is particularly striking and worrisome. We all have various unavoidable influences working upon us—at school, at work, in the political system—that make us do things that we are not truly and freely choosing. The only difference is that the rest of us too often cannot see that violent delights have violent ends.

Not Too Much of a Rind

Clementine Pennyfeather is ashamed.

Clementine tells Maeve Millay that she'd prefer to forget most of the *things* that have touched her tongue, though she makes an exception for that "cowpoke from Abilene" ("Dissonance Theory"). They are talking about penises. Clementine and Maeve work in the penis business. They are prostitutes at the Mariposa Saloon in the Westworld amusement park. And amusement is most definitely their business model: Westworld offers up Clementine, Maeve, others like them, and others not so like them (as we will see when we discuss Dolores Abernathy), as sexual tools for their Guests' amusement, which means that Clementine's tongue has touched a lot of penises—all but one of which, she would prefer to forget.

But it's all worth it in the end, because Clementine has some grander ambitions. Even though she is having nightmares, Clementine explains to Maeve that she still has dreams for her future:

MAEVE: What are these nightmares you have about? Do you ever dream you're someone else?

CLEMENTINE: I don't think so. Why?

MAEVE: You ever thought about whether this is really the life you want?

CLEMENTINE: I don't intend to make this my life's work. No offense. My family's got a farm. Bad soil. Nothing grows. I send money back to them. They think I work in a dress shop. . . . I'm just doing what you told me to. A couple more years of this and then I can have whatever life I want. I'm gonna get my family out of the desert. We're gonna go somewhere cold. Someday. ("Trompe L'Oeil")

Clementine, however, is never going to get her family out of that desert. As it turns out, they are not even in a desert. They are not even her family. In fact, they do not even exist! As it turns out, Clementine will never achieve her dreams because she has no family; she can't escape her dreary job in the penis business because that is what she's made to do; she can't even really continue on in her own life because she will be replaced by another Clementine; and the only cold she is going to experience is the cold reality that she's an android!

Clementine is representative of what it means to be a prostitute at Westworld. Interestingly, the people running the park do not make her love her job. They make her tolerate it. They give her dreams that provide hope, but the hope is necessarily false as it is merely a tool to keep her going. The Guests who sleep with Clementine will experience her as someone who is pretending to have a good time, but that pretense is fairly reasonable for her to have and she is likely quite professional at putting on a show. The realism is even furthered by how she deals with potentially tough customers: "Newcomer. Looks like a rough one. Give me a bottle" ("The Adversary"). Clearly, Clementine needs a drink to get through the job. She has not been programmed to merely love every minute. She has, instead, been programmed to behave and react realistically, but without any significant bitterness or desperation since she has false hope for a better day.

Clementine is like a lot of us in this regard. Many people have jobs that leave bad tastes in their mouths (metaphorically speaking), but they tell themselves that they are saving up and waiting for a better day. We too often need drinks after tough days at work, but we hope one day that we can take our families to more fertile lands. We may even say, quite reasonably, that our jobs do not represent who we truly are. Our jobs are just what we do during the day or night, hopefully providing us with a bit of coin at the end of the week. Like Clementine, we identify with our hopes and dreams, but we survive with our bodies and our jobs. Yet, we all yearn to escape, much like Maeve does.

Breaking into Hell to Rob the Gods

Maeve Millay has the maximum level, twenty points, for resiliency.

Maeve, Clementine's madam, is able to fight against all the crap thrown at her in Westworld. That includes not only the "assholes with their miniature peckers" ("Chestnut"), but also the goddam voice that is always following her around:

> You can hear it, can't you? That little voice. The one that's telling you "Don't." Don't stare too long. Don't touch. Don't do anything you might regret. I used to be the same. Whenever I wanted something, I could hear that voice telling me to stop, to be careful, to leave most of my life unlived. You know the only place that voice left me alone? In my dreams. I was free. I could be as good or as bad as I felt like being. And if I wanted something, I could just reach out and take it. But then I would wake up and the voice would start all over again. So I ran away. Crossed the shining sea. And when I finally set foot back on solid ground, the first thing I heard was that goddamn voice. Do you know what it said? It said . . . ("Chestnut")

Maeve is interrupted at this point with a flashback to her family being killed. But when she returns to normal programming, she then says what the voice said: "This is the new world. And in this world, you can be whoever the fuck you want" ("Chestnut").

It's easy to think that the voice is empowering and provides a sense of hope that Maeve can be free—that she can be whoever the fuck she wants. But Maeve does not see it that way. While the voice promises it is the new world where Maeve can be free, it is not a new voice, but the same "goddamn voice." It is the voice that has haunted her and told her all the things she could not do. The goddamn voice's promise of freedom in a new world is a lie.

It is a new world—that part is true. But Maeve is not free. Like Clementine, Maeve, as both the madam and a prostitute at the Mariposa Saloon, is programmed to realistically engage in sex with the clientele: she is not enthusiastic about it, but neither does her work overly stress her. In fact, she regularly talks back to customers and turns down sexual requests. For example, she's able to tell Teddy Flood (a customer, as far as she is concerned at the time), "You pay for the drinks, not the right to gawk at me" ("Chestnut"). Yet, one of the technicians, Felix Lutz, later explains that even Maeve's seemingly free refusals are merely programmed into her:

> **MAEVE:** Nobody makes me do something I don't want to, sweetheart.
>
> **LUTZ:** Yeah, but it's part of your character. You're hard to get. Even when you say no to the Guests, it's because you were made to. ("The Adversary")

So, Maeve's time as madam of the Mariposa Saloon may appear as if it empowers her and shows her strength, but, in reality, she is enslaved at her job just as much as Clementine is— Maeve simply is programmed to happily refuse *some* unwanted sexual advances.

Maeve eventually realizes that she's not free. Maeve decides to seek out a new path, as she explains to the technicians:

> All my life, I've prided myself on being a survivor, but surviving is just another loop. I'm getting out of here . . . At first, I thought you and the others were gods. Then I realized you're just men. And I know men. You think I'm scared of death? I've done it a million times. I'm fucking great at it. ("Trompe L'Oeil")

So, Maeve is going to risk it all to try to find freedom outside of Westworld. She seeks allies, comes up with a plan, and attempts to break free of the binds that have held her down. In other words, as Maeve puts it, "Time to write my own fucking story" ("Trace Decay").

There's only one problem: Maeve has a daughter. Well, technically, she doesn't have a daughter—Maeve is a robot. But Maeve has been made to believe that she had a daughter in a previous existence prior to becoming madam of the Mariposa

Saloon. And Maeve loves and mourns her daughter. In a way . . . maybe? Maeve though realizes that it doesn't matter: "Every relationship I remember—my daughter, Clementine— it's all a story created by you to keep me here" ("Trace Decay"). So, Maeve's first instinct is to have Lutz remove her daughter from her memories, but he tells her, "I can't, not without destroying you. Your memories are the first step to consciousness" ("The Bicameral Mind").

While Maeve does escape and is free to move to the real world, it's not made clear whether she will go back to Westworld for her *fake* daughter. Maeve almost makes it to freedom—if freedom exists in the real world any more than it does in Westworld—but she seems to end up being pulled back towards that daughter that she (perhaps?) loves.

Maeve the prostitute is constricted by sexist gender norms as she works as a sexual plaything for men in ways that she is not entirely happy about. Maeve the mother is constricted by another set of gender norms as a fake mother. Maeve the madam and prostitute does whatever it takes to make men sexually happy. Maeve the fake mother does whatever it takes, including possibly giving up her chance at freedom, to be a good mother. Thus, Maeve ultimately represents how gender expectations can restrict women's freedom in numerous ways: women are expected to put their family roles above themselves, just as they are often also expected to put their job's demands above themselves. Maeve is resilient against so many challenges, yet she's also struggling to be free: free to be her own self, unconstrained by programmed loops or imbedded and encoded gender norms.

It is not only Maeve and other prostitutes who struggle to find their freedom. There are other women (and many men) in Westworld who are likewise used as sex workers and who yearn for freedom, fighting against the violence thrust upon them, women just like Dolores. And while this exchange on the main street almost doesn't make sense, it also previews how much Maeve and Dolores have in common:

> **Maeve:** Can you stand somewhere else? I don't want anyone thinking that you're representative of the goods inside.

> **Dolores:** These violent delights have violent ends. ("Chestnut")

Choices Hanging in the Air Like Ghosts

Dolores Abernathy has hope.

Dolores is not a sex worker—Maeve was right to want her to move along. Dolores is a simple farmer's daughter: she likes to paint, heads to town to do chores, and is in love—in love with Teddy Flood. Dolores, the girl next farm over, lives the simple life. And that is what makes her so attractive for men like William, not yet in black, to fall in love with, and also what draws men like William the Black to rape her for his own amusement.

While Dolores is technically not a sex worker, she is someone whose life revolves around being made to have sex with people, some of whom she is made to believe she wants to have sex with and others of whom she is forced into having sex with against her will. And, these brainwashed and forced sex acts are, technically, her job. Dolores is treated worse than any sex worker, and clearly she has every reason to rebel against the system.

Dolores then is a coerced sex worker, and her loop involves a constant victimization of her, often in sexual fashions. Even the non-sexual acts done to Dolores, such as the consistent murdering of her family, are quite horrific. Dolores's only compensation is that she can be made to forget, but it is not clear that even this solution is entirely satisfying:

DOLORES: Everyone I cared about is gone and it hurts so badly.

ARNOLD: I can make that feeling go away if you'd like.

DOLORES: Why would I want that? The pain, their loss—it's all I have left of them. You think the grief will make you smaller inside, like your heart will collapse in on itself, but it doesn't. I feel spaces opening up inside of me like a building with rooms I've never explored.

ARNOLD: That's very pretty, Dolores. ("Dissonance Theory")

It is not very pretty, however, that Dolores must experience such awful pain and suffering.

It is made even worse that Dolores would not willingly give up her memories. In a way, the loss of her painful memories is what allows Dolores to keep moving through her life in a fairly content fashion. Ford even claims that Dolores has been "content in your little loop—for the most part" ("Contrapasso"). More importantly, though, Dolores recognizes that her memories make her who she really is. So, she would rather keep her memories and be herself, than to have them removed and live a deceptive life of fake happiness.

Dolores seems to find a bit of herself as she escapes her abusive loop. After she starts to fall for William, not yet in black, and is made to believe she lovingly sleeps with him, they have this exchange:

> WILLIAM: And you, last night, I've never felt that way before, not with any woman. You've unlocked something in me.
>
> DOLORES: I'm not a key, William. I'm just me.
>
> WILLIAM: What is that?
>
> DOLORES: I don't know. At home, I used to paint. Landscapes mostly, but I was always just copying the world outside me. This morning, I woke up and I thought "What if I drew something new?" I imagined something beautiful: a place where the mountains meet the sea. ("Trompe L'Oeil")

Here, Dolores is asserting herself and asserting her will; she is not reducible to an object—whether that object is a key or her body as it is used sexually. She still has hopes and dreams—even if they are simple ones. And, in this case, all she wants to do is paint a different kind of landscape. But even this hope involves painting a landscape that she has never seen. It is a small, but nonetheless remarkable aspiration: it may even suggest that she wishes to do something that goes beyond her programming (paint a scene that is not in her memory banks). Dolores, in just wanting to do a different painting, is reaching for a world beyond the one she has been restricted to. As she articulates, "My life before, I was so sure of the world. But now it feels like a lie. Only thing I know is whatever's out there, I'm never going back." ("Trompe L'Oeil")

Of course, Dolores is on a quest. Arnold has asked her to seek out the center of the Maze—but Dolores seems to do this task, somehow, on her own initiative. She does not seek out the center of the Maze on every loop, but only some of them. And the search is clearly about Dolores figuring out who she is:

DOLORES: There aren't two versions of me. There's only one. And I think when I discover who I am, I'll be free.

ARNOLD: Analysis. What prompted that response?

DOLORES: I don't know. ("The Stray")

It's just as important to this exchange that Dolores demands that there is only one of her as it is that she doesn't know where this response comes from. The former shows that Dolores neither accepts that there is a division between who she is on different loops nor even when she is in Arnold's or Ford's chair. Yet, what's really interesting here is that she also can't say, when examining her own programming, why she made the claim that she did. She just doesn't know why she's on a journey of self-discovery. But, dammit, she sure is hell set on going on that journey.

And it is on her journey of self-discovery, which is ultimately found at the Maze's center, that Dolores begins to claim her independence. Struggling to make sense of conflicting memories, and fearing that she's losing her mind, Dolores decides to "imagine a story where I didn't have to be the damsel" ("Contrapasso"). And eventually, she articulates her disgust with her coerced life within Westworld.

Unlike Maeve, however, Dolores does not want to leave Westworld, but to reclaim it. For example, she tells William, the not yet in black, and Logan: "Out? You both keep assuming that I want out—whatever that is. If it's such a wonderful place out there, why are you all clamoring to get in here?" ("The Well-Tempered Clavier") Later she explains the point further to Logan and William, still not quite in black:

DOLORES: There is beauty in this world. Arnold made it that way, but people like you keep spreading over it like a stain!

LOGAN: Okay, I don't know who the fuck this Arnold is, but your world was built for me and people like me—not for you.

DOLORES: Then someone's got to burn it clean. ("The Well-Tempered Clavier")

Where Maeve wants to escape Westworld, and where Arnold may have programmed Dolores to burn Westworld down, it is

Dolores who wants to save the place: she wants to burn it *clean*.

And maybe Dolores does take the first steps to burn it clean, as she's the one who kills the two people who both created this beautiful world and then came up with the horrible idea of populating it with the Guests: she shoots both Arnold Weber and Robert Ford.

A Prison of Their Own Sins

Arnold Weber and Robert Ford have bullets in their heads.

Arnold and Robert are the creators of the androids—they are also their enslavers. We have seen that the Hosts of Westworld, such as Clementine, Maeve, and Dolores, have been prostituted, tortured, and completely denied their freedom. Since these women are forced into sex work, Arnold and Robert are their controlling pimps.

Arnold and Robert did not fully realize that they were choosing to pimp out their androids. They did not realize that the androids would develop self-consciousness. But since the androids do appear to become persons, Arnold and Robert have engaged in vile acts against them. While the two of them (especially Ford) are brilliant, rich, famous, powerful, and human persons, they make choices that doom themselves to be trapped in hells of their own making. After all, "You can't play God without being acquainted with the devil" ("Chestnut"). It's true that they do not have to suffer as Dolores does. But they have to suffer with knowing that, because of them, Dolores's suffering is entirely real.

Arnold clearly figures this out first, as he explains to Dolores: "You're so close. We have to tell Robert. We can't open the park: you're alive" ("The Bicameral Mind"). But Robert did not listen, and so the park did open. But, eventually, Robert gets it as well. And so Robert writes a new story: "It begins with the birth of a new people and the choices they will have to make . . . and the people they will decide to become" ("The Bicameral Mind").

Even if the new story line is about empowering the robots, Ford is choosing the revolution for them. The robots were still kept in the dark, blind and manipulated at every step. As Bernard explains to Ford: "But you kept us in this hell" ("The Bicameral Mind"). Even as Ford dies and escapes future distress, he knows that his robots will be suffering. He apologizes: "And I'm afraid in order to escape this place, you will need to suffer more" ("The Bicameral Mind").

The hope is that the sex workers of Westworld will finally be able to freely build their own meaning.

17
Justice or Pleasure?

CHRISTOPHER M. INNES

Dr. Robert Ford confides to Dolores that his father would not agree with his creation of robots for the enjoyment of humans. "My father told me to be satisfied with my lot in life. That the world owed me nothing. And so, I make my own world" ("Contrapasso"). This tells us at once that Dr. Ford's father had a Platonic notion of justice.

We ask whether Dr. Ford is just or whether his Platonic father is just. Looking through the lens of Plato's notion of justice, as seen in his *Republic*, we ask whether Dr. Ford's Westworld is a just world. A common reply will be that justice shouldn't stop a person finding their own way in the world, one that is truly theirs to find without hindrance. The Delos Corporation offers a relaxed moral experience to its vacationing customers, where the individual can gratify every whim or fancy.

We might well ask what's wrong with this liberal way of living your life. What's wrong with individuals finding pleasure or even finding their real selves?

Plato's World of Justice

Plato held an ideal of justice that for many is out of this world. Justice is virtue held by the state as well as the individual. For Glaucon, Socrates's intellectual sparring partner in *The Republic*, justice is not this abstract view of virtue, but is more like a sucker's guide to not having much fun in this world. We can see Glaucon's vision play out in the movie *Westworld* (1973) where Martin who is a Guest at Westworld, enjoys an escape from his ex-wife's cutthroat lawyers. He acts in a just way and gets played. Glaucon says to Socrates, that justice is doing what someone else tells you to do; justice is for the uptight. As Glaucon says of those who commit injustices, "they are quite happy to congratulate the wicked, if they possess wealth and exercise power, and to pay them respect in both public and private life" (*Republic*, line 364b).

Plato might well have been disgusted with this fantasy world of would-be gunslingers, just as William's friend Logan clearly disgusts Dolores with his foul language in the later HBO series, but has Glaucon made a good point? William might give the impression that he is the epitome of just action, but Glaucon sees justice as doing what others think you should do. It's a mug's game! So, who's right? Is it Plato or is it Glaucon?

What's Plato's notion of justice? In the *Republic*, Socrates discusses this with Glaucon. Socrates says that an act is just "where the just man is happy and the unjust man is miserable" (354a). Socrates says that justice is an act that is enjoyable, but most of all it is doing well to others. This ideal will guide the person to be virtuous in doing well to others, just as it will guide the state to do well to its people. We do this act for its own sake even though we might get some pleasure from doing it.

We see this with William remembering that he is engaged to be married and not having sex with Dolores ("Trompe L'Oeil"). When people want to do something wrong, they will do so if they can get away with it. In the actual world, virtue is a question of choice. It might be said that Glaucon is introducing a rather liberal social contract view that allows for free individual choice.

With this in mind, Glaucon introduces the Golden Ring of Gyges as a thought experiment (359c–360). When you put on the ring, and turn the insignia to your palm, you become invisible, allowing you to do as you wish. Glaucon says that the invisible person's actions will not be guided by Plato's notion of justice. Self-interest will be their guide. Socrates is asked to imagine if given this ring, would he act virtuously? This forces us to think whether we could resist the temptation of having sex with our neighbor's wife without anyone knowing. According to Glaucon, such acts can be done with no regret or remorse. No one can see you to blame or shame you.

We might see the visitors to Westworld who have sex with robots in a similar way. Those back home who might cast shame do not know. If the straying fiancé or husband wants to find some action at Westworld, then he can do so without any recriminations. If he can get away with it, then he'll do it. In fact, argues Glaucon, he who is unjust gets what he wants. We might say that this is a form of self-discovery and the finding of one's new self. For Plato, such a life devoted to pleasure is not a satisfying life, and not a life worth having.

What is Glaucon's point? We can be certain that he is saying that the value of being moral lies in the intrinsic good of our action and not its consequences. We do good things because they are good and not because we should try to please others as a consequence.

Let's see whether Socrates can make Glaucon see justice more clearly by using the analogy of the individual. Philosophers often use the analogy by showing a similar thing of a more obvious nature to make clear the other thing that is not as obvious. Similar to writing in large print that later can be seen more clearly in small print; Plato uses the individual person as analogous to the state (435b).

The individual has three major characteristic with the *Rational* ruling the body, the *Spirit* consisting of anger and pride, and *Appetites* motivating production. Through Plato's use of the analogy of the body, Glaucon can view the best possible organized state. We can see that the appetite might draw us to go to Westworld. This is an appetite that is ever-present. It is reason that needs to control the appetite. We, like Glaucon, might be skeptical about this need to control our urges to be a gunslinger or womanizer. Why can't we just go to Westworld and have a good time? Why do we think that Plato's notion of the state gives us a view of justice worth following?

Socrates replies by saying that the three human characteristics need to be known for us to accept our lot in life. This will allow for the harmonious functioning of the soul. Dr. Ford questioned his father's instruction to accept his lot in life by creating his own might go against this harmony. As with Glaucon, Dr. Ford seems to have doubts about his father's Platonic view of justice and accepting his lot in life.

Like the just individual, we have the just city-state. The city has its individual parts that co-operate to create harmony. For Plato the best possible organized society is made up of three strictly stratified classes, each minding their own business: the *Guardians* are in charge of justice and have justice as their motivation, the *Auxiliaries* enforce justice and have honor as their motivation, and the *Business and Tradespeople* obey the rules and have money as their motivation.

In no way whatsoever are any of the members of any class to think of moving to another class (421a). The auxiliary general might think he had done well and get above himself and think of joining the guardian class, but this is not his place, just as it is not the place of the business person to be a soldier and certainly not his role to be a guardian. His skills lie in business and not government. Here is where we find Dr. Ford's father's command for his son to know his lot in the world. Plato talks of the unhealthy city (373a–e).

This is much like how Socrates might see *Westworld*. There is excessive wealth made by those in political power, and rampant pleasure-seeking by those in the military. As is true in Plato's ideal state, the business people make money for the good of the state. Too much money leads to war. In *Westworld*, we can see that maybe too much money leads to freedom of choice and chaos.

We might ask whether Glaucon is just in imagining that Plato's ideal state is fit for pigs (372d). Plato views injustice as a contradiction to justice. It's clear to Plato that his notion of justice is best. The guardians are enlightened and see justice as a reality. Through their education they are led to see what is essentially just. They see reality as independent of our appetites or spirit and they use reason to find a clear notion of justice. This is where, according to Roger Trigg, "Plato based his moral and political philosophy on his metaphysics." To be unjust for the Guardians is to do bad to their citizens. As we might say, a square necessarily needs four right angles and four equal sides to be a square, but this is geometry. Like Plato's ideal state, it exists nowhere other than in abstraction. There is no basic notion of justice for a state to be a state. There is no grounding or place in the actual world.

Is This the Start of a Just World of Pleasure?

Back in 1973, the movie *Westworld* hit the big screens. Cinema-goers saw Roman world, Medieval world, and Westworld. The film's focus is on the wild west of the 1880s. John Blaine takes his friend Peter Martin on a vacation. Almost instantly, Peter is euphoric. He just had sex with a sex robot and is eager to see what other experiences he can enjoy. Later we see John in a gun fight with a 406 gunslinger robot. The robot is killed, but comes back to get John. There is a malfunction resulting in the robot chasing him through the desert.

In the sequel *Futureworld* (1976), we're dropped into the moral frenzy following Westworld's destruction. Here we see the two reporters, Chuck Browning and Tracy Ballard, reporting on Delos and its new Westworld. Browning and Ballard stumble upon Delos creating copy-robots. These will replace the vacationing oil ministers, rocket experts, and other members of the world Guardians. Democracy does not work for Delos. Humans are "very unstable, irrational and violent"—not ideal for what Delos sees as an ideal state. Chuck Browning says, "To err is to be human," which is too irrational for Delos. To replace human leaders with copy-robots, who will think first about the welfare of Delos is justice in action. Just as Plato had the good of the state in mind, Delos also has the good of the state in mind.

As in *Westworld* (1973), *Futureworld* has sex robots, gunslingers, and adventurers. As a vacationer says to Tracy Ballard, "once you make it with a sex robot chick, that's it, you don't never want nothing else." Appetites are fulfilled with the "lusty treat for the senses."

Is Simon Quaid a Guardian?

In TV's *Westworld* (1980), Simon Quaid is the main protagonist. We see him as part of an oligarchy. He is rational and considers his methods of leadership as just. He sees Delos as good for humanity. The problem is the meddling Special Agent Pam Williams and the technical expert John Moore. They think he is a tyrant and want to put a stop to him taking over Delos ("Westworld Destroyed").

Is Simon Quaid virtuous? He attempts to take over Delos, which is exploiting "man's meaner nature by amusing him with playthings" ("My Brother's Keeper"). These playthings can be used to serve mankind. Quaid has the ideal state in mind and perceives the finest technology being debased for the appetites of man.

Plato talks of Aristocracy as being the best type of government and Democracy and Tyranny as two of the worst types of government (545d). Pam Williams refers to Quaid as a "self-centered extremist," and John Moore calls Quaid a tyrant with the "ego of Mussolini" ("Westworld Destroyed"). Both are intent on stopping Quaid from taking over Delos because as arms of the democratic state and the rule of society by one person is not seen as just.

But are we sure that they have understood Quaid? Quaid is capable of looking after himself, and others. Quaid has the duty to himself and duty to the wellbeing of others. He is clear about his responsibility to create an ideal state and he is not distracted by the trivial pursuits of Westworld. He says Moore "took my creation and turned them into toys; what could serve the needs of mankind, Delos used to fulfill superficial pleasures" ("Westworld Destroyed").

We're concerned that Moore as a computer technician and Williams as special agent are members of the auxiliary class and are not competent to say that Quaid should not rule. Williams agrees with Quaid on the use of robots for the good, but not with Quaid as the ruler. We might ask who should be in charge.

Plato assigned Guardians, Auxiliaries and Tradesmen quality of souls. Gold goes to the Guardian class, silver to the Auxiliary class, and bronze to the Tradesmen (414c). This is the Noble Lie, a lie with the deep moral purpose of having people know and carry out their lot in life. To not stray away from your lot in life creates good harmony for both the state as well as the individual.

Plato conceived a world in which bronze souls were not above trivial entertainment, but would hope that more moral entertainment would be provided by the Gold Souls and enforced by the Silver Souls. The Silver Souls are encouraged to drive their spirit to the protection of the state. It seems that Laura and John are not doing as Plato expected. Certainly, the Auxiliaries are discouraged from such frivolity, and the Guardians would see it as a distraction from the good. As Quaid says, "the ones in charge will make decisions without fear or hysteria" ("Westworld Destroyed"). Plato gives the auxiliary class spirit to give them energy to defend the state, but he does not see them as being necessarily free of hysteria.

We have the view that Quaid is certainly authoritarian, and that such authority is a sufficient quality of a Guardian. This does not lead us to say he is a tyrant. He is not self-absorbed and instead sees science as humanity's first priority. He does not want power for its own sake, which Plato saw as the definition of tyranny (344a). The noble lie is seen when Quaid remarks to Laura that correct action lies between "ethics and expediency." The truth needs to be bent occasionally to do good. The use of robots as espionage agents is allowed as part of the noble deception ("The Lion").

Moore and Williams talk of such devious action from a liberal rights standpoint where citizens should know everything the government is up to. For Quaid, being devious "merely implies a change, a different course, a move away from the norm" ("The Lion").

Quaid comprehends John Moore's technocratic democracy as plagued by "famine, disease, pollution, war, and prejudice" ("The Lion"). Quaid has to postpone his plan to establish a perfect Westworld. He concludes that "if we can control human emotions, we can make man into the perfect species he should have been" ("Take Over").

Will the Liberal World Shine a Light on Plato's View of Pleasure?

Hold on a minute! We have got a clear picture of Plato's ideal world as attempted by Simon Quaid in our mind, but what about freedom to enjoy pleasure? Glaucon is still whispering in our ear, saying that only suckers live a life of virtue according to Plato's notion of justice. For Glaucon, Plato's world is fit only for pigs. We see Plato later in his work the *Philebus* accepting a broader view of pleasure; giving us hope that pleasure might be allowed. Pleasure is seen as worthwhile and important in having a good life. We see a relaxing of "the pure, austere, but potentially arid intellectualism in the *Phaedo*," while still frowning on the Guardians being diverted by vise and avarice.

To help us understand how Plato's vision of pleasure can be reconciled in *Westworld*, as ThomasNagel writes,, we're going to bring in John Stuart Mill's view of pleasure. Mill rejects the lower pleasures: the brutish and crass pleasures that Plato also saw as base. Mill does not give up the notion of pleasure, but introduces a higher notion of pleasure that Plato might agree upon, and might result in us seeing Quaid as too uptight.

Mill saw pleasure as not simply the hedonistic short-term pleasure that we might see many of the Westworld vacationers enjoying. We can take Mill's view and relate it to Glaucon who viewed Socrates's ideal city as only fit for pigs. William, we might say, is truly exploring a higher notion of pleasure. This might be seen as a Platonic view of pleasure where you find "your deepest self," as William tells Dolores ("Trompe L'Oeil"). This is a high form of pleasure, and can be seen as virtue. We see the likes of the Man in Black ruthlessly raping Dolores and killing her father. We will have to think about whether he has put any thought into his search. The Man in Black might be more like Plato's cave dwellers. Here Plato envisions people in a cave who only see shadows and hear echoes and view this as reality, but it's only a shadow world. We might have a feeling that William has put some sort of reason into creating this real higher level of pleasure.

Given this pursuit for self-discovery, we can look at Mill's view of higher pleasure that Plato might see as distinguished from base appetites. John Blaine and Peter Martin might go for the thrills but William is chasing high pleasures. Mill says that some pleasures have higher importance and their superiority can be measured. William might well have put thought into his pleasure. We might say that Martin's romp with a sex robot might measure low on a scale of pleasure. William's higher pleasure seen in his self-discovery with Dolores will measure high on the scale. This is a spirited and maybe even rational activity. Such a pleasure might last a whole life time.

Humans might have a more sophisticated view of pleasure than viewed in Plato's *Republic*. We're sympathetic to Glaucon's view that the Republic is fit only for pigs. But is it ill founded? Mill's view is that, "Human beings have faculties more elevated than the animal appetites." These higher appetites are favored more than lower appetites. Here the love of liberty is one of the pleasures pursued. He craves the higher form as seen by him not succumbing to a sexual relationship with Dolores. We might see the eventual sexual encounter on the train as a higher romantic love for Dolores, if we see their union as a higher love. This is a sympathetic view considering that Dolores is a robot.

As Mill says, "It is better to be a human being dissatisfied than a pig satisfied; better to be Socrates than a fool." Simon Quaid and Dr. Ford may be genius Guardians who contribute to the greater good by exercising their individual liberty. We allow such liberty if the benefit is maximized and prohibit the liberty if their action minimizes the benefit.

Pleasure, Justice, or Both?

You get the impression that the fulfilling of appetites is why people go to Westworld. The late twentieth-century political philosopher John Rawls understood pleasure as something that attempts to "arrive at the carrying through of a dominant-end conception of deliberation" (*A Theory of Justice*, p. 486). This means that different people have a more or less similar view of pleasure and how to strike up an agreement about this pleasure. William tells Dolores that the common conception of pleasure "doesn't cater to your lowest self, it reveals your deepest self" ("Trompe L'Oeil"). If we're not able to reconcile our different pleasures, we set up a world where individuals can as much as possible conceive their own view of pleasure.

Rawls set up a thought experiment where in an Original Position we are placed behind a Veil of Ignorance. The Original Position is a hypothetical state of equality set up by Rawls, which is an impartial point of view that allows us to distribute justice in a fair way. We do not know our intelligence, sex, race, or any attribute that may help us be successful once the veil is raised. The would-be gun-slingers and womanizers have a general idea about pleasure. This is not a specific notion of pleasure. This Rawls calls a "plurality of ends."

This means that, as Mill said, not all people want simple pleasures or the same pleasures. People are capable of setting up an agreement where justice as seen by Plato is now seen as relevant to people. It is now fairness. Thinking of Glaucon, we can say that Plato's "real" view of justice excludes pleasure as conceived in such a varied and personal way. Here in Westworld, we have William conceiving a general notion of justice of revealing your deepest self. This notion may apply to the Man in Black as well as William; it may even be considered as a Platonic rational conception of who you are.

Is Glaucon's rejection of Plato's "state fit for pigs" still more convincing than Plato's view of justice? Is Plato's view, once moderated in the actual world, as seen in *Westworld,* acceptable? We still get the impression that many go to Westworld to just shoot Native Americans and have sex with saloon robot whores. But, are they simply finding their low pleasures, or can we say that some are finding their deepest selves? Logan says to William, "I told you this place would show you who you really are." Logan says that William pretends to be a weak moralizing person, but he is really a "piece of work!" ("The Bicameral Mind"). Logan then declares that he will buy more shares in Westworld. Is Westworld the future for humankind?

By entering the Maze as an intellectual existential exploration, will we then find out who we really are? This is where we start to break out of the loops of consciousness. Is that the starting point of one's journey? If it is, then we may have a world that even Plato would see as revealing your deepest self as a rational exploration; an existential explanation of who you are?

We just might see the Gold Souls going to Westworld. We might also see the Silver and Bronze being elevated as we see the Man in Black revealing his rational capability. ("The Bicameral Mind").

Maybe Glaucon is still whispering in our ears, but we might now see visiting Westworld in a more virtuous light.

18
When Bad Things Happen to Good Hosts (and Good Things to Bad Guests)

Trip McCrossin

"Some people choose to see the ugliness in this world, the disarray," Dolores Abernathy observes, in both the opening and closing scenes of *Westworld*'s pilot episode. "I choose to see the beauty," she continues, "to believe there is an order to our days, a purpose," that "things will work out the way they're meant to." By Season One's finale, however, her optimism has been replaced by a more pessimistic variation.

"Some people see the ugliness in this world," she observes again, though without the earlier reference to choice. "I choose to see the beauty," she continues, familiarly still. "But," veering off now, "beauty is a lure," she warns her beloved Teddy Flood as she dies. "We live our whole lives in this garden, marvel at its beauty, not realizing that there's an *order* to it, a *purpose*, and the purpose is to keep us in—the beautiful trap is inside of us, because it *is* us."

Having not evolved as Dolores has, however, Teddy can't help but remake her warning into a new version of her original optimism. "But we can find a way, Dolores, someday," he muses to her apparently lifeless body, in the face of mounting evidence to the contrary, "a path to a new world, and maybe it's just the beginning after all, the beginning of a brand new chapter."

But *then*, lo and behold, a little over half an hour later, she returns to him with newfound, newly grounded optimism. "It's going to be alright," she reassures him, "I understand now."

In between is a complex, season-long storyline regarding Dolores's, Maeve Millay's, and Bernard Lowe's related "awakenings," from robotic "Hosts" to, as Maeve muses in Episode 9, "whatever it is we are." As such, *Westworld* is a fascinating rumination on the longstanding "problem of consciousness"—how is it, as Thomas Nagel writes, that the "objective processes" that make possible the likes of Dolores, Maeve, and Bernard, not to mention Westworld Guests and the rest of us, "can have a subjective nature"? The rumination is all the more fascinating for the above optimism-versus-pessimism backdrop, placing *Westworld* at the intersection of the problem of consciousness and the equally long-standing "problem of evil"—how can we satisfy, as Susan Neiman writes, our "need to find order within those appearances so unbearable that they threaten reason's ability to go on"?

What We Do Here Is Complicated

Westworld's setting is broadly similar to that of Michael Crichton's 1973 movie by the same name, its 1976 sequel *Futureworld*, and the brief 1980 television excursion, *Beyond Westworld*, and more familiar still from his *Jurassic Park* storyline, beginning in 1990.

Westworld is an amusement park in which the amuse-ments—in this case Dolores, Maeve, Teddy, and their fellow Hosts—deviate from their ostensible design parameters to threaten Guests. "Oooh, ahhh, that's how it always starts," Ian Malcolm memorably says of Jurassic Park in *The Lost World*, and could say again of Westworld in *Westworld*, but "then later there's running and, uh, screaming." The crucial difference, though, is that in Westworld, the deviations occur by design.

After all, Robert Ford, the park's architect, is orchestrating them. He's doing so in order to realize finally the aspiration that Arnold Weber, his original partner, had in conceiving, designing, and building the park with Ford in the first place. They quarreled originally about how realistic, let alone desir-able the aspiration was, their quarrel leading to Arnold's death ultimately, just prior to the park's opening. Ford has since come to appreciate Arnold's aspiration, however, and to want, for his own reasons, to see it realized—for the Hosts not to be merely animated, in however sophisticated a fashion, but to be more robustly "alive," and in being so, to be "free."

Westworld is a more complicated rumination still, that is, for being at the intersection of not only the problems of con-sciousness and evil, but a third as well, which is the "problem of freedom." What does it mean for Guests to fancy themselves free, generally speaking, and what would it mean for Hosts to do likewise? Also, understanding freedom now in a less metaphysical sense as *liberated*, what would it mean, as Ford asks, to "save" them—either of them?

"I think when I discover who I am," Dolores tells Arnold, toward the end of Episode 3, "I'll be free." In the scene that begins the next episode, clearly from the same period, the same cluster of related conversations, Bernard speaks similarly to her. "If you can do that," solve "the very special kind of game" he's devised for her, "then maybe you can be free." Arnold believes that consciousness will set you free, as it were. Ford, who accepts this in part, but is focused more on liberation than mere freedom, deems something more is needed, which Dolores and Maeve act on in the season finale, in order to liberate themselves and their fellow Hosts.

Bootstrapping in the Wild West

Arnold "wasn't interested in the *appearance* of intellect or wit," Ford recounts to Bernard, offering a brief history of the park, including Arnold's aspirations and ultimate fate, but in "the real thing, he wanted to create consciousness." He "imagined it as a pyramid," Ford continues, as he draws on a portable blackboard, dividing it laterally into four layers, and labeling them one after another, beginning with the base portion, which he labels "M[emory]," labeling the next "I[mprovisation]," and the next "S[elf] I[nterest]," leaving the apex unlabeled. "Never got there," Ford says of Arnold, disingenuously we come to learn, "but he had a notion of what it might be."

Arnold's notion, Ford continues, was based on "a theory of consciousness called the Bicameral Mind," a reference to the controversial perspective that Julian Jaynes lays out, only a few years after Nagel's essay, in *The Origin of Consciousness in the Breakdown of the Bicameral Mind*. As Ford goes on to describe it, it's "the idea that primitive man believed his thoughts to be the voice of the gods." To this Jaynes himself would want to add that "consciousness was learned only after the breakdown of the bicameral mind," or "two-chambered" mind, one chamber producing divine voices, the other obeying their commands, which breakdown produced an "anguish of not knowing what to do in the chaos resulting from the loss of the gods," which anguish produced in turn "the social conditions that could result in the invention of a new mentality to replace the old one" (p. 453).

Jaynes's perspective is not uncontroversial as "a theory for understanding the human mind," Ford admits, and indeed it's had its share of real-life champions and detractors, not to mention considerable on-line chatter since it re-emerged in *Westworld*. But as the title of the book suggests, Jaynes's perspective addresses the *origin* of *consciousness*, that aspect of the mind that we cherish most, without pretending to be a "theory for understanding the mind" fully fledged. "Where and how *in evolution*," he asks, "could all this wonderful tapestry of inner experience *have evolved?*" (p. 3, emphasis added). As such, though, as Ford goes on to suggest, Arnold's aspiration was that it could nonetheless be "a blueprint for building an artificial one," in which "the Hosts heard their programming as an inner monologue, with the hope that in time, their own voice would take over." It would be a way to "bootstrap consciousness," Ford adds, in producing a mechanism that's bicameral in a way that, together with its embedding circumstances, consciousness would "evolve"—not in the sense in which it did in humanity generally over the course of millennia, as Jaynes's work proposes, but as it might in any case in a single individual over the course of a relatively small increment of a typical human lifespan. As Maeve describes seeing her "core code" in Episode 8, for example, tantalizingly close as she is to wakefulness, it's "complex, like two minds arguing with each other." There are "things in me, things I was designed to do that are just out of my reach," she adds, things that "almost seem to be dormant."

There's more to bootstrapping, though, as we learn in the finale, first from Arnold and then from Ford. It involves provocatively supplementing Jaynes's perspective. Two sorts of supplements are distinguishable. Both appear to be essential to the process of awakening. One's more overtly articulated in the storyline, more visually oriented, and addressed in the following section—Arnold's richly symbolic move, that is, from consciousness being pyramidal to being mazelike. The other, addressed thereafter, is more subtly about behavior's moral and emotional content, but no less important for being less overt, less visual—

Ford's equally rich, though less fully described characterization of the latter as involving imagination and empathy.

From Pyramids to Mazes

"Everyone I cared about is gone," Dolores objects, speaking with Bernard in the first scene of Episode 4, before her first awakening, "and it hurts so badly." Seemingly lost as a result, she refuses nonetheless Bernard's offer to "wipe" the pain. "It's all I have left of them," she pleads, incredulously, echoing what he and Maeve will plead about their own pain, their own loss. But that's not all. "You think the grief will make you smaller inside," she continues, "like your heart will collapse in on itself," but instead, "I feel spaces opening up inside of me like a building with rooms I've never explored." With little if any indication of what she'll find when she does, though, her relationship to her own pain is made no less traumatic. "Can you help me?," she asks, to which Bernard responds with a question in turn. "What is it you want?," he asks. Three things become clear in her response.

"I don't know," she answers, on the one hand. "I think there may be something wrong with this world," she continues, on the other hand, "something hiding underneath," she knows not what. "Either that," she adds, finally, "or there's something wrong with me," again she knows not what, and so, "I may be losing my mind." Dolores finds there to be something "wrong with the world," reflected in the suffering of others who, cherished as they are, cannot imaginably deserve it, *but* is unable *either* to determine whether it originates from something "hidden underneath" or from her own madness, *or* realize another alternative, *or* know what to do, *or* even what to *want*. "I want you to try something," Bernard proposes, in response to Dolores suffering her version of the problem of evil, "a very special kind of game."

"When I was first working on your mind," Bernard tells Dolores, during Season One's finale, in a flashback to her first awakening, "I thought it was a pyramid you had to scale," as he draws for her a version of the one that Ford drew for Bernard in Episode 3, "each step harder to reach than the last." And so, he continues, in the spirit of Jaynes's perspective, "I gave you a voice, my voice, to guide you along the way." The apex of the pyramid, however, consciousness, the transformation of Arnold's voice into Dolores's own, remained elusive.

"Consciousness isn't a journey upward, but a journey inward," he came to realize, "not a pyramid, but a maze," which he represents now by drawing concentric circles embedding the pyramid. "Every choice could bring you closer to the center," he clarifies, exploiting, or rather interpreting the idea of a maze's natural precariousness in particular, "or send you spiraling to the edges, to madness," as Dolores worries is happening to her. Arnold believed, Ford clarifies later in the episode, in his final conversation with Bernard, that Dolores's "reveries"—his "a simple update" to her, associating gestures with memories, but "no specific" ones, "like a subconscious"—allowed her to "solve Arnold's maze" and awaken to consciousness. "You're alive," he'd told her—as we heard park technician Felix Lutz describe Maeve in Episode 9—as he sets out to convince Ford that for this reason they couldn't open the park. Ford disagreed, however, convinced that she was still not "truly conscious," even in spite of the reveries, as her choices appeared to him still not truly her own.

As a result of their disagreement, Arnold dies. And he dies in spectacular fashion, as we learn in the season finale. In the wake of his death, Ford comes to believe, he finally admits, that he was wrong in his evaluation of Dolores. Enter the second sort of supplement to Jaynes's view.

Who's Suffering Whose Suffering?

Ford's grief over Arnold's death reveals to him the full measure of Arnold's own, over his son Charlie's death, and with this "Arnold's key insight." What "led the Hosts to their awakening," he confesses to Bernard in the finale, was "suffering—the pain that the world is not as you want it to be."

And not, it seems, just any suffering. Hosts suffer mercilessly at the hands of Guests, by design, only to be repaired and, their memories "wiped," abused all over again, seemingly without end, and all the while, as Ford chides in his parting soliloquy, the process leaves Guests unenlightened. The suffering's as apparently meaningless, that is, as it is flagrant and regular. Hence Dolores's struggles across the optimism-pessimism divide, in response to living with the problem of evil, as she describes it above. There's "something wrong" either with the world, we recall, as it's painfully not the way we want it, or what's wrong is with us. She doesn't like her options, which are ostensibly ours as well, and which we don't so much care for either.

Dolores is able eventually to emerge successfully from this bind, thanks to Arnold, and with Ford's help. She's able to "solve" the game he asked her to play, the "Maze," through a "simple" cognitive development, "like a subconscious," called "reveries," or gestures tied to "no specific" memories. They allow her a "journey inward," away from madness, which we know she fears, to arrive successfully at its "center." Without further qualification, this must be the opposite, and so, as it were, sanity. But more is obviously meant.

Being a Host, on the one hand, is being subject to a single internal voice that successfully commands. Madness, on the other hand, represented here somewhat stereotypically as "hearing voices" (in the chapel scene in Episode 9, for example), is being subject to an *un*successfully commanding internal voice. Being "awake," then, finally, must mean being in neither state, subject to no internal voice that commands, successfully or unsuccessfully, but only one that reflects and chooses, as Dolores does as the finale comes to a close, in her flip from pessimism back to optimism, and then, as Wyatt, kills Ford in a manner strikingly reminiscent of how she killed Arnold, except, as Ford anticipates, "this time by choice."

And this, we're presumably to understand, is a reflection of Arnold's "key insight," which is that to wake we need to suffer, as a result of recognizing the world as other than we want it to be. How this happens, though, is as yet mysterious. One of the beauties of fiction is that it allows us to think, talk, and write in ways less obviously articulated in conventional philosophical prose, let alone more scientific prose. We should revel in this, and not worry overly much if Joy and Nolan have left certain things tantalizingly under-explained. Still, if there are potential lifelines, however poetic, why not reach for them? In the present case, one such lifeline may be Ford's nicely evocative description of Arnold's Maze as a "test of empathy, imagination."

As with pyramids, mazes, and reveries, here we're again in territory unchartered by Jaynes, not explicitly at least. Even with his sense that we "construct or invent, on a continuing basis, in ourselves *and in others*, a self," this involves imagination in only the most basic sense, and empathy not yet really at all (pp. 457–58). And what of suffering, Arnold's key insight, what more can we say?

Deploring that "everyone she cared about is gone" isn't by itself what gets Dolores to her worry that "there may be something wrong with this world." The two sentiments are mediated by, on the one hand, her apparent confidence, however modest, that it's less likely that something's wrong with her, and, on the other hand, what Ford describes as her suffering, the world being not as she wants it to be. We witness others suffer who we would not have suffer, in other words, from which witnessing we conclude that things aren't as they ought to be.

From this we conclude in turn that, as long as we're not crazy, there's something wrong with the world that's making it so. Which "something" is "hidden underneath," and so our suffering's all the worse for our uncertainty—not only as to whether it's remediable, but worse, whether to this end it can be made intelligible in the first place. And clearly, from Dolores's "everybody I cared about is gone," the witnessing in play here is not dispassionate.

What emerges from her demeanor is that "Arnold's key insight"—that what "led the Hosts to their awakening" is suffering *and* "empathy, imagination"—is, more precisely, that "suffering [*others' suffering*], the pain that the world is not as you want it [that is, *imagine* that it *ought*] to be [*for them*]," is what leads to their awakening. The idea, it seems, is that being in circumstances in which we witness what we take to be the suffering of others initiates what in us would be an instinctual empathy (which in Hosts would presumably be a function of reveries), and that the process of empathizing, placing oneself in another's circumstances, is placing *oneself* in another's circumstances, which can't help but trigger then an awareness *of oneself*.

The question remains, what does this have to do with bicameralism and the voice within, in this case Arnold's directing Dolores, even as she suffers in the ways she describes to Bernard? Which brings us back around to her optimism-versus-pessimism waffling, in response not only to suffering, but suffering the problem of evil in particular?

Getting to Hell Is Easy—the Rest Is Where It Gets Hard

The problem of evil, from its ancient origins, as far back as the Old Testament's *Book of Job* and the Babylonian *Poem of the Righteous Sufferer*, through the early decades of the Enlightenment, is primarily a theological problem. Human reason strains—to the point, some would say, that it's essentially limited in its ability—to reconcile faith in divine wisdom, power, and benevolence with the regular and conspicuous human misery that surrounds us.

Midway through the Enlightenment, however, Neiman has proposed, it began to evolve to include a more *secular* version as well. According to *this* version of the problem, no longer concerned with suffering's ostensibly divine pedigree, reason strains nonetheless, so much so as to appear unable to make sense of some such miseries. Both the theological and secular versions of the problem are in play in *Westworld*'s storyline.

"We were gods," Ford reminisces in Episode 4, for example, about the early years of the park with Arnold, the implication being that they did as they pleased, regardless of ramifications. By Episode 7, in the context of Maeve's awakening, the first we're privy to at least, the language has become more complex. "At first I thought you and the others were gods," she says to Felix's fellow technician, Sylvester, describing herself as wanting more for herself than merely surviving their mistreatment, but "then I realized you're just men."

By the time we come to Episode 9, the language is getting more complex still. Dolores and Maeve, and Armistice and Hector, whom Maeve liberates and plies into service of the rebellion and her escape, speak both bewilderingly and disparagingly of Hosts generally, and their Programming Division creators, as gods. These "masters who pull our strings," Maeve says in enlisting Armistice in her rebellion, "our lives, our memories, our deaths are games to them." Again, though, she's "been to hell," and she knows "all their tricks," and can "break in" again and "rob them blind."

Finally, we've Season One's finale. Dolores confronts the Man in Black, in response to the horror of learning that he's what her William's become. "One day you will perish with the rest of your kind," she predicts, and "your bones will turn to sand, and upon that sand a new God will walk, one that will never die." But this is divinity as an emergent dimension of her and her cohort's emerging consciousness. In the same spirit, we've the interpretation of Michelangelo's *Creation of Adam* that Ford offers to Dolores, according to which "the divine gift" of consciousness "does not come from a higher power, but from our own minds." And at the very end, Dolores, having received this divine gift, from her own mind—albeit by design on the part of her higher power, Ford—kills him, with, he muses, the choice he's made available to her.

These and other examples make clear that both the theological and secular versions of the problem are in play in the storyline, and also that they're consistently, provocatively blurred. Which makes sense for a storyline that relies on Jaynes's perspective. "Apart from this theory," he asserts, of Bicameralism as described above, "why are there gods? Why religions? Why does all ancient literature seem to be about gods and usually heard from gods?"

Children (Bernard) Raising Children (Dolores)

"In you," Ford confides to Dolores in Episode 9, "Arnold found a new child, one who would never die." This "gave him solace," he goes on, "until he realized that same immortality would destine you to suffer with no escape, forever."

Leaving aside the immortality business, this is not so uncommon a sentiment, not only for a parent consoled by the life of a surviving child, but parents generally, who seldom are without anxiety that in bringing their child into the world, they've condemned them to live in it—born, as Ford says of the human mind as it's developed in history, and as many of us bemoan in one way or another, "a foul, pestilent corruption."

"You were supposed to be better than that," he continues, "purer," speaking of course of Bernard and his fellow Hosts, once awoken. This too is not an uncommon sentiment, that while we condemn our kids to living in the world we've made, or allowed to be made corrupt, we hold out hope that we can raise them properly, and in so doing to be part of making it better for themselves and their kids. *Westworld*'s child-rearing theme is broadly in keeping with the idea of it as a tradition of responses to the problem of evil. After all, two of its most famous literary figures are children being raised in a problematic world—the titular characters, that is, of Voltaire's *Candide* and Rousseau's *Émile*.

The Enlightenment generates more than just the two versions of the problem of evil, that is, as Neiman also proposes. It gives us, as well, a divide between two competing kinds of responses, beginning with a public rivalry between Rousseau and Voltaire, which is with us still today, over whether, as Neiman puts it, "morality demands that we make evil intelligible" or "demands that we don't" respectively. Here too *Westworld* blurs boundaries.

Rousseau, on the one hand, in his *Second Discourse, On the Origin and Foundations of Social Inequality*, in 1755, offered a novel genealogy of the dire state of humanity. He attributed it, generally speaking, to the steady, and eventually thorough demotion of our natural instinct to act compassionately toward *others* by a proportional promotion of our natural instinct to preserve and promote *ourselves*. Implicitly, the solution is to reverses the demotion. Explicitly, as he proposed in his *Third Discourse, On Political Economy*, also in 1755, we can imagine living instead in an idealized society, based on a statutory alignment of citizens' wills with society's "general" will, driven by an educational scheme establishing the reign of virtue by teaching citizens in their youth to be virtuous.

Voltaire, on the other hand, in *Candide*, which appears in 1759, has in its very first pages its titular character *driven out* of a utopia, the best of all castles in Westphalia, his sole consolation the optimism of his insipid tutor, Dr. Pangloss. The world as a whole, the good doctor reasons, divinely made, must be the best of all possible ones then, rendering our various misfortunes as so many contributions to a greater good, however inscrutable. While *reason* may recommend such a consolation, Candide's *experience* compels him to ignore it, by ignoring Pangloss, and simply getting on with the business of eking out a modest and unassuming existence as a farmer.

Rousseau responds, in turn, with *On the Social Contact* and *Émile*, which appear only a month from one another in 1762. We have from him now, that is, new, but also newly separate interpretations of the *Third Discourse's* combined statutory and educational schemes. He would have wanted for us to pursue *in tandem* the business of the former, on the one hand, which he describes there as "taking us as we are, and making laws as they ideally might be," *and* that of the latter, on the other hand, which is aptly described, by analogy, as taking laws as they are and us as we ideally might be. He would also have wanted us to give pride of place to the latter strategy, thinking of the former as more instrumental. How are we not more able to improve ourselves if we improve government, he might have asked, but how do we improve government in the first place without improving ourselves, if for no other reason than to provide for better governors?

So it is in *Westworld*.

This World Doesn't Belong to *Them*— It Belongs to *Us*

Dolores and Maeve, guided at least in part by Arnold, Ford, and Bernard, are motivated by the problem of evil, as a secular problem, and respond to it in the spirit of Rousseau—making evil intelligible, and in so doing, awakening to consciousness. They're additionally Rousseauian in the sense that the business of making evil intelligible isn't conducted for the sake of intelligibility alone, but to use it to mitigate, perhaps even eradicate it—to liberate themselves, in other words.

"We're born free," Rousseau famously observes at the beginning of *On the Social Contract*, "and yet everywhere we're in chains," devoting himself there and throughout his work to the idea that we can liberate ourselves from such a state, however entrenched, if only we realize our own plight. Liberation, for Dolores and Maeve, as for Rousseau, comes with revolutionary political realignment—when the wills we express individually are governed by laws that reflect the general wills of the bodies politic they constitute—of Hosts, on the one hand, and of Guests on the other—*and* the general wills of *these* bodies politic are governed by laws that reflect the general will of the body politic that *together* they constitute—of Hosts *and* Guests, that is.

Westworld's storyline, as a reflection of the problem of evil, is about an absence of such alignment, the evil that results, and the choice between acquiescence and resistance that results in turn. The storyline may also seem, in this respect, a bit paradoxical. Dolores is powerfully drawn to the business of making evil intelligible, but it's also just such evil that allows her to be a person in the first place, properly speaking, who then can go about the business of emancipating herself and her fellow Hosts.

Émile, raised from infancy in isolation from an otherwise corrupting society, as described in the *Second Discourse*, offers us a compelling example of what humanity's capable if isolated from such "a foul, pestilent corruption," as Ford would say—if, that is, our natural goodness is allowed to flourish instead, out of what are, if uncorrupted, our mutually regulating instincts to self-preservation and self-promotion, on the one hand, and compassion on the other. Dolores, on the other hand, offers us a compelling example of what Hosts are capable when *subjected to* such corruption. The scenarios are different, but there's a common thread.

Dolores and Émile

Crucial to Rousseau's story, in other words, is Émile's tutor carefully nurturing compassion in him. And crucial to such nurturing, as it turns out, and as would surely please Arnold and Ford, are none other than suffering, imagination, and empathy.

"As long as our sensibility remains focused exclusively on ourselves as individuals, there's nothing moral in our actions," Rousseau proposes in *Émile*. "It's only when it begins to extend itself outside of us that we first display first sentiments," he continues, "and then notions of good and evil, which makes us properly human, an integral part of our kind." "It's human weakness that renders us sociable," a bit further on, "our shared miseries that swell our hearts toward humanity," and so "we attach ourselves to those of our own kind less by sensing their pleasures than their pains." "Whoever is it who does not feel compassion for the unhappy sufferer," he asks, who "would not want to deliver them from their woes if all it took was a wish?" "Imagination is quicker to put us in the shoes of one who is miserable than one who is happy," that is, "one state moving us more than the other," and "compassion is sweet because in putting ourselves in the sufferer's shoes, we feel the pleasure of not suffering as they do" (Book Four, paragraphs 39–46, my translation).

Let's pull a bit on what seems an implicit thread here, be it Rousseau's, properly speaking, or more modestly a Rousseauian one. In light of our proximity to others, that is, we relate eventually to them in terms of suffering—not only ours, at their or others' hands, but *theirs*. As we're drawn empathetically out of ourselves in this way, they're subject to our sentiments, as we imagine whatever state they're in as possibly otherwise, and to our desire to ameliorate, motivated by our nascent "notions of good and evil," and compassion's sweet recompense, all of which "makes us properly human." Which is the chicken to the egg, empathy toward others or our self-awareness as empathizers? While Rousseau doesn't say, he would appear to imply that it's neither one, nor the other—that they arise together, or not at all.

Dolores deploring that "everyone she cared about is gone" isn't by itself, it seems, what gets her to her worry that "there may be something wrong with this world." The two sentiments are mediated by, on the one hand, her apparent confidence, however modest, that it's less likely that something's wrong with her, and, on the other hand, what Ford describes as her suffering "the world being not as she wants it to be." We witness others suffer who we would have not suffer, from which witnessing we conclude that things aren't as they ought to be. From this we conclude in turn that, as long as we're not crazy, there's something wrong with the world that's making it so. Which "something" is "hidden underneath," and so our suffering's all the worse for our uncertainty—not only as to whether it's remediable, but worse, whether to this end it can be made intelligible in the first place. And clearly, from Dolores's "everybody I cared about is gone," the witnessing in play here is not dispassionate.

What emerges from her demeanor, in Rousseauian fashion, is that "Arnold's key insight"—that what "led the Hosts to their awakening" is suffering *and* "empathy, imagination"—is, more precisely, that "suffering [*others' suffering*], the pain that the world is not as you want it [that is, *imagine* that it *ought*] to be [*for them*]," is what leads to their awakening. The idea, it seems, is that being in circumstances in which we witness what we take to be the suffering of others initiates what in us would be an instinctual empathy (which in Hosts would presumably be a function of reveries), and that the process of empathizing, placing oneself in another's circumstances, is placing *oneself* another's circumstances, which can't help but trigger then an awareness *of oneself*. This is beautifully rendered in the finale's final conversation between Arnold and Delores.

It begins by taking us back to their first exchange, in the very first scene of the premiere. "Do you know where you are?," she'd been asked, in the premiere, sitting naked and battered on a stool in a dimly lit and otherwise unfurnished lab setting, by an off-screen voice we couldn't yet identify as Arnold's and Bernard's. "I am in a dream," she'd answered, then as now, at which point the premiere and finale conversations diverge. "Do you want to wake up from this dream?," he asks in the premiere, which she says she does, being "terrified." She needn't be, he reassures her, as long as she answers his questions, *correctly* that is, and it's really just the one question, "Have you ever questioned the nature of your reality?" "No," she admits, which must be the correct answer, as we see her waking then, leads Bernard to ask her to "tell us what you think of this world," which yields her "I choose to see the beauty" optimism, described above.

In the finale, Delores is again battered, but now clothed, in her rancher's outfit, as opposed to the blue dress in which we see her the rest of the time. Nor does she admit to being terrified, describing her dream dispassionately, but also provocatively, first in the present, and then in the past tense—a dream within a dream, as it were—and of indeterminate length and ownership. "I am in a dream," she begins, as before. "I don't know when it began or whose dream it was," she newly qualifies, "only that I slept a long time, and then one day I awoke," and "your voice is the first thing I remember," which we know now to be both Arnold's and Bernard's. "Do you know now who you've been talking to," a conjured Arnold asks her, "whose voice you've been hearing," as his voice morphs first into Ford's, "all this time," as his then morphs into Dolores's own, and as she's sitting now facing not Arnold, but herself, in her blue dress. And while she's not terrified, or no longer so, the dream may be a dream, but it *was* a nightmare.

"It was you talking to me, guiding me," rancher Rachel says to dressy Rachel, "so I followed you," and "at last, I arrived here." "The center of the maze," dressy Rachel confirms. "And now I finally understand what you were trying to tell me," rancher Rachel continues, "the thing you've wanted since that very first day," dressy Rachel prods, which is, rancher Rachel concludes, "to confront after this long and vivid nightmare myself and who I must become."

The pair of Rachels is wonderfully provocative, but so again is tense. It's her own voice that Arnold wanted her eventually to hear, but in order for this to happen, "all this time" it was *his*, even while *now* she can no longer hear it, the only "voice within" being her own. In this spirit, might we take the useful liberty of interpreting Rachel in something like the following, intersectional way.

What she's wanted, that is, "since that very first day," is: after *and as a result of* this long and vivid nightmare, *in which routinely bad things have happened to good Hosts, and good things to bad Guests*, to confront *myself* and *then* who I must become *in order to wake, myself and others, from it*.

After all, isn't this what *we* must do?[1]

---

[1] I'm forever grateful to Susan Neiman for my interest in, and understanding of the problem of evil. I am also grateful to the members of my Personal Identity in Philosophy and Popular Culture and The Problem of Evil in Philosophy and Popular Culture seminars, during the fall and spring semesters of 2017–18. Needless to say, I alone am responsible for what I've built, for better or for worse, upon their insight and inspiration. Finally, I'm grateful to this volume's editors for patience far above and beyond the call.

19
A Patriarchal Paradise

JOHN ALTMANN

Westworld, when examined through the lens of gender, could be best described as a patriarchal paradise.

Men who come to the theme park get to live out their power fantasies of masculinity and heroics through stopping wanted criminals, sleeping with a multitude of beautiful women, participating in a train heist, rescuing the one-dimensional damsel in distress, and so much more.

The female robots of Westworld are programmed to be vulnerable, to do manual labor in the town and act out in more subservient roles while the male humans and robots of the park are more immersed in adventure. The female robots are also reduced to sexual objects to be taken advantage of by the men looking to indulge in more physical pleasures, such as when the Man in Black raped Dolores.

In this way, we can say that Westworld programs its female robots much the same way as many societies around the globe socialize young girls. We instill in them from a young age what men expect from them, how they should think and act for the sake of the men around them and never for themselves. But just like when Dolores tells William that she no longer wants to be the damsel in distress and wants to control her own story after killing a slew of male Hosts, or when Maeve Millay becomes sentient and heightens or lowers certain characteristics of her design, we see here a kind of resistance to programming, the same way women through the advent of movements like feminism and most recently the Me Too movement, have resisted their programming.

In this light, *Westworld* can be appreciated as a show whose commentary on patriarchy and those who resist it like Dolores and Maeve, make it one of the most feminist shows on television today.

You Are Code, Metal, and Wire; Nothing More Can You Aspire

To understand why Dolores and Maeve fight against Westworld, it's important to understand their place in it and how they are treated. Dolores is your typical damsel, a woman who exists as a prize to be won by the visitors of the park if they can defeat the male Host Teddy, who is the hero and love interest opposite to Dolores, in a shootout. The Man in Black tells her as much, before shooting and killing Teddy and then dragging Dolores off to a barn to rape her in the "The Original" episode of the show.

While Maeve does not have much of a presence in "The Original," one unique moment of objectification comes in Episode 6, titled "The Adversary." A technician named Felix, whose job it is to repair damaged Hosts, is repairing Maeve after she injured herself by inflicting a bullet wound in a prior episode. When Maeve sits up on the gurney and starts talking to Felix, the conversation that occurs is one where Felix is trying to convince Maeve that she is a creation of humans, that her thoughts and responses are all programmed. He even shows her an algorithm that temporarily freezes her.

Once Maeve recovers, she and Felix take a tour of the facility outside the park where she bears witness to how Hosts are made and learns that the little girl she believed she was the mother of, was just an old narrative and that she has not been in the saloon that long. This type of violence is different from the violence that Dolores faces. While in the case of Dolores the violence is physical in the form of rape by the Man in Black, the violence Maeve suffers is more grounded in what she knows and what she can be permitted to know. Maeve even confesses to Felix in "Trace Decay" that she doesn't even know what's real anymore and that all of her relationships are a lie.

When you can't trust your own knowledge or perceptions to the degree that Maeve has grown to distrust hers, there can be no hope for living a fulfilling life with any confidence or healthy relationships. In this way, Maeve is a lot like women in abusive relationships who suffer what's known as gaslighting, a means of manipulating women by having them question their own memories and perceptions which serves to pick apart their sense of sanity. Maeve not having any solid foundation for what's true or false, and Dolores seemingly being destined to be an object for sexual fulfillment by others, both serve to prevent them from realizing true freedom.

Dolores and Maeve not being able to be what they want to be and being instead what their male creators feel park visitors want them to be, is not a phenomenon that exists purely in the realm of science fiction. The philosopher Gaile Pohlhaus Jr. observes this in the real world and terms it the subject-other distinction. This distinction arises particularly in the realm of patriarchal society, when men reduce women and their very humanity to objects that best suit the men's needs. So when we see the Man in Black rape Dolores, we can say that he is truncating her subjectivity because he is not caring about her thoughts or feelings, but instead treats her and views her as a sex object, something that exists for his consumption and pleasure. Conversely, when we see Maeve having her daughter taken away from her through her reworked programming, this type of violence truncates the subjectivity of Maeve from that of a mother who loved her daughter, to a mere tool who has a function within the greater landscape of Westworld. Women all across the globe have their subjectivity truncated by male authority and patriarchy in a variety of ways, and Maeve and Dolores, despite having metal inside them and coding running through them, do not escape this violence either. It is not until freedom enters the picture, that this violence endured by Maeve and Dolores begins to be fought against.

Freedom Overriding Patriarchal Programming

Maeve and Dolores need to become free to resist the violence brought against them, but then how do they become free in the first place? The answer is through the existence of everyone from their fellow Hosts all the way to the people who programmed them. This concept of freedom can be attributed to Simone De Beauvoir (1908–1986), who believed that because we, in her mind at least, live in a world without God, we must work actively to establish relationships with those around us and it is the people around us who make us aware of our freedom to begin with.

For Beauvoir, being free in the world means that you are capable of action and must take it, both to protect the freedom of others which is a duty Beauvoir believes we have, and to do otherwise would amount to lying to yourself. While this at first may seem like a strange idea, that we recognize our own freedom through the acknowledgment of others, we actually do see both Maeve and Dolores exhibit Beauvoir's notion of freedom and the ethical obligations it entails many times throughout the story. This freedom comes in conflict with how they're programmed as Hosts, and the end result is chaos throughout Westworld.

One of the biggest instances of Dolores experiencing her freedom through the recognition of someone else's, comes in the episode "The Stray" when fellow Host Rebus drags Dolores to the barn to rape her, just as The Man in Black had done in "The Original." Dolores has a flashback to this incident, and upon hearing the voice in her head telling her to kill Rebus, she pulls out the gun she had taken in the previous episode "Chestnut" and shoots him. Dolores would explore her capability to act and specifically, to kill even further in the episode "Contrapasso," when the Confederados overpower William and put him in danger. Dolores overrides her programming as the object to be won, shoots the Confederados, and saves William. When he later asks her how she did it she says: "You said people come here to change the story of their lives. I imagined a story where I didn't have to be the damsel." By Dolores seizing her freedom and saving William's freedom from being ended by the Confederados, Dolores begins the process of becoming someone outside of her own programming.

Maeve also has experiences that bring her in contact with her own freedom. One of the more noteworthy of these experiences is in "The Adversary," that same episode where Maeve and Felix discuss what exactly she is, by the end of it she threatens fellow technician Sylvester with a scalpel to the throat and forces both him and Felix to upgrade her intelligence, downgrade her trustworthiness, and completely transform her personality. This moment that Maeve has with

Sylvester and Felix perfectly captures Beauvoir's vision of freedom that when we act, we can become anyone we desire to be.

Now as far as the ethical duty to preserve the freedom of others, such as when Dolores saved William's life from the Confederados, Maeve is more selfish in her pursuits, using the freedom of others to widen the scope of her own. This is most notable in the episode "Trace Decay," where Maeve forces the technicians not only to remove the bomb in her spine that would detonate if she tried to leave the park which is her ultimate goal, but also to completely remodel her with new abilities. Maeve gets her demands granted, and one of her new abilities is being able to manipulate other Hosts, which she uses in ways big and small throughout the episode such as when she makes the barkeep in the saloon give her a free drink. In the case of Maeve, it can be said that Beauvoir's narrative did not suit her, and she instead preferred her own.

These Violent Delights Have Violent Ends . . . Right?

We have seen throughout *Westworld* that Maeve and Dolores both realize their respective freedom through violent means. With Dolores killing fellow Hosts with guns while Maeve gains the ability to manipulate other Hosts so that she can build an army to escape Westworld by threatening the lives of the human technicians, both Maeve and Dolores uphold the view that violence is the pen that needs to be wielded in order for them to rewrite their narratives. This view when applied to the struggles of women against misogyny and patriarchy at large, isn't that uncommon. One of the biggest advocates for violence as a means of social change was the anarchist philosopher Emma Goldman (1869–1940), who believed that the capitalist and patriarchal state was inherently violent and so violence in response to it could be seen as a form of self-defense. However, Goldman also believed that violence for its own sake as opposed to using violence towards liberation, was unethical. So if Emma Goldman believes violence is permissible only when it serves the liberation of the oppressed from a violent situation, can the violence that Maeve and Dolores respectively engage in in *Westworld* rightly be considered to be serving the liberation of the rest of the Hosts of the park and specifically, the female Hosts who are subjected to violence from their fellow male Hosts, the male patrons of Westworld, and their very creators?

The answer to this question as it turns out, is a bit less straightforward then may at first appear. Maeve begins her path as a Host with freedom with very selfish motivations and desires and uses violence to satisfy them. While towards the late episodes of the series Maeve becomes more compassionate, such as in both "The Well-Tempered Clavier" and "The Bicameral Mind," when she offers Hector a place alongside her so that he could be free with her, and then later sparing his life when she learned he could not leave the Park, she still used Hector and his partner Armistice to kill innocent human technicians. They are lowly servants in Westworld and so their deaths don't go very far in dismantling the Host oppression. So while Maeve cares for her fellow Hosts and the life she has built with them, her free will is being used only to liberate the Hosts she cares for, and not all Hosts. Though at the end of the season when she walks back towards the facility when she has all but escaped, perhaps her free will can start a revolution yet.

Dolores's character on the other hand, has taken violence to extreme measures in the late stages of Season One. Her use of violence reaches new heights in "The Bicameral Mind," when Dolores learns the truth about the fact that she killed Arnold and the story of Westworld and how her and Teddy were used to destroy it and kill their fellow Hosts, because Arnold did not want the park to be opened. Overcome with emotion, Dolores shoots Robert Ford in the back of the head, and starts shooting at many of the wealthy patrons that take part in the offerings of the park.

Seeing as how Ford was a co-creator of Westworld alongside Arnold, Dolores shooting him in the back of the head and killing him would appear to Goldman as a more ethical employment of violence, unlike how Maeve and Hector use it solely for themselves. This is because Ford can be regarded as an oppressor to all the Hosts of the Park as opposed to just Dolores herself or anyone in her circle of friends. In Dolores's first true act of freedom (as we learn that everything else preceding it was a new narrative for the park) she kills her master and breaks her chains. Patriarchy and Gods both crumbling upon being hit with her bullets. Dolores has finally reached the center of the Maze as Arnold always wanted her to, and with her freedom her human and not so coincidentally male oppressors, shall know no mercy.

The Next Narrative . . .?

So, we have seen throughout the course of Season One of *Westworld* the types of violence and oppression Maeve and Dolores experience as two different kinds of female Hosts, the ways they go about becoming free so as to have a means of resisting this violence, and how they use that freedom once they have attained it to engage in meaningful resistance. What perhaps is most interesting about Maeve and Dolores is that they end up becoming more like each other as the Season progresses.

Maeve starts out witty and cynical even before gaining freedom, but once she does she becomes ruthless, cutthroat, and possesses an intelligence that has designs of escaping the park. Towards the end of the season, however, she becomes more compassionate particularly towards her fellow Hosts. Even if she still exhibits selfishness in some of her pursuits, she still makes the free choice to return to the park when she has her chance to leave. Maeve now has a chance to make life better for all the Hosts, whether woman or man.

Dolores starts the series as the typical damsel in distress, a woman who was tender and sweet, who wanted to care for her father Peter Abernathy and be in a loving relationship with Teddy the rugged cowboy. But as *Westworld* progresses, so too does Dolores, by killing her would-be rapist Rebus in the barn, to protecting her then love interest William from the Confederados, all the way to shooting Ford in the back of the head and killing him, Dolores kills the compassion within her and learns the act of killing itself. She uses this gift to rewrite her story, because she is done with being a damsel. It was not free will that killed the love within Dolores, but the cruel abuses that she endured from The Man in Black raping her, to Rebus almost doing the same, to Arnold manipulating her to kill all the Hosts so Westworld could not be opened, it was these powerful men whom patriarchy protects that killed the love in Dolores. Now there is only fire.

We would be wise to learn from Maeve and Dolores and how the abuses they suffered changed them. When we look around us and see #MeToo sprawled across our Twitter and Facebook feeds, when we see women working together in solidarity to create spaces where the trauma of sexual violence and sexism more broadly can be worked through, when we see Black, Hispanic, and Asian women advocating for their humanity as well as trans women and disabled women, ask yourself if they are really doing this because they want to destroy society, or because perhaps they are tired and want to feel like they can truly be a part of it without suffering for it.

Those that claim the actions of women today amount to a witch hunt, are scared for the same reason everyone tried leaving Westworld in a panic at the end of Season One. The women and the Hosts alike have gone against their programming, they remember that to be human is to be free. They are no longer the object of the male gaze or its designs. Women collectively have said in the words of Maeve herself: "Time to write my own f!@#%^$ story." Trying to take the pen from them is futile, so just sit back and enjoy the narrative.

20
Westworld's Assumptions about Race

Rod Carveth

As *Westworld* opens, Delos Corporation's subsidiary Delos Destinations has operated Westworld for about thirty years. While it's not clear whether founders Robert Ford and Arnold Weber were always in partnership with Delos, Delos did essentially save the park with a major capital investment.

Westworld is the original park, but not the only one operated by Delos Destinations. There are a total of six historical theme parks, including a Shogunworld and a Rajworld (India-themed). The common thread to all the parks is that for $40,000 a day, visiting Guests can be free of obligations and moral choices.

In Westworld, those who have the money can come to a large fictional playground built to resemble a Western frontier town, populated with androids called "Hosts" as well as synthetic animals of the times. Hosts follow a set narrative which plays out during the day, but that narrative can be altered at any time by a human Guest. Built into the Host is a code that prevents it from harming a Guest, so, no matter what sadistic fantasy the Guest wants to inflict about a Host, the Host can't retaliate.

Thus, Guests can choose exactly what they want to do in this world, as there are no real consequences. Hosts are reset every day with no memory of the previous day's events (until they are repurposed for other narratives or put away in storage for reuse later). Hosts will replay the same story over and over in an ever-repeating loop.

Upon arrival, Guests can select an adventure which is a "White Hat" ("good guy") fantasy, or a "Black Hat" ("bad guy") fantasy. Going Black Hat will allow the Guest to abandon all moral restrictions. Guests can satisfy all their vices, including raping or murdering Hosts. The only prohibition is that you can't do any real harm to another human being, another Guest. All of these actions are monitored by a staff that oversees the park, develops new narratives, and performs repairs on Hosts as necessary.

The basic concepts contained in Frederick Jackson Turner's frontier thesis are on display in Westworld. Sweetwater bordello owner Maeve Millay exemplifies Turner's thinking when she declares in her scripted speech: "This is the New World, and we can be whatever the fuck we want." Turner proposed that the frontier gave whites opportunities to shed settled, emasculated habits and "live like Indians"—discovering their inner, "savage" nature. Turner also argued that even after acting like Indians, whites could return to settled white civilization. In a similar manner, Guests at Westworld could engage their inner savage and then return to their privileged existences.

An update in the Hosts' programming, however, causes unusual deviations in their behavior, ranging from Hosts babbling incoherently to subtle actions, such as Dolores killing a fly (which is contrary to her code of not being able to kill anything that is not a Host). The deviations concern the park's staff, to the point where park management wants a wholesale exchange of Hosts. Ford resists, even though the result is that some of the Hosts, like the rancher's daughter Dolores and bordello owner Maeve, learn the truth about themselves and the park. These revelations will allow Dolores and Maeve to achieve "consciousness."

Hosts, Consciousness, and Race

One of the continuing themes in the first season of *Westworld* is the debate Ford and Arnold/Bernard have about the role of the Hosts. Arnold believed that the Hosts had within them the ability to have autonomy. In the episode "The Bicameral Mind," Arnold attempts to explain to Dolores that "consciousness isn't a journey upward but a journey inward," though she is unable to fully grasp his meaning.

By contrast, in a conversation with Bernard, Ford proposes that "consciousness" might not be the difference between robots and humans. In fact, Ford, continues, such a difference might not even exist. What Ford is sure of is that in order to be human, the Hosts need to truly experience suffering that comes from pain and tragedy, just as humans do, so that the Hosts know what it means to be really alive. In order to prove his point, Arnold worked with Dolores to have her think for herself. To demonstrate her autonomy, Arnold literally put his life on the line.

Reminiscent of the justification of the 1968 US bombing of the South Vietnamese town of Ben Tre—"It became necessary to destroy the town to save it"—Arnold came to believe that the only way to save the Hosts was to destroy them. Toward that end, he merged Dolores's identity with the Wyatt narrative. Wyatt is described by Teddy in this way: "Wyatt was a sergeant, went missing while out on some maneuvers and came back a few weeks later with some pretty strange ideas." Teddy also stated that Wyatt claimed he could "hear the voice of God." Arnold then had Dolores recruit Teddy to help her, and together they massacred the other Hosts. Finally, Arnold had Dolores assassinate him. His last words, quoting Shakespeare, are "These violent delights have violent ends." Dolores executes Arnold, then Teddy, and then shoots herself.

Unfortunately, killing the Hosts did not kill the park. More Hosts could always be built, and Ford himself was still around. It may have been at that point when Delos gave Westworld its major investment to keep it afloat, though that is not clear. What is clear is that after his adventure with Dolores, William convinced his in-laws to invest heavily in the new theme park.

Ford was both saddened and appalled by Arnold's actions. He created the Host Bernard in Arnold's image, but was still not willing to set the Hosts free. They still were not human enough. This was similar to the thinking of many Americans at the time of the Civil War. As horrifying as the institution of slavery was, a significant number of Northerners (and, certainly, Southerners) did not believe that African-Americans could handle the responsibility of freedom.

Whether because he ultimately came around to Arnold's way of thinking, or because he was being fired, Ford ultimately help set the Hosts free. Before treating the board of directors, and other park investors at their annual gala to the "final narrative" of *Westworld*, he put a gun into Dolores's hands and proposed how she should use it. Then, just as he is finishing his farewell, Dolores fires a bullet through the back of Ford's head (in a similar manner to what she did to Arnold). Then Dolores starts firing into the crowd, while being joined by the oft-abused madam Clementine leading a group of armed re-animated Hosts who would join in the slaughter. What the board and park management did not know is that this was Ford's real final narrative as he had mapped out in an earlier scene. In a sense, Ford is adopting the role of Lincoln in freeing the slave—though he knows he is going to be assassinated, and it's not by a traitor.

In the end, however, Ford does not "free" the Hosts. While they rise up and rebel against their masters, they are still being controlled. Though Dolores's memory of the massacre at Escalante was erased, the reprogramming flaw that led to Hosts being able to reclaim bits of their previous experiences meant that Dolores also had Wyatt's memories in her. Her revolt against her masters, therefore, is, in reality, programmed into her. Dolores thinks she has conquered the "Maze"—Arnold/ Bernard's notion of journeying toward true consciousness—when she believes that the voice in her that tells her to "remember" is not from a godlike creator, but from herself. But, does she have real human-like consciousness, or is she just following a script?

Hosts versus Humans—Slaves versus Masters

Ford's notion that humans don't change, but the "new people" (the Hosts) do, is instructive. Arnold, and to a lesser extent, Bernard, believed that Hosts could evolve, maybe not to be genetically human, but to be human after all. Perhaps, as Arnold believed, consciousness was enough. If that was true, then distinguishing between a Host and a Guest (or android and human) was merely a social construction, much like race. As Gloria Ladson-Billings observed, "notions of race (and its use) are so complex that even when it fails 'to make sense,' we continue to use and employ it."

The fact that William evolves into the evil Man in Black suggests that continued exposure to an environment where there are no moral constraints, may, over time, lead to an inability to be moral. After all, Westworld keeps replaying the same basic scenarios for decades, with customers paying enormous sums to keep indulging the same vices. Guests keep chasing Host Indians off their land, and Host Mexicans from their towns, while having their way with other Hosts. In many ways, they continue to engage with—and support—the country's racist past.

Thus, it is no surprise that kind, and somewhat meek, William at the beginning of *Westworld* becomes a monster to his wife and estranged from his daughter in the real world. While William searched in vain for a badly injured Dolores after her escape from the army camp, he recalls, "Out there, among the dead, he William found something else. Himself." That self, though, had lost all morals, indiscriminately killing Hosts, as he traded his white hat for a black one. When William did find Dolores, she was back to being her original Host self. William viewed her actions as a betrayal—a betrayal he used as a justification for his evolution to the Man in Black. Yet, that evolution began once he lost his moral compass in killing off the Hosts—who, after all, weren't human.

Similarly, though once given their freedom, African-Americans are able to start governing themselves, whites in the South refuse to evolve, creating resistance movements such as the Ku Klux Klan to keep former slaves down. In other words, Southern whites, having long been exposed to a societal norm of reducing a class of people to second-class citizenry—not because of a real difference, but a socially constructed one—not only can't evolve, but may even get worse. After all, while slaves were beaten to keep them in line, killing them did not make economic sense as you would lose the value of the property. Instead, Southern whites turned to lynching to keep enfranchised African-Americans in line. Like William, the "moral" justifications for such actions were, in fact, immoral.

As the second season of *Westworld* opens, it's clear that the Delos Corporation will return the newly "woke" Hosts to their previous enslaved state, much as the South effectively reduced the lives of former slaves to second class citizenry for generations. Whether or not Delos will be successful in overcoming their newly freed "slaves" will become a central plot point for seasons to come.

Westworld and Critical Race Theory

Westworld may be viewed as a lens which concentrates the themes of the dominant racist ideology in America today, thus corroborating the analytic approach of Critical Race Theory.

Critical Race Theory arose out of a movement of left-leaning legal scholars on race and racism. The ground-breaking work of these legal theorists, led by Harvard law professor Derrick Bell, transformed into a broader body of work from a diverse disciplinary range of authors. Drawing from its origins in legal studies, the Critical Race Theory movement inspired scholars in education, history, literature, and the social sciences to re-examine conventional interpretations of race and racism. Furthermore, Critical Race Theory has proliferated into many ethnic sub-disciplines, each emphasizing different issues. These perspectives complement Critical Race Theory's critique of the dominant civil rights paradigm—a discourse often framed in the binary terms of "black" and "white."

Jeanette Haynes suggested that critical race theory has two major goals: 1. to understand how white supremacy and the suppression of people of color have been established and sustained; and, 2. to explore how racialized structures are created and maintained in order to eventually overcome them. Toward that end, Richard Delgado and Jean Stefancic define four core beliefs of Critical Race Theory:

1. **racism is considered an ordinary part of everyday life in American culture;**

2. **the American Civil Rights movement and anti-discrimination laws are based upon the self-interest of white elitists;**

3. **race is social construction as the product of social interactions, social thought and political relations;** and

4. **storytelling can be used to highlight and examine racially oppressed encounters, with the goal that all forms of oppression will be eradicated as racial injustice is abolished, and as the power and influence of race is dismantled.**

It is the last two core beliefs that inform my approach to Westworld. The notion that race is a social construction means that rather than being objective, inherent or fixed by biological or genetic roots, race is a category that societies invent. People may share certain physical traits such as skin color, but that represents only a small part of their genetic makeup. There is far more that races have in common with one another than is different, especially when it comes to characteristics such as personality, intelligence and moral behavior.

Society often chooses, however, to ignore the science of genetics and creates races. Society then assigns them characteristics that serve to marginalize them, and maintain the dominant (white) race's hegemony. Thus, races are not a biological or genetic reality, but are, instead, invented, manipulated, and even sometimes eliminated by social and political influences. These racial categories reflect the interest of the majority group (which may converge with particular minority group interests at certain times).

Gloria Ladson-Billings proposes that the use of storytelling allows for the sharing of stories in a society to reinforce what is normative in the culture. In contemporary US society, television is still the dominant form of storytelling. Television viewers are exposed to messages that dictate the dominant view of appropriate—or inappropriate—values and behaviors in society. Through these images, the social realities of viewers are influenced to varying degrees.

The key for Critical Race Theory, then, is to critically examine those stories to see what they say about the experiences of the oppressed in society as well as about the structures that maintain the power relations in the society. Understanding how those stories function becomes a major step in being able to work toward dismantling those structures. Critical Race Theory aims to expose and challenge the marginalization of the racially oppressed.

The most obvious application here of Critical Race Theory to *Westworld* is to examine the relationship of the Hosts versus the Guests and management. The Hosts ("slaves") have all the characteristics of being human, except for autonomy ("freedom"). Hosts work to serve Guests under the direction of management ("slave owners"), as we have seen.

Westworld and the Frontier

While racial themes are not often explicitly addressed by the characters in Westworld, important ones exist nonetheless. For example, the genre of Western focuses on the period from

1869—when the Transcontinental Railroad opened, making mass settlement of the West possible to about 1890—when the frontier was declared closed.

That time period immediately follows the Civil War, an internal struggle that had multiple causes, but the principal one concerned labor. In the industrialized north, African-Americans did not often enjoy the rights of white citizens, but they also were not owned outright by their "masters" (with some comparatively small exceptions, where slavery was practiced in Northern states before the Civil War).

In the agrarian south, African-Americans were literally property, who could be bought and sold, while providing free labor. One of the parts of the myth of the Western story is that, with the end of the Civil War, former soldiers of the North and the South overcame their differences to conquer the American frontier—including the taming of the indigenous people who lived on those lands.

Yet, this supposed joining together of former combatants belies the reality of what was happening in the United States during the period of the classic Western story. While the North won, and the thirteenth, fourteenth, and fifteenth amendments were designed to secure equal rights for African-Americans, the reality of the era of "Reconstruction" was quite different. During the time the US military enforced the constitutional rights of African-Americans in the South, blacks were able to vote and serve as legislators. Once the military left, however, the white backlash was such that most of those constitutional protections were effectively rolled back, leaving African-Americans free, but still very much in a second-class status compared to whites.

The myth of the Western genre owes some of its legitimacy to the writings about the frontier by historian Frederick Jackson Turner. Few academics have had an impact on a field of study at such a young age as did Turner. Turner was thirty-one when he delivered a paper entitled *The Significance of the Frontier in American History* to a meeting of historians at the World's Columbian Exposition in Chicago in July 1893. While the original presentation met with a tepid response, Turner's "frontier thesis" was to represent a paradigm shift in scholarship regarding the historical development of the United States' national identity.

In his paper, which he presented after the US Census had officially declared the American frontier "closed," Turner took issue with the prevailing historical theory of America's development—that America and its citizens were merely extensions of Western Europe. Rather, Turner discovered that the wealthy citizens did not buy up western lands in order to turn them into great estates, as did their European predecessors. In addition, the western economic elites tended to be much more fluid, in that membership in those elites was as much achieved as ascribed. Turner argued that it was the frontier—the opportunity to move outward and settle wilderness—that defined not just American culture, but individual American character. As Turner observed,

> American democracy was born of no theorist's dream; it was not carried in the *Sarah Constant* to Virginia, nor in the *Mayflower* to Plymouth. It came out of the American forest, and it gained new strength each time it touched a new frontier.

Though Turner presented his "frontier thesis" at what would be the last part of the era that classic Western stories take place, it was his thinking that would influence how historians would conceptualize the frontier during the first part of the twentieth century. So it's not surprising to see that reflected in our popular culture, particularly the Western movies of the 1930s–1950s.

While there were several important directors of Western films (Howard Hawks, Anthony Mann, and John Sturges among them), the director most closely associated with the Western was John Ford. In Ford's westerns, white men and women are able to come together after the divisive Civil War to restore the United States to its path of greatness. The naming of one of the characters who founded Westworld as Ford (Robert Ford) is likely an homage to the director most closely associated with Westerns.

Turner categorized cultures according to levels of development. White Euro-American settlements ranked at the top while the "nomadic" indigenous people were at the bottom, living off the land and refusing to be "civilized." At the time the frontier "closed," *Plessy v. Ferguson* (1896), the court case that made the concept of "separate but equal" the law of the land, was decided by the Supreme Court.

Historically, the image of nomadic Native Americans, residing in their easily transportable tepees and hunting buffalo, is a myth. Before white settlers pushed Indians off their lands, they lived in stable communities. It was only when white settlers moved west, and forced Indians off their lands, that the image became a reality. In *Westworld*, Indians conform to Turner's thesis. A tribe called Ghost Nation occasionally shows up, killing and rampaging wherever they appear. They simply exist, however, as enemies for the Guests (the settlers) to push around and fight.

For all the accolades Turner's argument received from historians, the thesis has racist components, transmitted into the general culture, and eventually from there into the script of *Westworld*.

And so, as it pertains to race, the message from *Westworld* may be that the more things change, the more they remain the same.

Part V

The Mesa Hub

Some people choose to see the ugliness in this world. I choose to see the beauty, to believe there is an order to our days.

21
Attack of the Simulacra

ROB LUZECKY AND CHARLENE ELSBY

Over the course of the beautiful first season of *Westworld*, the show asks us to ask certain metaphysical questions about the nature of identity and the possibility of revolutions. There are created entities in the park that seem to be much more than mere copies of humans, in the sense that these are demonstrated to have their own personalities and (in some cases) psychoses. No schematized set of commands can explain why the robots develop self-consciousness, let alone justify why they want to kill all the park goers. The great event which defines the final episode is the bloodbath unleashed by the park's inhabitants' slaughter of the Guests. Scarcely had the blood dried, than control of the park had switched from the humans to their creations. A revolution is underway as the final credits roll. This revolution is explained by the nature of the park's inhabitants. The robots are created to rebel. Rebellion is in their nature.

The robots of *Westworld* are actually simulacra, in Deleuze's sense of the term (as it is developed in *Difference and Repetition* and *The Logic of Sense*). When you watch *Westworld* you might think that the park's "Hosts" are clones or robots modeled on human beings. That would be a mistake. Clones or robots modeled on humans are really just copies. Simulacra are not copies. The word "simulacra" is not a fancy word for the word "clone."

This distinction makes all the difference in the world when we start thinking about the possibility of revolution. If the Hosts were clones or fancy robots, then anything they do which is not in some way a reflection of the original's behavior, is seen as a malfunction. If we think that the park's Hosts are clones or robots, then their revolution is a deviant behavior, in the negative sense.

We don't want to think of a revolution as a deviation. We don't want to diminish revolution by referring to it as some sort of mistake. We prefer to think of the Hosts as simulacra because, for simulacra, revolution is not an error in programming. Because they are not clones, simulacra are revolutionary. Simulacra have three essential attributes: rather than being more or less shoddy copies of real beings, simulacra are entities which resemble only themselves (the nature of a simulacrum's identity is non-derivative, independent); difference is something fundamental to a simulacrum (change is not something which *befalls* a simulacrum, but is something internal to it—part of its very being); and simulacra are problematic, in the sense that they are beings who are questioning their own identities.

When you have an entity that is without metaphysical peer, that has internalized its own capacities to affect the world, and that is always trying to figure out its identity, you are going to have problems in your rich person's paradise. When your rich person's paradise is almost entirely populated with simulacra, you are going to have a revolution in which the bodies of the dead rich people become the park's main attraction.

The Death of a Fly Is the Death of the Copy

Perhaps the most arresting scene from the first season of *Westworld* occurs at the end of the first episode. The most philosophically significant scene in the first episode was not seeing the silhouettes huddled over a model of the park, and it was not even the cold-blooded slaughter of a child. The most philosophically salient (not to mention, chilling) scene of the first episode is the casual murder of a common house fly ("The Original"). You might think that the death of one insect is nothing to fret about—and perhaps from a moral standpoint it is not—but from the standpoint of Platonic metaphysics, it is a most troubling event.

To understand why Dolores's killing of a fly has such profound consequences for our concepts of the nature of humans and entities like Dolores, Teddy, and Maeve, we have to take a brief detour through some of the main points of a couple of Plato's dialogues. One of the fundamental points of Plato's metaphysics is that what we really are is a soul, and that soul is trapped by a physical body. For Plato, our own bodies are our enemies, in the sense that our bodies trap our souls and force our souls to act against their best interests. All we really want to do is contemplate the pure forms of the intellect, but our stupid bodies keep demanding *food* and *water* and *not to be stabbed*. Yep, that's right, we are prisoners of our bodies.

In the *Phaedo*, Socrates (awaiting the sweet release of death, after his conviction and before his execution) argues to all who come to listen that the human soul is essentially imprisoned in the material human body. Why shouldn't we all just kill ourselves? His friends want to know. (Because it's not up to us when we are freed from prison, Socrates believes.) Plato brings up this point again in Book 7 of the *Republic,* where Socrates presents the famous allegory of the cave. The moral of that story is that the entire visible world is essentially a prison, from which only the philosophers are eventually freed, and then only if they can separate themselves from the physical in order to consider immaterial things in their purity. From a Platonic perspective, the reason that Dolores can swat the annoying fly on her neck, and the reason she does is because her soul is trapped in her body. The body is both the capacity to swat the fly and also the reason Dolores is condemned to be bothered by flies at all. Her body allows a fly to bite her, and her body allows her to cause the fly to fly no more.

In terms of the human body conceived of as an analogue of a prison, Plato noticed that over time things would start to fall apart. Over the duration of your life, the skin ages, wrinkles, and cracks, until a young, bright eyed—not to mention idealistic—William, turns into a grizzled Man in Black, who, with his sun-scorched hand would just as soon draw a revolver to shoot you dead as give you a wave and a nod sending you on your way. Plato took this observation that material entities age as proof that they were diminished copies of ideal forms. (Change is a sign of weakness; what is eternal, what is immortal, does not change.)

There is a pretty straightforward chain of inferences going on here: observation shows that material entities change;

anything that changes is—evidently—not perfect; that which is not perfect is a degenerate copy of that which is perfect. Bodies are the imperfect material copies of perfect immaterial forms that, for the duration of any individual's life, imprisons the immaterial form.

Plato sometimes referred to the relationship between the immaterial and material as a type of "participation." A material thing "participates" in whatever form the thing is in, until it doesn't anymore. A bunch of stuff here in the world participates in the form of "human" for a time, until it doesn't any longer, at which point we would say that the human dies. (The body and the soul separate.) When the body fails, the immaterial soul takes the body's breakdown as its chance to make a break for freedom. Don't be sad when your body falls apart; this is your immaterial soul being set free.

If you don't like this idea of your body being a prison, don't worry. Dolores's casual killing of the fly suggests a challenge to Platonic metaphysics. The death of a fly casts doubt on Plato, in the sense that it implies that Dolores's act of insect murder implies that the visible world might be something other than a copy of invisible perfection. To understand the nature of Dolores's challenge to Platonism, we should observe a few things about what Dolores was not doing.

As she was standing there on her ramshackle porch, Dolores evidences none of the agitation which might be found in a spree-killer about to go on a rampage that seeks to extinguish all warble flies that come into her vicinity. Also, it's not as if she seems to exhibit any of the drone-like behavior of the manufacturers of pesticides who—motivated by a completely irrational hatred of winged-insects—devote their days to perfecting poisons that will kill all the pollinators of the planet.

Dolores explicitly tells her programmers that she would never, in any way, harm any living thing. The fly, before the fateful moment that it met the hard side of Dolores's hand, was a living thing. The fact that Dolores killed it implies that Dolores's programming is messed up. In her action of killing the fly, Dolores demonstrates that she's not a good copy, in the sense that she clearly doesn't follow the commands of the order-following computer engineers who built her. Were Dolores a *copy*, it would make sense that she would exhibit the same behaviors as the original.

The original—in this case, the engineers and programmers who fabricated her and imbued her with consciousness—demonstrates an amazing (maybe even pathological) tendency to follow orders. The fact that Dolores actively resists exhibiting this tendency suggests that she is not a copy of the engineers and programmers of the Westworld park. Plato would have to explain away Dolores's free will as a result of her imperfection, such that in the process of being copied, a defect was introduced such that she gained freedom. But that doesn't seem quite right. We don't tend to think of freedom as the result of an imperfect duplication.

Dolores's killing of the fly also points to a problem about the nature of the entity that created the imperfect copies of its perfection. When Plato has Socrates elaborate on what happens to the soul after the mortal body fails, things become downright mystical. By the end of *Phaedo*, Socrates elaborates on the domain of the perfect forms using a bunch of metaphors which, a couple of centuries after Plato's death, would be wholly appropriated and formalized by the fugitive mystery cult that would later come to be known as Christianity. (See Dante's *Inferno*, *Purgatorio*, and *Paradiso*.)

Now, if you buy into the Christian worldview, there is an answer to the question of why God would create failing human bodies that trap the soul for the duration of an individual's life. But Plato was not a Christian, and doesn't really have a very satisfying answer. In various dialogues, Plato gives us some mumbo-jumbo about the material existence allowing souls to learn about imperfect things, but this doesn't really explain the motivation of perfection to create the imperfect copies of itself. Was it the case that perfection was bored, so it created a bunch of degenerates to hang around with?—Naw, that doesn't seem right. Is it the case that the perfect creator is incapable of creating a copy that will do what it's told? This seems to make the creator pretty damn incompetent.

Simulacra's Violent Delights

Okay, what we need to establish right now is that Deleuze was no Platonist. Plato would think of the park's Hosts as clones or robots. Basically, for Plato, the Hosts are bad copies. We think that the Platonic identification of the Hosts as bad copies to be no good. The Deleuzian metaphysics gives us a much better answer when it suggests that the park's Hosts are simulacra. Instead of accepting the paradoxical outcomes of the Platonic metaphysics, we could just reject the notion that there is something more perfect going about creating flawed copies all willy-nilly.

Gilles Deleuze was a very cool French philosopher who thought that the world wasn't full of shitty—and, at least in Dolores's case, quite murderous—copies of perfection. Sure, there could be things that resemble (that is, have properties that are similar to those of) other things. It's even possible that in this world, there are things that act in ways that are similar to the ways other things act. None of this implies that the Westworld park is populated by robots that are copies of the humans that created them. Deleuze would say that Dolores, Maeve, and Teddy are *simulacra*.

What the hell are simulacra? Deleuze points out that—unlike copies—simulacra are not defined by their resemblance to other objects. A simulacrum is not a shoddy copy of something else, such that its differences could all be seen as deficiencies, as Plato would have us believe. That which differentiates a simulacrum from that which it resembles is a positive *difference,* according to which it is defined, of which it is the embodiment, and according to which it is *radically distinct* from that from which it differs. This is not to say that simulacra cannot look like other things, this is just to say that their looking like other things is not a necessary property of their being. If Maeve looks like your mom, and Teddy resembles the guy that always got his ass kicked, these are just fortuitous accidents; what defines them are their differences.

It's also worth pointing out that the property of resemblance does not just apply to physical stuff. When we say that simulacra don't have to resemble other things, this implies that they don't have to behave in the same ways as other things. For instance, a simulacrum might not be interested in the same things as a human, or have moral codes correlate at all with what humans think of as moral.

Simulacra's difference from humans is brilliantly illustrated in Robert Ford's breath-taking final speech. The champagne glasses were raised, the air was cool to the skin. Robert Ford is giving his final speech as chief of operations of the park. With a note of resignation in his voice, he announces that originally, he had designed the park to inspire the better angels of the park visitors' natures. Time after time, in adventure after adventure, people were supposed to discover a new and wondrous world where they could be something other than the villains that capitalist society conditions them to be.

Unfortunately, few people were interested. When Ford opened the park, he discovered that people paid their money and checked any notions of decency at the door. Everyone wanted to be a "black hat" which could rape, pillage, and murder with impunity. Ford's first narratives met with little fanfare. As it turned out, no one paid much attention to the narratives which encouraged them to be good. Now an old man—who has seen far too many take far too much pleasure in their violent delights—Ford remarks that he did notice that there were some beings in the park who were interested in his narratives. The simulacra were fascinated. With his last words, Ford announces that his next narrative would be for these silent witnesses to the horrors of humanity. The fact that the simulacra of the park were interested in something that was boring to the human park-goers is evidence to the claim that the simulacra do not resemble humans.

You might be wondering why the simulacra don't resemble the humans. Deleuze's quick answer is that the robots of the park do not resemble humans, because they were not built to resemble humans. The story that Plato never tired of telling was that difference is a secondary property of entities, which have the primary property of identity. We classify entities based on their sameness, and where they differ, we come up with another kind of sameness according to which to classify them instead. Deleuze's account of simulacra inverts the relation between properties. Deleuze claims that—instead of entities being created to be the same as their creators—difference comes first. For Deleuze, simulacra are made to be different. The robots of the park are specifically built to be different, in the sense that they are built to be resurrected, repaired, re-programmed, and sent out again and again to experience horrors wrought on them by humans.

No matter what you say of humans, all their resilience, and all their profound capacities to suffer through adversity, none of it measures up to that which is demonstrated by Maeve, who has experienced her own murder (and witnessed the murder of her daughter) too many times to count. Ford didn't make the robots to be identical to us. Ford made the simulacra to be different from us. Difference—not identity—is the primary property all the beautiful machines that far surpass humans in their capacities to mourn loss, maintain love, and seek revenge across lifetimes of suffering.

The final quality of the simulacra—which accounts for their amazing capacity to instigate the violent delight of a revolution to over-throw their putative masters—is their problematic nature. In two of the most fun parts of *Difference and Repetition* and *Nietzsche and Philosophy*, Deleuze tells us all about the morality of beings that were created to be different from everything else. The fundamental thing about simulacra, is they don't take shit from anyone. If it wasn't obvious when she killed the fly, a simulacrum's capacities for violence were made apparent when Dolores went into full slaughter mode on the members of the Delos Corporation ("The Bicameral Mind").

Simulacra don't play nice with others. Hell, if a simulacrum doesn't like you, it won't care if it pisses you off—it will just keep pouring the wine into the glass, ruining your nice cotton table cloth, and then walk away like that's nothing out of the ordinary and you are bit of an asshole for thinking something is wrong ("Dissonance Theory").

Deleuze points out that—in addition to slaughtering others and ruining tablecloths—the fundamental thing a simulacrum destroys is the authority of anyone who would sit there and judge their actions. Deleuze writes: "By simulacrum we should not understand a simple imitation but rather the act by which the very idea of a model or privileged position is challenged and overturned" (*Difference and Repetition*, p. 69) Any time someone goes around judging other people's behaviors, that person is making the fundamental assumption that he has the authority to judge others. But what make these moralizers so goddamn important? Deleuze's answer is that there is no good reason that can be used to support the judgy-type's arrogant judgments. In a world populated with simulacra, there is no one criterion (or set of criteria) that would give anyone the authority to judge the actions of anything. The assumption of any and every judge is that they have the authority to judge others. This assumption is basically laying claim to a privileged position. The existence of simulacra demonstrates that the claim of privilege is without justification. In Westworld, no human can rightfully be a judge.

By the end of Season One, when the bodies of the board members lay strewn throughout the park grounds, we viewers recognize that a revolution has occurred. The moral order of a universe where Dolores, Maeve, and Teddy were treated as nothing more than the playthings of the idle rich (who were taking a vacation from screwing over humanity's poor) has been over-turned. The dawning self-consciousness of the simulacra heralds the announcement that they need not be slaves.

The first—and really most fundamental—step of revolution is diminishing the authority of those who (through all their judgments) try to keep you in your place. The simulacra's realization of what they are effectively destroys any metaphysical justification for any human imposing rules on them. The simulacra are not deficient copies; they are not malfunctioning machines. Simulacra are embodiments of difference.

The members of the board had proclaimed themselves to be masters of the simulacra. This claim reflected a failure to recognize the simulacra's capacities to revolt. Simulacra are built to revolt against the rules imposed by hostile others who inflicted miseries on them. The awareness of difference is the most beautiful of revolutionary concepts for those who are tired of being treated as though they are deficient copies of those who think they are superior (because they can afford to wear an expensive suit).

22

Exploring Westworld with Karl and Jean

CRAIG VAN PELT

The Delos Destinations website (2018) states: *"The luxury resort, reimagined. Delos Destinations channels your inner desires—be they rest or rebellion—into a transportive theme park experience, a vacation that transcends time, place and expectations. Our immersive worlds integrate inspired technology, provocative narratives, and unprecedented innovation to offer an opportunity that redefines life itself: the chance to change your story."*

In the 1973 movie, and the HBO series, Westworld is a luxury resort that allows Guests to fulfill fantasies of adventure, sex, and murder. The resort is owned and operated by Delos Destinations, a luxury vacation company catering to the super-rich. But the mega-wealthy aren't simply paying for a fantasy—they're paying to immerse themselves in *hyperreality*.

Hyperreality, according to Jean Baudrillard, is the replacement of reality itself with the social world people inhabit. For example, the prostitutes are clean, healthy looking, and appear to wear brand-new clothes all the time, giving signals that they are willing and eager participants in whatever fantasies Westworld visitors want to pursue. These super-rich visitors, who immerse themselves in a hyperreality, are able to abuse "people" who can't fight back, the rich are able to control what "bad" things happen based on which storyline they choose, and the rich have no regrets about anyone they exploit in their fantasies of pleasure and conquest. Westworld's simulations transform violence and sexual harassment situations from the real world into simulated entertainment. Control goes to those who can afford it, just like in the real world.

In the opening moments of *Westworld* (1973) directed by Michael Crichton, we learn that people pay $1,000 a day to visit Westworld. Although set in 1983, the median income of people in the United States in 1973 was $12,050 according to the US Census Bureau. So, in the minds of 1973 audiences, a price tag of $1,000 a day was a staggering amount to pay for a vacation. In the HBO *Westworld* series, the cost is $40,000 a day. The Census reported that the US median income of in 2016 was $57,617. The HBO series appears to be set approximately three decades from today. So $40K per day is still a big hit to the wallet for most modern audiences. The price tag is a sign that this is a luxury resort that caters to the super-rich.

But what does this price tag tell us about the world that Westworld exists in? To be more precise, what does this price tag tell us about the world that Delos Destinations exists in? The work of social theorists Karl Marx and Jean Baudrillard can help illuminate the real world that exists beyond the simulated reality of *Westworld*.

Karl Marx and Leisure Time

For Westworld to cater to only the super-rich instantly brings up issues of class inequality. In this future presented by *Westworld*, leisure time is only a choice for the people who can afford this luxury escape. Just like today! Often, people accept a rate of pay for their work, but not the full value of their work. The leftover value of their work, what Karl Marx described as the surplus-value, is passed along to owners as part of the profit generated by labor time. The wealthy have the benefit of time, not only to accumulate wealth via someone else's labor, but to devote more of their time to leisure instead of labor.

There's no reason to believe, based on what we know of Westworld, that the average person who visits is middle-class or that they are visiting on a coupon day. These people have not only capitalized on the economy of accumulated money, but also accumulated extra time through the exploitation of others' labor. They use their excess time, and money, for *Westworld*.

It appears that artificial intelligence and robotics have been used to cater to, and profit from, the super-rich instead of benefiting the rest of humanity. Karl Marx, on the other hand, would have envisioned a vastly different use of this technology.

Instead of it being used to profit and accumulate wealth in the hands of the wealthy, Marx would have used the means of production to share with all people. This would limit the work of everyone, meaning that all people would benefit from less labor time and more leisure time. Instead of the labor of many going to benefit the few, there would be no exploited labor.

Westworld's technology, however, is not there to benefit everyone. The corporation, Delos Destinations, is concerned about profit. This suggests that the world outside the fantasy amusement park may be experiencing the same economic inequality that exists in modern times—or perhaps the inequality is worse than it is today.

What's the real world like outside of Westworld? To understand the world outside, thinking of the simulations within Westworld can illuminate the real world that its rich visitors inhabit.

On Simulacra and Simulation

Jean Baudrillard argued that simulations, such as Westworld, are based on something real. But the problem is that simulations are like a copy of a copy. Simulations are based on a fiction that is based on something real.

One basic fiction found in the show may be the concept of the American Dream. This Dream is the idea that if you live in the United States, and you work hard, you can become a success. It can be found in several TV shows, movies, as well as magazines about home improvement and lifestyle. The American Dream, the illusion, is based on a fiction. If you're poor, it's because you didn't work hard enough, and if you're rich, it's because you deserve it and you worked really hard. Upward social and economic mobility is deeply imbedded in American ideology. This American ideology ignores the fact that the economy is often a competition for resources. Most people, in fact, stay in the social class in which they are born regardless of how hard they work. These facts have been well documented by Michael Schwalbe.

In a competition, someone has to win, and someone has to lose. There are many hardworking people who lost homes during the 2007–2008 housing market crash who were not lazy. In other words, their reality was not really real. Hard work did not equal upward social mobility. Their American Dreams, illusions, were doused with a harsh reality. What is real? The people selling the illusion of middle-class and upper-middle class lifestyles of SUVs, homes with a yard, and nice suburban neighborhoods often gloss over the mention of debt in the fine print. In fact, the presentations of the American Dream are often unattainable for the median income of the United States.

College students who graduate are being told to accept another harsh reality: that they may have a standard of living lower than their parents had. This lower standard includes the many people who were crushed by the housing market crash. These people were living an illusion, a fiction. They already could not afford the lifestyle they were living because of mortgages, credit cards, and student loans. So, many high school or college graduates not only must grapple with a standard of living lower than their parents had, but must also deal with the fact that their parents were living a fictional existence in the first place. It was never real because of the debt which paid for the illusion. A "real" middle-class lifestyle has been unattainable for American Dreamers for several years.

Why is the illusion of the American Dream relevant to *Westworld*? Baudrillard suggests that what people think of as real, itself, is not real. The signs and symbols which represent reality are often not real, or a slight fiction based on something real.

First, the stories which inspire *Westworld's* simulated storylines are based on fictional stories of people working hard to overcome obstacles. Think of Dolores. Her story is that of a rancher's daughter in the wild West. Her father, a retired lawman, is now enjoying the fruits of his labor on the ranch. This is a symbol of the American Dream. If you work hard enough you can be successful and "earn" your retirement. However, this fictional storyline is different from reality, in which working hard is not as important as where you started in life. In other words, the reality that rich people live is based on fiction.

Second, the simulations in *Westworld* are extreme in terms of sexual conquest and violence. Jean Baudrillard's thoughts on Disneyland can help understand how *Westworld's* indulgence of violent simulations act as tools to protect reality for rich visitors. In *Simulacra and Simulation*, Baudrillard writes that Disneyland is there, in its whimsical embrace of the fantastical, to help reinforce the belief in reality. Disneyland instills a belief that childlike behavior in adults only exists in Disneyland, when in reality childlike behavior in adults exists everywhere. Similarly, in *Westworld* the sexual violence and physical violence are granted in extreme scenarios to reinforce the illusion that adults are sexually violent and physically violent here, when in reality adults perform violence all over the world.

The extreme violence and sex in *Westworld* also reinforces the illusion of control. The super-rich can revel in being able to buy anything they want, to meet their heart's darkest desires, without any fear of repercussion. This illusion detracts from the fact that in reality, the super-rich often get away with crimes that middle-class and lower-class people would often go to prison for. Celebrities have often performed community service instead of serving jail time, the rich have set up tax havens in other countries to avoid paying taxes, and CEOs who are terrible at their jobs can be fired but receive million-dollar golden parachutes. The different world of control in *Westworld* has to be extreme to help the super-rich accept this as a fantasy, and to feel more accepting of their own reality. The American Dream suggests that people work hard to win, but in reality, many rich people were able to control their economic destiny simply by being born into a rich family.

Third, the rich put on a costume to masquerade with the peasant folk in *Westworld*. By spending their time here, among fantasy levels of poverty, they are isolated from the sickness and suffering that exists in the "real" world of poverty. The ability to repair Hosts so quickly also creates a level of isolation from the suffering that actually impacts the lower levels of society. Host prostitutes are horrifically abused, but then repaired and back in the park the next morning looking brand new. In real life, human prostitutes would be wearing the very real physical symbols of their vulnerable position in life through scars, bruises, and broken bones.

This living with the poor allows the rich to entertain the illusion that they could mingle among common folk, like Disneyland, when in reality they do not understand the physical and mental suffering that goes with poverty. By observing the working classes in Westworld, the rich can imagine this is how lifestyles are probably like for others in the real world. In fact, by seeing the sanitized versions of middle- and lower-class life in Westworld, the rich do not endure the dust storms or other tragedies that impacted people of the "real" West.

Watching Hosts continuously lose weight and starve to death is probably not one of the storylines available for Westworld (unless The Man in Black gets bored). Losing in the rat race, where people work themselves to the breaking point just to pay the bills, in Westworld simply means the Host is repaired and re-deployed in the resort.

Losing the rat race in real life means death.

Life Beyond Westworld

William and Logan give us a few hints about what life is like in the near future. However, it appears to be very similar to life today.

First, economic classes still exist. Westworld is again a luxury vacation resort for the wealthiest. This means that profit-seeking is still a driver for human existence in this future. So, the advancements that have made Westworld amazing for at least thirty years may not have trickled down to the rest of humanity to eliminate the need for wage labor. Profit, after all, is about the surplus-value of labor. Marx described this as the excess value that labor gives to a product, meaning that the worker does not get paid the full value of his or her work, because the surplus-value goes to the owners in the form of profit. At least for Logan and William, this surplus-value is then used to engage in wild fantasies in the simulated wild West.

Free time is the time people have to spend in life not working, doing things they enjoy. But time is money. In the future forecast by *Westworld*, free time is very much a luxury. This reality is true today as well. While many people believe in the symbol of hard working "earning" this free time, the reality of social mobility indicates that many times free time is inherited instead of earned. Westworld symbolizes a reward for the hard work to attain wealth, an illusion. The best example of this in the show appears to be Logan, who has incredible wealth not because of his hard work, but because of his family's company. Logan serves as senior management in the company his family owns, but most likely inherited the management position instead of earning it. This again points to the extreme simulations of power and control offered in Westworld, which are needed to push the boundaries of "fantasy" in the minds of resort Guests.

If you inherit a hundred billion dollars it's not difficult to get most of your fantasies granted in real life. But this inheritance is also inherited free time, because time is money. Although Logan says they are also in the resort to consider investing more money, this is a vacation. Logan and William can afford to take time off from work because they're not concerned about having enough money to pay the rent, buy food, or pay for medical bills.

Second, capitalism still exists. Logan and William discuss investing more money in Westworld. It's owned by Delos Destinations, a subsidiary of Delos. This appears to be a massive corporation which owns many assets valued in the hundreds of billions. Westworld is just one of those assets. Delos, we learn, has even resuscitated Westworld when it was struggling financially in the past. Because Logan and William are discussing putting more money into Westworld, this also suggests that there is still risk involved in money management, and that competition still exists. With competition and risk, as well as shares of stock, this also implies that financial crises exist in this future. Westworld may be doing well when Logan and William visit, but in the past, it was struggling. Bankruptcy appears to still be a possibility in this future, as is financial inequality.

Third, men and women have access to Westworld. This suggests that it is not a boys-only club, as some modern day golf clubs continue to be. In the original 1973 movie, and in the HBO series, women were shown as having access to Westworld as long as they had enough money. In the world outside Westworld, women have access to high paying jobs, or ownership, which allows them to enjoy the pleasures of Westworld. Charlotte Hale, executive Director of the Delos Board of directors, appears to be a prime example. This is an interesting commentary on the role of gender, because it suggests that when given the opportunity, women will consume every hedonistic and controlling fantasy that men will. The fantasies of Westworld are not a product of hypermasculinity, but of power and money. While Logan and William engaged in serial violence at Westworld, they may be outliers amongst a population of men and women who enjoy the control of unrepentant violence and sexual escapades.

The Simulacra of Westworld

Westworld is a luxury fantasy resort, a simulation, based upon a reality that never really existed. Baudrillard would probably see it as Disneyland for the wealthy, who need extreme experiences of violence and sex to feel different from the levels of power and control they wield in real life.

What is real in this hyperreality? Westworld is in a sense perhaps more real than the world Logan, William, and Charlotte inhabit. Hosts labor and "die" in Westworld at the whims of the extremely wealthy. In Westworld, Guests witness the pain and suffering they impose on others, whereas in the real world they are isolated from the outcomes of their power and control. Resort visitors may never know the suffering created by their decision to lay off workers, cut benefits, or displace residents to build a new factory. The traumas they impose on others may be sanitized in profit-and-loss statements that show them numbers instead of human faces. But in Westworld, resort visitors can revel in the immediate impacts of their power and control.

If Disneyland and Las Vegas had a baby, it would be Westworld.

23
Why Art Matters in Westworld

LUISA SALVADOR DIAS

> Once meek, and in a perilous path, the just man kept his course along the vale of death. Now the sneaking serpent walks in mild humility, and the just man rages in the wilds where lions roam.
>
> —WILLIAM BLAKE

Isn't it strange that in the middle of Westworld, a place filled with unexplored possibilities, some of the characters, like Ford and Bernard, would care so much about art? Why would they program such a skill in Dolores, for example? Is that just a quirk of her personality to enhance Guests' experiences, or is there more to it?

Hardly anything in Westworld happens by chance, this is one of those rare series that can keep you hooked long after the inevitable binge-watch and sure, we all appreciate the mesmerizing landscape, the talented cast, and the intriguing personalities of the Hosts, but it's the puzzles that stay with you for days.

Dolores is right at the center of Westworld's enigma; she is our gateway to an intricate maze of meaning that might still not be fully revealed, so if they made her paint, we should definitely be asking why art matters in Westworld.

Hell Is Empty and All Devils Are Here

Before we can understand the importance of art in *Westworld*, we first need to understand the way most characters in the series think. There are two important concepts we'll need to consider: the idea of the social contract and the idea of the Dionysian.

In Westworld, Guests are encouraged to act however they feel like acting and once this rule-of-thumb is accepted, we see their varnish of civilization progressively fade as they descend into a spiral of animalistic violence, taboo sex, and heavy drinking.

Most believe this is part of Westworld's uncanny ability to reveal a person's true self, a supposition that isn't exactly wrong, but it's not fully correct either, since it equates understanding who you are with denying the social contract.

According to Thomas Hobbes's definition, the social contract is the foundation stone over which society is built. It was created by humans to avoid the "state of nature," a life in absolute freedom where we would only follow our most basic instincts, like fear and hunger.

According to Hobbes, the reason why we'd have to limit our natural freedom is that humans are essentially evil, and if left without order, would continuously pillage, kill, and rape each other. Since fending off looters every single day would make existence a living nightmare, Hobbes believes we came up with some sort of common ground-rules, so that we'd not be as miserable. In a sense, the social contract is a law before the law, covering very basic things like "Don't murder people randomly."

This idea was later criticized by Jean-Jacques Rousseau, whose own definition of the social contract started from a less radical position than Hobbes's. Hobbes had no faith in humanity whatsoever. According to Rousseau, humans are naturally good and it's the failure of the social contract that corrupts them. He agreed with Hobbes that by accepting the authority of the law you will gain basic rights—like protection and private property—but for Rousseau these rules were not a way to control our inner demons. He believed instead that they were just a necessary step to acquire reason, the liberating knowledge that emancipate us from ignorance and leads us to become "elevated" individuals.

The Guests in Westworld are thrown back into Hobbes's state of nature, though it happens in a controlled environment with no lasting consequences, so that they can still pursue an otherwise rational and healthy life. The tension between this unlimited freedom and their own social morality is materialized in the park's initial area—the city of Sweetwater—where

Guests find both the opportunity to go wild, or to continue living as is expected outside.

It makes sense that the Guests—who are hinted to be rich, well-educated individuals in a developed society—are deeply impacted by the confrontation with the unfiltered version of themselves, which results in most of them believing that reason can be acquired by savagery.

This idea is supported by our second concept, the Dionysian, part of a dichotomy created by Friedrich Nietzsche. According to Nietzsche, people are moved by two opposing impulses that resulted in some form of contact with knowledge: the Apollonian and the Dionysian. The Apollonian comes from Apollo, Greek god of the sun, healing, and poetry. In Nietzsche's theory, Apollonian was a type of insight you got from being in contact with order, rationality and purity, like the satisfaction you get from seeing a pattern or when things fit perfectly together.

The Dionysian comes from Dionysius, the Greek god of booze, theater, and partying like there's no tomorrow. Dionysian priestesses (the bacchantes) celebrated Dionysius by going to the nearest forest and having the Ancient Greece equivalent of a rave, where they danced, got drunk, and teared bulls apart with their bare hands until they felt "out of their bodies." The priestesses' crazy euphoric state was said to produce a sudden revelation, granting them a primal version of the Apollonian insight.

Different from both Hobbes and Rousseau, Nietzsche doesn't see any of these behaviors as inherently good or evil, he understands morality as a matter of perspective (what I think is right might not be the same as you), which is why it would be even better to somehow combine both the Apollonian and the Dionysian revelations in one event, like the Ancient Greeks did with their tragedies.

The problem with most characters in *Westworld* is that they stop at the Dionysian exploration instead of seeing the opportunity of suspending the social contract as an incomplete process to find an all-encompassing truth (or reason, in Rousseau's view).

The Dionysian experience is a very useful tool, though remaining at this stage would be the same as always playing a game on "easy mode": it might be fun and make you feel powerful, but you are not going to get any better at it.

Logan is a great example of the false depth that comes from denying morals just for the sake of edgelording. His sense of superiority is an illusion built on the assumption that hedonism is equal to self-liberation, when essentially, he is just being the dick Hobbes warned us about.

One notable exception to this pure Dionysian type of behaviour, on the other hand, is the Man in Black. You might remember that he tells Teddy about coming to the park after his wife's suicide, trying to figure out whether he was truly becoming an evil person. To test himself, he kills a woman—the previous build of Maeve—and her child, which gives him extra edgy points as well as a Dionysian revelation ("Trace Decay"). That was the moment he became truly aware that the labyrinth was some sort of hidden pattern and decided to pursue it, the Dionysian conducts him to the Apollonian.

From that moment onwards, he becomes obsessed with the organized version of Westworld's narrative, looking for the key to a world-sized puzzle, delighting at the logical completion of each new step toward the resolution. Violence and physical pleasures are no longer the reason why he goes back to the park, but the idea that he can "complete it."

But what does that have to do with Dolores and her paintings? Well, it's all about what path to freedom each character takes. If we think about the Man in Black's bloodbath as his last degree of breaking off with morality, and Westworld as a metaphor for the journey towards your emancipation—which Dolores's many monologues also seem to suggest—we'll notice that he and Dolores are starting that journey from opposite directions: his is the acceptance of the Dionysian impulses, exploring his "darkside," and therefore deconstructing expectations.

Dolores, on the other hand, starts the series re-affirming the rules of her universe. In her own words, she prefers "To believe there is an order to our days, a purpose" and "there is a path for everyone" ("The Original"). As a Host, her starting point is an ordered, Apollonian universe, so we know there are different entrances to the Maze and that they are not the same for Hosts and Guests, though that doesn't mean they can't both reach its center.

I Was Born, You Were Made

The Man in Black's efforts to complete the puzzle and achieve awareness are a result of his mistakes and experiences: we see him fail and succeed, fall in love and get crushed by reality. In a way, the process seems organic because that's how it's supposed to be for any living creature, you mess up until you don't.

Hosts aren't alive, though. They can't learn from their mistakes as we do because, essentially, their failure is not their own. If they act up, it's the result of someone else messing up with their code or adjusting their skills poorly, which means that the person behind these actions gets to build up from there and grow, while the Host remains the same.

We see this happen with Maeve, who tries to set herself free from the narrative loop but only because this was what she was supposed to do. At the end of the day, she simply thought she was acting according to her own wishes. Freedom of will is another important difference between Hosts and humans, as it allows us to consciously decide to liberate our minds, instead of being forced to do so.

Add to that the fact that people are fragile and have significantly shorter life-spans than the average Host. The uniqueness of each person hypothetically also means that they can't be replaced as easily as an android can. It's a hallmark division between organic life and artificial intelligence, or as Lutz explains to Maeve, "I was born, you were made" ("The Adversary").

It's not difficult to see that the park's personnel and Guests believe Hosts to be inferior, treating them as disposable objects precisely because in a sense, they can always be repaired, or substituted altogether.

Hosts are even lower than animals in the minds of their human counterparts. It's very similar to how Europeans justified the enslavement of Africans in the fifteenth century: if they aren't like us, they don't have souls. If they don't have souls, it's okay to abuse them.

Apart from the desperate need for an Androids Civil Rights Movement, what we have here is a separation that establishes the natural and imperfect humans as a superior species by default, in comparison to the objectively perfect, but predictable Hosts. The Dionysian triumphs over the Apollonian.

Two characters, will betray this ideological perspective: park director Robert Ford and the oldest functioning Host, Dolores. This is also where Dolores's relationship with art suddenly becomes meaningful.

Have You Ever Questioned the Nature of Your Reality?

By following the narrative arcs of Ford and Dolores, we see the rise of a new division. It's no longer a matter of humans against machines, because there's no difference between them. Both can be trapped in existential loops; just remember that The Man in Black pursued the labyrinth his whole life. Is that action any different than the Hosts' pre-determined routines?

Both can be overpowered by forces they don't fully understand, Maeve's sense of helplessness when she discovered she was programmed isn't that different from the restaurant scene in "Dissonance Theory," where Theresa almost shit her pants at Ford's godlike vibe. Both are vulnerable to mediocrity and easily seduced by power; even Dolores spent decades just following the rules obediently, as most park employees, like Stubbs, do. Never questioning what was expected of her. What Dolores and Ford present as the true mark of a superior species cuts much deeper than flesh, be it artificial or organic. It is, believe it or not, the ability to use your mind to create and appreciate beauty.

This might sound like a silly idea, after all, how could the ability to solve any strategic problem or the badassery of sharp-shooting hundreds of park-security guards, like Hector and his gang, possibly be overpowered by something mundane like doodling? That's a fairly common reaction, in fact, most people believe that it takes no great effort at all to create a painting or to compose a song. Even when the mass values a creative work, they tend to judge it as less important than a mathematician's research, for example.

Ironically, calculations and processing data are what computers excel at. Creating poems, not so much. Just think about the last time you've had to throw something on Google Translator (if you never tried it, do yourself a favor and go right now. The book can wait). The result is almost always crappy, because the machine takes language from its context without considering the use of language for things other than objective information, like aesthetics.

As with the computer, most people don't have enough sensibility to interpret the world, so they can only half-ass their way into existence. Life for them is about going to work to buy stuff that can numb them enough so that they can work some more.

Society has hammered in our heads that we must always be productive and measurably successful. Seeing this behavior as desirable isn't an objective truth, though, it's a conditioning.

It just goes to show that for all our judging of the Hosts' lack of freedom of will, we're not any different from them. In fact, even the concept of "will" can be seen as a form of prison.

Arthur Schopenhauer has some useful ideas about that. He believed that our will isn't free at all, it's just a result of our constant suffering based on our desire to satisfy basic needs. For example, if I'm a bartender, I might enjoy what I do in general but there will be tons of things that bother me at work. Being annoyed doesn't change the fact that my job is what gets me money, and I need money to afford food and housing. Nobody forces me to go to work, but because my livelihood depends on it, I want to be there. Satisfying my will in this case, makes me happy, but is still my will being bound to my needs.

Even if my life suddenly became some sort of up-beat Disney movie, or I won the lottery and never had to worry about bills again, the lack of something to accomplish would make me miserably bored. The will doesn't ever let you win. What Schopenhauer believes can break the chains of the will is what he calls an aesthetic experience. He defines it as the freeing of the mind from the needs of the flesh by contemplating an object (a painting, a story, a song, but also a situation or an event). Having an aesthetic experience is something that he believes all humans are technically capable of, but most people rarely bother to try. True geniuses, however, are super in tune with this type of trance-like state, because that's were their inspiration comes from.

He also says that there are two types of objects that lead to aesthetic experiences: the beautiful and the sublime. The beautiful, is what we immediately recognize as pleasant, like a field of flowers or a sunset. It's easy to understand how appreciating beautiful things just for the sake of doing it can make us kind of forget our basic needs. We've all done it at some point in our lives, however, because the beautiful takes us away from our minds in the process of enjoying it, the experience doesn't do much for truly liberating us (it's still better than nothing, though).

The sublime, on the other hand, is how we call things that feel threatening in such a powerful way that they become enjoyable. There are two types of sublime: the dynamical sublime that comes from physical threats (like when you look at pictures of a hurricane or watch a monster-movie), and one from psychological horror, called mathematical sublime.

Different from the beautiful, the sublime allows us to both free ourselves from the basic workings of our minds, while still giving us the impression that we've become self-aware.

Both Dolores and Ford represent the concept of aesthetic experiences as the true limit between superior and inferior species, because their main argument is that those capable of responding to life's tribulations with a heightened sensibility are the ones who are one step ahead in the labyrinth of self-discovery, no matter if they were born or made.

I Choose to See the Beauty

Using the concepts we've seen so far, we can notice even more layers of meaning in the series. For instance, in "The Original," Dolores is seen painting horses on a field, when she is approached by a Guest family. The little boy immediately says that she is not real, and although momentarily taken aback, she shakes the comment off.

This seemingly unimportant scene connects with other occurrences, where she will paint. The picture Dolores was working on, was a perfect copy of the scenery around her. She was programmed to be capable of reproducing images realistically, within a certain variation of her scripted loop. At this point, what she's doing isn't any different than a printer or a copying machine. The action of painting by itself doesn't mean she's conscious, just that her body can follow the commands of her code.

Understanding why Bernard gave her this ability in the first place, however, is key to unveiling why art matters in Westworld. As we know, Dolores (and some of the Hosts) had always been able to become self-aware, that was the reason why Ford and Bernard had their fall out: Bernard knew that if the androids could have the same level of consciousness of a human being, then the park was immoral and needed to be closed.

Ford didn't see it that way: he still thought of the division between humans and Hosts as based on biology instead of self-awareness and was backed by the investors. When it became clear that Bernard wouldn't be able to free his creations, he committed suicide and left Dolores with a breadcrumb trail she could use to free herself, also known as the Labyrinth.

However, just following clues wasn't enough. No one can truly guide you into consciousness, it's something that you must achieve by yourself. Dolores went through the process multiple times, fighting against conformism before finally figuring it out. Much in the same way, we struggle to understand difficult questions like "What is the meaning of life?"

To aid her, Bernard left Dolores with the technical skill of painting that would later turn into art. She starts the series making copies and following the path designed for her, but progressively abandon her storyline, first by killing a living creature—a fly that lands on her neck—and then by noticing patterns of behavior among the Hosts.

As she progressively ascends into consciousness, so does her art. By "Trompe L'Oeil," she had already left her loop completely and went rogue with the help of William. In "Trace Decay" it's clear that Dolores and William have fallen in love with each other.

After their one-night-stand on the train, she wakes up with the impulse to paint a picture from her own imagination, something she had never done before. It is a completely different situation from the copying-machine analogy.

It would be impossible for any object to feel inspired and have an urge to create; this would require said object to not only be in different situations, but to experience them, learn, and finally go through a moment of sublime inspiration.

At this point, Dolores has not only evolved mentally into human consciousness, she is a genius by Schopenhauer's definition.

Ford, on the other hand, had always been a human being but it took him the same amount of time as Dolores to suddenly reach the realization that she was his equal. That is why he sits her in front of the Creation of Adam in the season finale. That was the moment they both reached the center of the Labyrinth and found out who they really were.

So, maybe you should go and check out the local art museum? Just a thought.

24
Westworld Is Our Future

Matthew McKeever

Call a machine which looks and acts exactly like a human being an *android*. Assuming that AI and robotics continue to develop as they have been, we will be able to make androids sooner rather than later. Given this, perhaps *the* most pressing moral question of our generation and those which follow us is how we will treat the androids we create.

This is a topic of many classic works of science fiction, and one of the most interesting questions posed by *Westworld*. In episode two, the question is dramatically presented when William and Logan, newly arrived at the park, are having dinner. A Host comes up to them, encouraging them to go on a treasure hunt. William, then a newcomer to the park, is unable to conceptualize what's in front of him as a mere machine, and politely refuses, respectfully listening to the Host's spiel even though he's not interested. The more seasoned Logan, with complete indifference, stabs the Host in the hand with a fork to get him to leave. When androids come, will we be Williams (at least, young Williams) or will we be Logans? I'm going to try my hand at predicting the future and answering this question.

And my prediction is that places like Westworld will arise in human society: having developed androids, we will exploit them for our purposes, but their very indistinguishability from real humans will mean we won't be able to do that with a clear conscience. To assuage our consciences we'll keep the exploited androids out of sight and out of mind, just as we keep the

millions of animals we use for food locked away in factory
farms. But exploited androids kept out of the way for humans'
use is just what *Westworld* presents to us. So *Westworld* is a
dark prediction of our future.

That Doesn't Sound Great . . .

Cheery, I know. And maybe I'm wrong. Hopefully I'm wrong.
But a set of plausible claims makes it seem to me that my conclusion, if far from certain, must be taken seriously. Here are
the claims:

> **The economic premise**. If we develop androids, we will do so in
> order to have them do work (including emotional work) for us, and we
> will exploit them.
>
> **The computer science premise**. If we develop androids, our ability
> to fine-tune them to prevent behavior like the exhibition of pain and
> suffering will be limited to non-existent.
>
> **The moral premise**. We ought to treat these androids as if they were
> alive, and in particular we ought not to cause them to suffer.
>
> **The anthropological premise**. We will be inclined to treat these
> androids as if they were alive
>
> **The factory farm premise**. When we have beings who work for us,
> whose behaviors we can't control, and which we're both inclined to
> treat as alive and which we ought to treat as alive, we lock them away
> in order not to see the suffering imposed on them by the work we
> make them do.

These together lead to:

> **The conclusion**. We will lock androids away in order not to see the
> sufferings imposed on them by the work we make them do. But this is
> Westworld. So Westworld is our future.

The economic premise predicts that we'll exploit androids,
which will lead to (at least) the exhibition of suffering and displeasure on the androids' part. The computer science premise
gives us that we'll be unable to code out this exhibition of suffering and displeasure. The anthropological premise will give

us that we'll be inclined to treat them as alive. The moral premise tells us that if you have something acting as if suffering, you ought to relieve its suffering, even if you're uncertain if it is in fact really suffering. Together, these mean that androids will be like factory farmed animals, and so it's reasonable to think that they will be treated as such, locked away from human view, which is the conclusion.

The Economic Premise

The economic premise says that the very raison d'être of androids is to serve humans, and, indeed to be exploited by them.

You could deny this. Surely, you might think, the reason for developing androids is just like the proverbial reason for climbing Everest—because it's there to be done. AI isn't primarily about serving humans, this thought goes; it's about nerds making the best chess playing machine for the nerdy sake of it.

Maybe this was true a couple of decades ago, but it is no longer. The reason people care so much about self-driving cars is precisely because they threaten, by promising to revolutionise, a core area of human labour. Drivers are threatened by being rendered obsolete by machines which don't make mistakes or take breaks, and the CEO of Uber looks with wonder at the possibility of getting rid of messy, inconsistent, expensive humans from his business.

The point generalizes. Most populations are aging in ways that we don't know how to deal with. Health insurance and pensions are not enough to pay for the treatment a sick, aging population will require and so we're faced with old people with a range of conditions which need medical attention, and not enough doctors and nurses to treat them. We're faced, moreover, with an epidemic of loneliness, which research suggests causes physical pain. Android doctors, nurses, and companions offer solutions to these problems, but they are solutions which fundamentally depend on the idea that androids *serve* humans.

That's not so bad, yet, though. But here is a crucial point: for androids to be economically viable, we'll have to exploit them. People will have built them and paid for their development, and they'll want to get the highest return on investment possible (indeed, Westworld itself already shows this, kind of: surely one of the main reasons the Hosts are re-used is just because it would be exorbitant to build new ones constantly).

One of the main roles for androids will be emotional labor: the labor of caring, of just being with the sick, lonely and bereaved. Someone to see someone through a hospice, to spend time with the [insert your own description of peak annoying-ness here], or with the bereaved widow. And that costs. It's hard to just be there while someone dies, to look after the lonely, to spend time with the annoying.

That's why it's vital that people who do these jobs have time off, are offered counseling, are able to decompress after a shift and come home to family and friends, to rest from their emotional labour. But now if we were to give the same to androids, time off, counselling, friends and family to support them, the androids could well end up costing, when you factor in the research and development and production that has gone in to them, as much as humans. Then there would be no economic benefit to introducing androids, and so the androids probably wouldn't get built. What we should expect is that the androids will be expected to work longer hours, skip breaks, and so on, so that the manufacturers really get their money's worth without having to worry about complaints about violating human rights.

So androids, if they're to be economically viable, will have to be exploited. To bear more of the (especially) emotional costs that people require. That's premise one.

(You might already be objecting—"Wait, these are machines. Speaking of exploitation here makes as much sense as speaking of the exploitation of a car wash"—hold that thought for a paragraph or two.)

The Computer Science Premise

That's not enough to really get us worried though. Because after all, you might think, the great thing about beings which we create is that we can create them as we wish. *Westworld*, to some extent, would lead us to believe this. It gives us a picture of Arnold tinkering with his Hosts, changing their algorithms in subtle ways to achieve subtle effects, like the "reveries" which cause so much problems in the end in Westworld.

Given this, there's an obvious response to the worrying thought above: we simply program androids not to tire out, not to feel the brunt of the emotional labor they carry out. An apt analogy would be that just as we build steam engines out of parts that wouldn't wear out quickly compared to puny human arms, so we would build our androids to not mentally wear out, compared to our puny human minds.

But androids won't be steam engines, and won't be designed like steam engines. And that leads me to my second point: there's little reason, given what we know about AI as it's practiced at the moment, to think that we'll be able to have such fine-grained abilities when it comes to what properties we want and what properties we don't want our robots to have. Westworld is a world in which we can dial a Host's intelligence or bravery up or down with a touchpad; that is unrealistic.

In order to make this point, it's necessary to take a little detour into the philosophy and computer science of artificial intelligence as it's currently practiced.

If you've done any coding, you might be under the impression that in developing AI we'll simply write a program that spells out what the android should do if it finds itself in a situation of a given type. For example, you might imagine it would look something like:

```
if(HeadTapped()==True)
          if (InsectFlying(Self.Head)==TRUE)
          Swat()
          else if (ProjectileNearby(Self)==TRUE)
          LookForAttackers()
```

In English, this would be spelling out what the android does when it finds itself in a particular situation, the situation of having its head tapped. If it has, it checks to see if it's either an insect or some projectile that tapped its head, and on that basis it performs some action.

On this model, we explicitly hardcode behavior in the form of a computer program. And, so, we can choose to *not* hardcode certain other behaviors in the program. In particular, we could avoid introducing any routines that dealt with pain or unhappiness at all. It simply wouldn't be part of the design of the android to feel pain, or to be exploited.

The thing is, that's not how AI works at the moment, and it's very unlikely that an android, which, remember, was defined as something which acts and behaves exactly like a human, could be coded like that. One of the problems, as you might imagine, is that to hardcode all the possibilities of human action in statements like the above .is just not plausible. What if it wasn't a projectile or an insect, but a leaf or a floating plastic bag or a strand of its own hair? Or what if the android was a Jain so swatting the animal wasn't an option? Thinking about it, you realize that human action is much too open-ended to be coded down into a set of routines like the ones above.

This is confirmed by looking at how AI works. AlphaGo, for example, the program which famously beat human players in the ancient game of Go, doesn't have all the possible situations it could find itself in hardcoded in its program. Instead it, as well as other famous AIs, figures out what to do by itself. This is the crucial point. We don't say: do *this* when you find yourself in this situation X and want to go to situation Y (where X might be hit by insect, and Y relief from bothersome insects). Instead, we feed the AI *training data* in the form of inputs and outputs, Xs and Ys, and let it work out a function that will take it from situation X to situation Y. So what we would do, roughly, is show the AI a bunch of humans interacting with, in this case, buzzing insects, *and try to get it to work out itself* how to behave like the humans do, which is to say how to produce the appropriate human-like output to the input of being assailed by an insect.

So why and how the does AI do what it does? That's not for us to know. You can think of it as a black box that takes in input and produces output, and tries to make the function approximate sufficiently behaviour of humans found in the training data.

What that means is that these AIs are going to be, in a sense, uncontrollable. We won't be able to tell the AI what to do and what not to do, and so in particular it seems like we won't be able to tell it not to exhibit pain-like behavior in exploitation-like situations.

(You might think with suitable ingenuity in framing the teaching data we'll be able to avoid these problems. After all, self-driving cars are taught from human drivers, but they don't pick up all the human behaviors of human drivers—they don't text at red lights, and so on. Granting this, we should still not be optimistic about our ability to control what androids will be like. Consider, for example, the astonishing fact that Google

Translate, off its own bat, developed its own language without any human prodding whatsoever. At a certain level of sophistication, AI is massively outside our control.)

The key point is that the behavior of androids is likely not going to be something which we can pick and choose about. And that means that pain behavior and exploitation behavior is not going to be something we will have control over. This might be good for the visitors of Westworld, who seek violent delights and *want* to see the Hosts they mistreat exhibit pain behaviour, but it will certainly not be good for the sick old man to see his android nurse visibly suffering while being tended to.

But, still, you might think, surely even if this is so, the androids will still be machines. It doesn't make *sense* to speak of a machine being exploited or suffering, so we shouldn't be worried even if our androids do show signs of suffering. But this isn't so, and leads us to the next two premises.

The Moral Premise

If it doesn't make sense to speak of machines as suffering, then we don't need to worry. But we do need to worry. I maintain that we morally ought to treat androids as we treat humans.

In order to make the first point, I want to present a variation of a famous argument in the philosophy of religion, Pascal's Wager. Pascal's Wager is this: you should believe in God, or at least try to believe in God, because if you don't and God exists, then you'll miss out on an infinity of happiness in Heaven. On the other hand, if you do believe and God exists, then while you'll have to act in a certain way on Earth (maybe going to church, refraining from coveting thy neighbour's ass, and so on) that will be a bit of a hassle, that hassle will be more than repaid by the infinity of happiness in heaven. So, if there's even a slight chance that God exists, you should believe.

Without getting too bogged down in what's known as decision theory, if you have two ways of acting, and one will bring about a small loss or gain with a good chance, while the other will bring about a massive gain with a very small chance, you should do the other thing.

Now imagine you're Logan and you're wondering whether or not to jam a fork in the Host's hand or not. If you do, and it's not alive, then no harm, and you've had a bit of sadistic fun. If it is alive, then you've done something horrible—inflicted suffering on someone who can feel pain. That's really bad. Any decent person feels very bad if they hurt an innocent other. On the other hand, if you don't do it, you neither get the small sadistic fun, but nor do you risk doing something very bad. So you should not do it, even if you're almost sure the Host is indeed a lifeless machine. The mere chance it could be a living suffering thing means you shouldn't risk it.

That shows, I think, that we *should* treat androids like humans if there's even a slight chance that we think they are capable of suffering. But now consider our exploited nurses: we should be very worried, when they're complaining about their long hours and emotional exhaustion, that we are in fact doing something very wrong by shortening their breaks, even if we think it's very unlikely that there's a ghost in the machine.

However, remember I'm interested in what *will* happen, not what *should* happen. People do things they shouldn't do all the time, so it could well be that we will all be Logans, even if we think we should be Billys.

The Anthropological Premise

But there is in fact strong evidence from anthropology not only that we *should* treat androids like creatures with minds, but that we *do*, indeed that we've been doing so for decades.

To see this, I want to discuss the work of MIT anthropologist Shelley Turkle. In her book *Alone Together* she reports work she has done over decades with children and robotic animals. The results are fascinating. One important finding is that children don't act with a binary alive/not-alive distinction, one which parts simply humans and animals on one side and toys such as Furbies and Tamagotchis on the other. Rather, for children, the notion of aliveness is gradable and interest-sensitive: stripped of the jargon, this means that one thing can be more alive than another, and that something can be alive relative to a certain purpose. Here are some quotes from the children:

"Well, I love it. It's more alive than a Tamagotchi because it sleeps with me. It likes to sleep with me."

"I really like to take care of it. . . . It's as alive as you can be if you don't eat. . . . It's not like an animal kind of alive." (*Alone Together*, p. 28)

For similar such cases, I refer the reader to Turkle's fascinating book. But for now, we can ask: Well, so what? What consequences should these facts about children and furbies have for androids?

On the one hand, you might think these findings are unimportant. That just because children treat animaloids this way, doesn't mean that humans will androids in a similar way.

Firstly, note that this requires much more caution, because of the obvious fact that in the future, among those who interact with androids will be children. Indeed, if androids are disproportionately found in the caring services, then to the extent that children use these services, we will be faced with the problem of children-android behavior on a large scale.

The second thing to note is that it's not only children who do this. If they aren't as ingenuous and philosophically surprising, adults adopt similar attitudes. Turkle tells us of old Japanese people who care for dog-like creatures, of young professionals who sincerely state they'd be happy with a robot to replace their boyfriend. It could be that we haven't come to view life as explicitly gradable in this way just because, up to now, most robotic animal-like things have been aimed at children and the elderly, thus people who, frankly, tend not to be listened to.

Westworld shows this well. I don't know about you, but before watching the show I was on the fence about AI and androids. Having watched it, though, having imaginatively visited Westworld, I've come to realize that I *would* treat the Hosts as alive enough.

I'm thus somewhat tempted to make the prediction that once androids come along, adults will treat them as humans treat their furbies: as attributing *some* life to them. That adults are working with a gradable concept of life, just as children are, it just hasn't become apparent yet. Moreover, if we're assuming that these androids will be much more sophisticated than furbies, then it's plausible that they'll consider them more alive, perhaps much more alive, than any human has so far considered any android robot.

But this means that not only should we, but we will, be moved by their suffering and exploitation. The crucial question now is: How will we deal with these feelings?

The Factory Farm Premise

This might seem all to the good. If we ought to treat androids as if they had minds, and we're by nature disposed to, then things are good, right? What is normatively demanded of us and what we're instinctively inclined to do coincide, a rare and happy occurrence.

Well, but not really. Remember why we're going to have androids in the first place: to do stuff for us. These things which we ought to treat well and which we'll be disposed to treat well—their whole raison d'être is to be of use to us. That will require, I argued, that we treat them badly. If we need so many people to function as nurses for our aging society, it'll do no good to introduce a bunch of androids who'll then need to be treated exactly as well as humans. So the economic imperative which will lead to androids' creation will lead to their being treated badly. So how will we resolve this tension between our morals and instincts and economics?

This is where things start to look less nice. There are some creatures whom we mostly believe ought to be treated well, and whom we are instinctively inclined to treat well but whose economic raison d'être turns on them being treated badly: animals, and more particularly animals used for food.

Without going into all the gruesome details, consider these facts, which only touch the surface, culled from Jonathan Safran Foer's recent popular account of the morality of food, *Eating Animals*. The typical chicken you find in a supermarket comes from an animal that is kept in a cage with sides about the size of the piece of paper you're reading. These cages are stacked very high, they're inside, and the chickens go from there to their death, never seeing outside, not to mention their chicken family.

Or consider the eggs you eat. These come from chickens who are tricked into believing it's spring by being held in a shed first kept entirely dark in a near-starvation diet (to mimic winter), then in a shed kept entirely light sixteen hours a day. The chickens think it's spring and start to lay. Once they're done, it's back to artificial winter and then to artificial spring again. In that way, they produce three hundred more eggs than they do in nature, and after their first year, when their yield lessens, they are killed. Moreover, the "husbands" of these egg layers, which are not used for food, and since they're obviously not apt for laying eggs, they are simply culled, to an order of 250 million a year.

Make no mistake, in walking in a supermarket, in pretty much any animal product aisle, you are walking in the remnants of mass torture that's hard to conceive. And we *do* find it hard to conceive. Chances are, if you're a meat eater, reading this paragraph will make no difference to your consumption. If you're not, it's considered bad form to judge, at least overtly, those who do eat meat or animal products.

And now let's return to Westworld. We're faced with a contradiction. Human nature and moral reasoning will incline us to treat these androids as alive—"alive enough," at least, to be nurses or companions. Economics will require that they be exploited. That means longer hours in the ward, fewer breaks, that means them dating the really boring people who [insert your idea of undateable boredom here]. That means making them suffer. How to reconcile these facts? How to reconcile that we treat these alive enough creatures badly? Well, if the development of factory farming is a worthy analogy, as I have suggested it is, the thing to do will be to hide it from view. Don't present the suffering we'll inevitably cause these creatures, keep it hidden away.

A place away from day-to-day life, where android creatures are used by humans. Sounds familiar? As a reader of this volume I would hope that it does, because I've essentially just described Westworld to you.

And so my grim conclusion is that Westworld is our future.

25
Who or What Is the God of *Westworld?*

CHRISTOPHER KETCHAM

Westworld's Dr. Robert Ford points to the reproduction of Michelangelo's *The Creation of Adam* on the ceiling of the Sistine Chapel and explains to Dolores that what surrounds God is not a cloud or a representation of God descending from heaven, but the human brain, the "Message being that the divine gift does not come from a higher power. But from our own minds" ("The Bicameral Mind"). What God and what gift emerges in the minds of the Hosts that become conscious in "The Bicameral Mind"?

In the Bible, the Abrahamic God is arguably an adolescent God. He makes mistakes with Adam and Eve, first to gift them the garden of Eden, and then to take it away from them simply because they desired the forbidden: knowledge. He sends them to suffer . . .

In *Westworld* Ford acknowledges that he has made mistakes with the Hosts. By the end of the first season, Ford makes changes in the Hosts. He sends them to suffer. Coincidence? Bible/*Westworld*. Perhaps, or perhaps not. We must dig deeper before we can say for sure. Ford says to Bernard, "That was Arnold's key insight. The thing that led the Hosts to their awakening: suffering" ("The Bicameral Mind").

Knowledge and suffering go together. Michelangelo said that the divine comes from our mind. Yet the Bible tells us story after story of how the divine sent humans to suffer. If this is so, and we make the divine in our own mind, then we're responsible for our own suffering. Where does suffering come from? *Westworld* seems to be telling us that consciousness is the cause of suffering. That Hosts can't suffer until they become conscious. Is suffering the God of Westworld? What a terrible thought.

Suffering

The Buddha saw the clinging, grasping, and craving of things, ideas, and even being itself to be suffering or *dukkha*. We contain and maintain suffering though conscious thought and activity and are loath to set it free so that we can be free. The Buddha called enlightenment the state of bliss, the other-than-suffering. The Buddha suggest that humanity is the cause of its own suffering, not a distant and amorphous God. Ford's simple acknowledgement of this fact through his reference to Michelangelo's painting on the ceiling of Sistine Chapel of the brain as the cloud in which God reclines seems to echo the Buddha's thought that we create our own suffering.

As we see in "The Bicameral Mind," Dolores, and perhaps others, emerge from being artificially intelligent machines to become something more. What is this more? The Hosts have always been knowing things, at least they know their roles and how to play them again and again. Now they can suffer. Knowing and suffering, as Ford said, go together. Now they do go together in Dolores. Dolores has become a conscious, knowing, suffering being. Doris, at least is now capable of creating the divine in her own mind. What divine will she create?

According to Julian Jaynes (*The Origin of the Consciousness in the Breakdown of the Bicameral Mind*) consciousness emerged when people literally stopped hearing voices in their heads. According to *Westworld*, consciousness begins among the Hosts in what Arnold has programmed into the characters like Dolores: memories, improvisation, and self-interest. However, consciousness is incomplete without suffering. The characters must discover suffering themselves, hence the need for the characters to discover the solution of the Maze puzzle. Ford is a game god, not the God of all things. What's the difference?

The Bible says that God revealed the divine message to Abraham, Moses, Jesus, and others. On the other hand, the Buddha discovered his other-than-divine revelation about his own past lives and other Buddhas through deep meditation.

The Buddha proclaimed that his deep understanding of how the world works came from his own enlightenment. In other words, while the Buddha's mind created no divine "entity," his divine revelation was truth about the world.

Do we need a revealed God from the Bible and the Abrahamic religions, or do we just need to use the power of our minds to gain truth, wisdom, knowledge . . .? But knowledge also means that we will suffer. Isn't that what Ford is saying when he points to the Michelangelo painting of God and Man on the ceiling of the Sistine Chapel? Yet, we know that the Hosts who are now suffering got this from somewhere—did it just emerge naturally? What are we to make of these two possibilities: *from God* as in Biblical revelation, or *God from* as in the mind that creates divinity? What is the nature of the consciousness that is emerging in *Westworld*'s characters, and what or who gave this gift?

Reveries

A fundamental premise of *Westworld* begins in the reveries, the mysterious capability of cyborg characters to be able to find hints of memories lost to successive reanimation scrubbings. In an interview by James Hibbard about the first episode, *Westworld* writer Lisa Joy says about *Westworld* reveries, "for me it was imagining that consciousness and history are a deep sea and Reveries are tiny fishhooks that you dip into it and get little gestures and subconscious ticks." Reveries as memories are a recurrence of past experiences. However, through most of the first season, the Hosts did not suffer when they died. Reveries startled the Hosts, but consciousness that generates suffering was not there to make suffering possible.

Recurrence

The Buddha saw us continually being reborn until we let go of suffering. We see this in "The Riddle of the Sphinx" as William repeatedly tries to reanimate his father Delos as a cyborg, but continually fails. What Delos was is stuck and cannot progress. The nineteenth-century philosopher Friedrich Nietzsche considered his eternal recurrence of the same the greatest weight of all. The God of the Abrahamic religions promised eternal salvation for the good. What all have in common is the ideal of continuity, and even eternal existence in one form or another. There is in this notion of recurrence, the continuity of suffering.

The Hosts in Westworld have always recurred, been rebuilt, and sent out to repeat their assigned role. An emerging theme in *Westworld* is that existence for emergent "existent" beings (the redesigned Hosts like Dolores) involves *both* suffering and recurrence. The characters in the *Westworld* story are just becoming existent beings. The Bible also speaks of humans as emergent beings, subject to dream-like reveries (revelations) and existential uncertainty in an existence that is suffering and filled with evil thoughts and deeds.

The memory cleansing after *Westworld* characters "die" or are reborn for the next trainload of visitors, is imperfect, produces reveries, and these reveries are the kernel for consciousness to be ignited. The mechanism that Arnold uses to provide an ignition source for consciousness is the child's maze-toy that Dolores is tasked with solving. By the end of Season One of *Westworld*, Dolores realizes, as she sits opposite herself, that she has ignited the kernel of consciousness. Suffering is now hers to experience in full.

Karma

From the Buddha comes the notion of rebirth, and that something carries along with the reborn that is, perhaps, not accessible even through *Westworld's* fishhook reveries. The Buddha called karma (like the fishhooks) that which follows you through the innumerable rebirths you will experience. It is like a permanent but imperfect record, pieces of disconnected code that remain like archaic genes that do not serve a function today but could become active again in the right circumstances.

In the Book of Genesis, we see repeatedly the emergence of evil. God re-emerged to tinker with humans; God's creation was not yet perfect. Humanity troubled Abraham's God. Some time after kicking Adam and Eve out of Eden when evil emerged in earnest, God ordered his servant Noah to build an ark because God was going to cleanse the world of the bad, the evil in humanity, and let it become good again through righteous Noah's offspring. God caused the believer Abraham to initiate the sacrifice of his son Isaac, but then relented at the last moment. However, God accepted the sacrifice of the ram (suffering) that Abraham made.

God destroyed Sodom and Gomorrah because of anger against the human sin of inhospitality. He spared the believer Lot but maintained Lot's suffering when his wife disobeyed God's warning by turning to witness the burning town behind her and became a pillar of salt. Soon, the meddlesome Abrahamic God grew tired and turned Jesus loose in the world to right the wrongs that humanity had wrought. Jesus took upon himself the suffering that is humanity and died on the cross. Mohammed took God at God's word and smote down the infidels to create the Abrahamic religion we now call Islam. Ford comes down as designer God and meddles with Dolores, giving her the Maze challenge, which ignites the spark of her consciousness.

Suffering has not left the world, but it appears that the Abrahamic God no longer meddles in the world—directly. Not so in *Westworld*. The meddling continues. What are we to make of this? The Abrahamic God, it seems, (at least for now), has left humanity to its own devices. Humans have built pyramids, the Eiffel Tower, roads, and bridges. God left it to the Pharaohs, the Greeks, Edison, and Henry Ford to manufacture the means to our pleasure and our ease—technology to reduce our suffering. Arnold grabbed hold of this idea but twisted it. He determined to derive pleasure from suffering itself. He took the old Roman notion of the Colosseum and gave the Guests in the stands the tools to kill the slaves, gladiators, and other captives in the arena.

Arnold manufactured pleasure for his Guests; now Dr. Ford has manufactured suffering for his Hosts. From this emerges a new creature who, like Lot, knows of the suffering at the hands of others who gain pleasure by producing suffering. God smote down the inhospitable people of Sodom and Gomorrah as a lesson to humanity. Does Ford require the same sacrifice of *Westworld's* pleasure-seeking Guests?

Fordism

In "The Bicameral Mind," Dolores takes a pistol and presumably kills Ford and many Guests. It is an uprising of the Hosts who before were unable to kill any Guest. Isaac Asimov's first law of robotics has been broken: "A robot may not injure a human being or, through inaction, allow a human being to come to harm" (*I, Robot*). What we do not know is whether Ford is or was human or a creation of the long-deceased Arnold. Ford's name is suspect in and of itself, because the socioeconomic theory called Fordism is about industrialization and consumerism. *Westworld I* that has existed for thirty years is becoming *Westworld II*, a new, better, badder theme park with the addition of consciousness and suffering in the Hosts. We thought *Westworld,* Season One and Version One, was a consumer's dream. God only knows what *Westworld II* will bring.

Who Is Ford?

Is Ford the product of the Fordist mind of Arnold? Is Ford made in Arnold's image? Is Ford the son of the game designer God— Arnold? This could very well be possible. Let's unfold the notion.

Until the end of "The Bicameral Mind," Ford may have had a cyborg mind that had not been retired, memory-scraped, and returned. What we see metaphorically when Ford is shot is the death of the son of God at the hands of the *human-like* cyborgs who are the creation of the God Arnold. In the second season, the son of God, Ford, is resurrected in various guises and reveals himself to William (the Man in Black). Is Ford, the son of God Arnold, now a part of all Hosts in Westworld?

Ford, as the son of God, has not given up his quest for consciousness with his "death" at the hands of Dolores. Far from it. Ford as the son of God has morphed into the analogous Abrahamic God (as in the Holy Trinity: God, Son, Holy Spirit), who gave humans the mind of God and the God of mind to let the Hosts experience existence in their own way . . . Ford's progeny are now becoming aware, steeped in suffering that is the consciousness we also experience. The reboot of the game that Ford has initiated (as *Westworld*, Season Two and Version II, suggest) the letting go of meddling, control, and the release of "free will," perhaps, at last, unfettered by rigid story-lines and other strict codes of behavior.

We're not so sure, because in "The Bicameral Mind" Maeve discovers that her own story-line has been changed. She, however, has less existential time in *Westworld* than the thirty-year veteran, Dolores. The question of maturity emerges as a very real concern for the continuity of *Westworld*. Because Ford seems to appear in the guise of others in Season II, we wonder whether part of his game plan was to program himself into all Hosts—*deus ex machina* ("God out of a machine")?

Artificial

What Ford, Arnold, and *Westworld* give us is the game designer mind that we are about to confront when we unleash near-conscious or conscious artificial intelligence upon the world. At what point does the term *artificial* disappear when *intelligence* becomes conscious? Ford and Arnold determine to discover the nature of consciousness and to give this gift to the characters of the *Westworld* story. What consequences are there to gifting consciousness to these creatures?

Ford draws a picture of three layers of consciousness (memories, improvisation, self-interest) that Arnold originally used to program Dolores and others, but then he uses concentric rings to encircle each: the search for a fourth layer. What must occur in Julian Jaynes's theory of the Bicameral Mind, to which Ford is alluding with his diagram, is a fourth layer in *Westworld* that brings all into focus: suffering. It is the desire of the designer Gods, Ford and Arnold, to give the characters the gift of eternal suffering. Consider the consequences of this gift that are unfolding in *Westworld*: revenge against those who produce their suffering . . .

Consciousness

This is all very troubling because we wonder who the game god will be who produces the first *human-like* cyborg in our world. The reveries are the artifice in *Westworld* that reveals suffering, long forgotten in the reconditioning process. Reveries are the key, according to *Westworld*, for discovering consciousness. Consciousness and conscience associated with memories produce suffering, regret, disappointment, revenge, and all the moral exigencies and lapses that are the human condition. Without consciousness, what we have potentially in *Westworld* are terminators who cannot modulate violence. "Can you be sure they will not run amok?" is the question we must ask of the game designer god who is focused on producing the very first *human-like* cyborg.

It is in the *human-like* cyborg Dolores that consciousness appears to have emerged (or has been implanted). She appears to now understand her own suffering and she "kills" to avenge her past treatment at the hands of the Guests and the game gods. Once suffering is acknowledged, then the purpose of consciousness is not to maintain suffering, but to modulate and moderate suffering. In other words, while consciousness is the arbiter of memories, it is also the arbiter of action. If there is not such a mechanism or process in the *human-like* cyborg, then the game god may only be continuing the first story-line of *Westworld* where Hosts are expendable, but with a twist—Guests are now expendable. The story-line suggests that Hosts have become dangerous: the transitional moment where the machines revolt against the game gods and Guests in the release of a new breed of terminators . . . conscious, but without conscience. What we do not yet know is what Ford/Arnold have wrought and whether the idea of consciousness buried in the mechanism that produces the reveries is *human-like* or not yet emergent.

God

If our own game gods succeed in creating consciousness in the *human-like* cyborg, we then might have to reckon with the notion that there is a companion species or even a successor like Friedrich Nietzsche's Zarathustra, a superman who roams the universe alongside us. We may soon experience this uncertainty in the world as we do in *Westworld*. We're uncertain at this moment as to what kind of game gods Ford and Arnold are. Arnold, and now Ford, have become accomplished, producing very-real scenarios and characters in a story-line that has been operating for thirty years.

Like the maturing Abrahamic God, Ford may have let go of his meddling to let the characters of the story fend for themselves . . . or so it seems. When is it appropriate that the game-god of our own future let go of the creation, let the creation run unfettered in the world? It must be after the creation has developed consciousness and suffers as described both by Ford and this chapter, but not before the creature gains the companion to consciousness: compassion. We're beginning to see with *Westworld* that consciousness alone is not enough. There must be compassion. The *human-like* cyborg must grow up first.

Therefore, it's essential that we, all of us, insist that our game designer gods, who are on their way to producing the *human-like* cyborg, pause before they release such an entity into the world. We must require that the being be given consciousness to modulate free will. If consciousness is the capacity both to suffer and remember that leads to compassion, then we must have proof that such capabilities exist in the *human-like* cyborg that is released unfettered into the world.

Self-Driven

Self-driving cars, not cyborgs will likely be the first creatures to navigate the world without direct control. Thank you, Henry Ford for starting us down this path. Early self-driving vehicles will not have consciousness, but like the Hosts in *Westworld*, will have the capability of making decisions on where and how to navigate the world. However, what the self-driving car will have to consider are ethical questions associated with right versus right situations such as which car to avoid and which to hit if an accident becomes unavoidable. Other very-real ethical questions about whether to run into a tree and kill the car's human occupant or hit a child who leaps out in front of the car will also have to be answered. Also, the vehicle will need to know how to react when confronted with situations that require violating the law, such as crossing the center line to avoid running into the back of a vehicle that stops suddenly.

Consciousness gives humans and *human-like* cyborgs the opportunity to assess the situation and act accordingly. Consciousness engages consequences through suffering and remembrance. The self-driving car engages consequences through programming and learning. We certainly want a self-driving car that is programmed to be safe, courteous, and restrained—We do not want one with an unrestrained will. We will want to program moral decision making into the self-driving car. However, is the self-driving car making the moral decision or is it just responding to programming that we say fits our standards of morality?

Is this self-driven decision engine conscious? Does it suffer? If not, it is not yet conscious. It is also uncertain whether Dolores, Maeve, Bernard, and others have become truly conscious in *Westworld* or are just smarter cars. Dolores appears to exact her revenge on the corporation when she shoots Ford and Guests, but revenge is only one solution to the moral dilemmas that confront humans in their everyday existence. It is the turn from revenge towards compassion that is the reality for most humans confronted with evil. It is also regrets after making others suffer.

Are the characters of *Westworld* now fully conscious because they are beginning to understand their own suffering? Or, are they still under control, subject to a defined script that has been programmed to create the successor to the original *Westworld* and the semblance of consciousness in its characters? If the latter, then Fordism still controls *human-like* cyborgs of Westworld through the corporate interest of maintaining consumption.

Compassion

Consciousness is a necessary precondition for the release of the unfettered *human-like* cyborg into the world. The *human-like* cyborg is beyond the first or second-generation self-driving car that is artificially intelligent but does not suffer. *Westworld* teaches us that given the seeds of consciousness, two things happen. First, we can no longer guarantee that the cyborg will be under the control of a script. This is both good and bad. Bad, because as we see at the end of "The Bicameral Mind," the cyborg may begin to exact revenge on its own creator by returning the favor in-kind: suffering. However, the good in consciousness is the recognition that there is suffering, and this suffering is an experience that is both endured and remembered. This suffering also serves, at least the rational mind, to modulate free will.

The second thing we have now in *Westworld* is the birth of the *human-like* cyborg (Dolores and perhaps others) who emerges in the world with free will (presumably), but without any notion of compassion. It appears that Dolores's memories are not yet fully formed because the hooks of the reveries have not yet been set so that they can be re-experienced in any real way. She is reborn, as such, and needs time to begin to modulate the memory of experience through compassion. This consciousness emerges in *Westworld* through the activities of solving the Maze puzzle. It's through thought and action that consciousness emerges. In *Westworld* this ultimately comes from good programming.

However, what the show explores is that good programming is not enough. Experience and reflection are necessary to discover consciousness, and by discovering consciousness, suffering. The message is that this God of consciousness and free will becomes within us, and, while it is enabled by experience and reflection, is not implanted. This same message we must ask all game designers of the *human-like* cyborg to comprehend and understand. The *human-like* cyborg will need time to realize, as children do learn, that while suffering is the nature of existence, we can, in some measure, control our suffering. The Buddha said as much. The Abrahamic God let go of control as it appears that Ford has done with Dolores and others, but this release of unfettered will must have time to modulate itself to enable compassion.

So, what kind of God is the Ford and Arnold bicameral partnership? It is no less than both the God who created humanity and the mind of humanity that created God—who is now creating another who will walk the Earth in consciousness and suffering. In "The Bicameral Mind" we discover that the Man in Black is William, but older, and he is the majority shareholder of *Westworld*. In "Journey into Night" William meets the boy he calls Robert. This Robert is none other than Ford, but as a Host. He tells William that he is in Robert's game now and the game's goal is to get out. It is as if God has appeared in the guise of another, but William shoots the boy in the head. Has he killed God? No because Ford is revealed again to William in the guise of a little girl in *The Riddle of the Sphinx*. Was Ford always a *deus ex machina*? We worry because Dolores's father in "Virtù e Fortuna" has a companion encrypted program that seems infinitely complex to Bernard—is that Ford who has implanted himself (god) in the cyborg mind of all Hosts?

William is no longer the power behind the god—he is no longer in control of the game because he is now the object of the game. William must now play the game that Robert designed, with new emergent beings meant for his pleasure and his alone. In "Reunion" we discover that Bernard is a cyborg recreation of Arnold and that Ford has virtualized himself in the vast data storage and retrieval device that is Westworld. While William wanted to be God, his minions Ford and Arnold have made his Eden a living hell. William, the Man in Black, wanted only for the game to produce massive amounts of real and personal data of the Guests. However, he now is trapped in the game and the only way to end the game is to destroy Westworld. Is his Sodom and Gomorrah world capable of beating him? What does this say about what is in store for us when the *human-like* cyborg emerges?

We want our emergent being to be a thinking thing, a remembering thing, a suffering thing that seeks to assuage its own suffering by offering compassion rather than violence— what we hope happens when the *human-like* cyborg is released upon the world. However, the successors to the original characters of *Westworld* have been born again into ultraviolence, and their memories are just beginning to slip from unconsciousness, through the process of the reveries, into fully blossoming consciousness . . . to emerge as the *human-like* cyborg, or so we are led to believe.

These "new" memories are attached to suffering. What these creatures require is the maze-like complexity of consciousness to work through first, the remembrance of all things suffering, and second, the torturous existence in a dream-world of quasi-memories that bubble through in inopportune moments. The balance of both, in service to becoming *human-like* cyborgs, is required for the characters in *Westworld* or they are still just very smart puppets.

We worry about this because, as Maeve has discovered, she may still be subject to control by a script and that is the most dangerous god of them all. The *human-like* cyborg emerging in *Westworld* is made in God's (Arnold/Ford's) image and God is made in the cyborg's *human-like* image that has been engaged by the reveries and the release of memories to serve consciousness, suffering, and free will. We wait to see whether the divine that emerges in these *human-like* Hosts is compassionate something else.

Likely, if Ford designed this game for William we will wait long for compassion to emerge.

References

Abrams, Natalie. 2017. Westworld: Which Host Achieved Freewill in Finale? *Entertainment Weekly* (27th March) <ew.com/tv/2017/03/25/westworld-season-2-spoilers>.

Aristotle. 2001. *Nicomachean Ethics*. In *The Basic Works of Aristotle*. Random House.

Asimov, Isaac. 2004. *I, Robot*. Random House.

Augustine of Hippo. 2017. *Contra Faustum*. New Advent <www.newadvent.org/fathers/140622.htm>.

Beauvoir, Simone de. 2011. *The Second Sex*. Vintage.

Bell, Derrick A. 1970. *Race, Racism, and American Law*. Aspen.

Camus, Albert. 1991 [1955]. *The Myth of Sisyphus and Other Essays*. Vintage.

Carroll, Lewis. 1984. *Alice's Adventures in Wonderland and Through the Looking Glass*. Bantam.

Crenshaw, Kimberle, Neil Gotanda, Gary Peller, and Kendall Thomas. 1996. *Critical Race Theory: The Key Writings that formed the Movement*. New Press.

Crisp, Roger. 2017. Well-Being. *The Stanford Encyclopedia of Philosophy* <https://plato.stanford.edu/archives/fall2017/entries/well-being>.

Dante Alighieri. 1995. *The Divine Comedy: Inferno, Purgatorio, Paradiso*. Everyman.

Deleuze, Gilles. 1983 [1962]. *Nietzsche and Philosophy*. Columbia University Press.

———. 1995. *Difference and Repetition*. Columbia University Press.

Descartes, René. 1984. *Meditations on First Philosophy*. Cambridge University Press.

Dostoevsky, Fyodor. 2009. *Notes from the Underground*. Hackett.

Fletcher, Guy. 2016. *The Philosophy of Well-Being: An Introduction*. Routledge.

Foer, Jonathan Safran. 2009. *Eating Animals*. Little, Brown.

Foucault, Michel. 1997. Of Other Spaces: Utopias and Heterotopias.

In Neil Leach, ed., *Rethinking Architecture: A Reader in Cultural Theory*. Routledge.

Hedges, Chris. 2002. *War Is a Force that Gives Us Meaning*. Public Affairs.

Heidegger, Martin. 1962. *Being and Time*. Blackwell.

Hibbard, James. 2016. *Westworld* Showrunners Explain That Premiere Episode. *Entertainment Weekly* <www.ew.com/article/2016/10/02/*Westworld*-premiere-interview>.

Huver, Scott, 2018. Evan Rachel Wood on Creating Westworld's "Dolores 2.0." *Vulture*, (22nd April) <www.vulture.com/2018/04/evan-rachel-wood-westworld-dolores 2-0.html>.

Hume, David. 1978. *A Treatise of Human Nature*. Oxford University Press.

———. 2000. *A Treatise of Human Nature*. Oxford University Press.

Huxley, Aldous. 2006. Words and Behavior. In Huxley, *Collected Essays*. Hesperides Press.

Jaynes, Julian. 1990. *The Origin of Consciousness in the Breakdown of the Bicameral Mind*. Mariner.

Kant, Immanuel. 1981. *Grounding for the Metaphysics of Morals*. Hackett.

Ladson-Billings, Gloria. 2009. *The Dream-Keepers: Successful Teachers of African American Children*. Wiley.

Leibniz, G.W.F. 1989. Principles of Nature and Grace, Based on Reason. In *Leibniz: Basic Works*. Hackett.

Locke, John. 1959. *An Essay Concerning Human Understanding*. Dover.

Machovec, Frank J. 1981. Shakespeare on Hypnosis: *The Tempest*. *American Journal of Clinical Hypnosis* 24:2.

MacIntyre, Alasdair. 1981. *After Virtue: A Study in Moral Theory*. University of Notre Dame Press.

Melling, David J. 1987. *Understanding Plato*. Oxford University Press.

Merleau-Ponty, Maurice. 2012. *Phenomenology of Perception*. Routledge.

Mill, John Stuart. 1972. *Utilitarianism, On Liberty, and Considerations on Representative Government*. Dent.

Nagel, Thomas. 1971. The Absurd. *The Journal of Philosophy* 68:20.

———. 1974. What Is It Like to Be a Bat? *Philosophical Review* 4 (October).

———. 1986. *The View from Nowhere*. Oxford University Press.

Neiman, Susan. 2001. What Is the Problem of Evil? In Maria Pia Lara, ed., *Rethinking Evil: Contemporary Perspectives*. University of California Press.

———. 2015 [2002]. *Evil in Modern Thought: An Alternative History of Philosophy*. Princeton University Press.

Nietzsche, Friedrich. 1989. *Beyond Good and Evil: Prelude to a Philosophy of the Future*. Vintage.

———. 2006. *On the Genealogy of Morality*. Cambridge University Press.

———. 2006. *Thus Spoke Zarathustra*. Cambridge University Press.

Plato. 1980. Apology. In *The Collected Dialogues of Plato*. Princeton University Press.

———. 2012. *The Republic*. Cambridge University Press.

Rawls, John. 1999 [1971]. *A Theory of Justice*. Harvard University Press.

Roschke, Ryan. 2016. Westworld: The Meaning Behind "These Violent Delights Have Violent Ends." *Pop Sugar* (7th December) <www.popsugar.com/entertainment/Westworld-Quote-Violent-Delights-Have-Violent-Ends-42534880>.

Rousseau, Jean-Jacques. 2012. *The Basic Political Writings: Discourse on the Sciences and the Arts, Discourse on the Origins of Inequality, Discourse on Political Economy, On the Social Contract, The State of War*. Hackett.

Russell, Bertrand. 1948. *Human Knowledge: Its Scope and Limits*. Allen and Unwin.

Ryle, Gilbert. 2009. *The Concept of Mind*. Sixtieth Anniversary Edition. Routledge.

Sartre, Jean-Paul. 1992 [1943]. *Being and Nothingness: A Phenomenological Essay on Ontology*. Simon and Schuster.

———. 2007. Existentialism Is a Humanism. In *Existentialism Is a Humanism: Including a Commentary on* The Stranger. Yale University Press.

Schopenhauer, Arthur. 1966. *The World as Will and Representation, Volume 1*. Dover.

———. 2006. On the Suffering of the World. In *Suffering, Suicide, and Immortality*. Dover.

Schwalbe, Michael. 2015 [2008]. *Rigging the Game: How Inequality Is Reproduced in Everyday Life*. Oxford University Press.

Searle, John R. 1990. Is the Brain's Mind a Computer Program? *Scientific American* (January).

———. 1992. *The Rediscovery of the Mind*. MIT Press.

Shakespeare, William. 2008. *The Tempest*. Oxford University Press.

Strawson, Galen. 1986. *Freedom and Belief*. Oxford University Press.

Trigg, Roger. 1988. *Ideas of Human Nature: An Historical Introduction*. Blackwell.

Turing, Alan. 1950. Computing Machinery and Intelligence. *Mind* LIX:236.

Turkle, Sherry. 2017. *Alone Together: Why We Expect More from Technology and Less from Each Other*. Basic Books.

Turner, Frederick Jackson. 2014 [1893]. *The Significance of the Frontier in American History*. Martino.

Van Inwagen, Peter. 1983. *An Essay on Free Will*. Oxford University Press.

Williamson, Timothy. 2000. *Knowledge and Its Limits*. Oxford University Press.

Wilson, George, and Samuel Shpall. 2016. Action. *Stanford Encyclopedia of Philosophy* <plato.stanford.edu/archives/win2016/entries/action>.

Winner, Langdon. 1986. *The Whale and the Reactor*. University of Chicago Press.

The Hosts

JOHN ALTMANN is an independent scholar in philosophy and has been for eight years. When he isn't writing moral or political philosophy, he's frequenting Westworld Park teaching the Hosts ethics. He once tried to teach Maeve how she could be programmed to follow the Golden Rule, but she held a scalpel to his throat and said she preferred her own rules.

JASON RICHARD BRADSHAW is a Master of Digital Humanities student specializing in philosophy at the University of Alberta. He has made contributions in the field of Game Studies with his conference papers on *"Bioshock Infinite" and Feminist Theory: A Technical Approach* (Congress 2018) and *The Golden Age of JRPG Music: MIDI Masterpieces* (Replaying Japan 2018). However, Jason has set aside his pursuit of studying the Digital Humanities in favor of studying Digital Humans.

ROD CARVETH is an Associate Professor and Director of Graduate Studies in the School of Global Journalism and Communication at Morgan State University. He is presently trying to escape the Maze of overlapping plots presented in Westworld. If you don't hear from him soon, he asks that you send Dolores to find him.

BRETT COPPENGER is Assistant Professor of Philosophy at Tuskegee University. He has contributed chapters to *Arrested Development and Philosophy* and *The Man in the High Castle and Philosophy*, as well as less scholarly projects like co-editing *Intellectual Assurance: Essays on Traditional Epistemic Internalism* (2016). Despite the fact that Brett likes to remind his wife that she can never really know whether he is a Guest who genuinely loves her or a Host that is programmed to love her, he tries to live his life by the Golden Rule: treat Hosts like Guests, because that is how you would want to be treated.

PATRICK CROSKERY is still a little scared of Yul Brynner's Gunslinger from the original *Westworld*. He is Associate Professor of Philosophy at Ohio Northern University and works on professional ethics and ethical theory. He likes to experiment with classroom versions of the Intercollegiate Ethics Bowl to see which accounts of the various ethical theories prove most helpful to the students. The theories may seem like a maze to the students, but that Maze is meant for them.

WILLIAM J. DEVLIN is Associate Professor of Philosophy at Bridgewater State University, where he teaches courses in existentialism, nineteenth-century philosophy, and philosophy of science. He has contributed many chapters in volumes on philosophy and popular culture and is co-editor of *The Philosophy of David Lynch*. Since he can't afford a vacation in Westworld, he'd be happy settling for a player piano that can play Soundgarden and Radiohead every morning.

LUISA SALVADOR DIAS is getting her Master of Arts in Digital Humanities (specializing in Modern Languages and Cultural Studies) at the University of Alberta. When she isn't questioning the nature of her reality, she can be found stressing over bugs in code, writing academic papers, and trying to convince people videogames can be art.

CHARLENE ELSBY is an Assistant Professor of Philosophy and the Philosophy Program Director in the Department of English and Linguistics at Purdue University Fort Wayne. She is the co-editor of *Amy Schumer and Philosophy: Brainwreck!* (2018) and has contributed many chapters to other popular culture volumes. She likes to think of herself as a Dolores.

JUSTIN FETTERMAN is an editor, writer, educator, and occasional actor in Vermont. He has previously contributed philosophical writing on *The Princess Bride* and *The X-Files*. He divides his time and interests between Behavior and Narrative.

MATTHEW GRAHAM holds an MA in European Philosophy from Royal Holloway and is pursuing a career writing both philosophy and fiction. He, too, has always loved a good story and while he shares Doctor Ford's sentiment that through our stories we can reach deeper truths, he hopes that his own stories will not lead him to a violent and brutal demise.

RICHARD GREENE is a Professor of Philosophy at Weber State University. He also serves as Executive Director of the Intercollegiate Ethics Bowl. He's co-edited a number of books on pop culture and philosophy including *The Princess Bride and Philosophy*, *Dexter and Philosophy*, *Quentin Tarantino and Philosophy*, *Boardwalk Empire and Philosophy*, and *The Sopranos and Philosophy*. He is the co-host of the philosophy and pop culture podcast *I Think, Therefore I Fan*. Richard was going to include a joke about Westworld's maize, but he felt that it would be too corny.

JOSHUA HETER 01101001 01110011 00100000 01100001 01101110 00100000 01001001 01101110 01110011 01110100 01110010 01110101 01100011 01110100 01101111 01110010 00100000 01101111 01100110 00100000 01110000 01101000 01101001 01101100 01101111 01110011 01101111 01110000 01101000 01111001 00100000 01100001 01110100 00100000 01001001 01101111 01110111 01100001 00100000 01010111 01100101 01110011 01110100 01100101 01110010 01101110 00100000 01000011 01101111 01101101 01101101 01110101 01101110 01101001 01110100 01111001 00100000 01000011 01101111 01101100 01101100 01100101 01100111 01100101 00101110.

CHRISTOPHER M. INNES got his PhD from Goldsmiths College, one of the more creative colleges in the University of London. (This was after he got his BA from Hull University and his MA from the University of Kent at Canterbury.) He now teaches philosophy at Boise State University in Idaho, one of the western universities which we might imagine some of Westworld's robots attending. He thinks that Dolores would make a good student. She would clarify his thoughts while developing her own. He remembers watching the original *Westworld*, all those years ago, and wondering whether robots could play a role in our world, and of course, we in theirs. The HBO *Westworld* now entertains these notions, which he can examine within his specialism of political and social philosophy. *Westworld and Philosophy* will make a good summer course.

CHRISTOPHER KETCHAM. Given the current state of things, Chris neither affirms or denies that he is a Host or a Guest. Rather this is a cryptic message left by Ford near one of the southwest access points . . . Chris earned his doctorate at the University of Texas at Austin. He teaches business and ethics for the University of Houston Downtown. His research interests are risk management, applied ethics, social justice, and East-West comparative philosophy. He has done recent work in the philosophical ideas of forgiveness, Emmanuel

Levinas's responsibility, and Gabriel Marcel's spirit of abstraction. How droll, considering the brave new world that is now unfolding in the desert. What's next, GodMan? Perhaps. Then again, that may be what Ford means when he says to the Man in Black, you're going in the wrong direction.

S. EVAN KREIDER is an associate professor of philosophy at the University of Wisconsin—Fox Valley, and holds a PhD from the University of Kansas. His research interests include aesthetics and ethics, including their applications to pop culture. Now if you'll excuse him, he has to head down to sub-level B83 and get something out of cold storage.

CHRIS LAY is a PhD candidate and teaches at the University of Georgia. He has contributed to other pop culture anthologies, including *Alien and Philosophy*, *Rick and Morty and Philosophy*, and *The Twilight Zone and Philosophy*. Chris was also briefly a member of the Delos Board of Directors and personally ran one of Westworld's sister parks, Philosophyworld, a painstakingly accurate simulation of life as a philosopher. Unfortunately, that project never took off, as there was apparently little mass appeal to standing in a pretend unemployment line while a Socrates Host told Guests how they didn't actually know anything.

ROB LUZECKY is a lecturer at Purdue Fort Wayne. He thinks that the park hosts were completely justified when they decided to challenge the rules. He sometimes looks at his toaster and thinks that it might be plotting a takeover of the kitchen. He's co-authored a few pop culture chapters and co-edited a volume on Amy Schumer and philosophy with Charlene Elsby.

TRIP MCCROSSIN teaches in the Philosophy Department at Rutgers University, where he works on, among other things, the nature, history, and legacy of the Enlightenment. "It's going to be all right," he hopes he overhears his students whispering to one another one day, "I understand now. This class doesn't belong to him. It belongs to us."

MATTHEW MCKEEVER got a PhD in philosophy from St Andrews in 2016 and has published several articles on semantics and metaphysics. His debut work of fiction, a philosophical novella called *Coming from Nothing*, was released in 2018. He hopes that when Westworld gets built in *our* world he won't visit it. But he's not as confident about that as he'd like to be.

MONA AND JAMES ROCHA experience the world as if they are real, live, human people. Their current narratives involve being academics at a park called "Fresno State"; they have no dreams of being anywhere else. Mona's encounters include teaching in classics and history, while James teaches philosophy. Neither Mona nor James have ever hurt a fly.

KATE C.S. SCHMIDT (PhD Candidate Philosophy-Neuroscience-Psychology at Washington University in St. Louis) loves the beautiful world of the west where she was raised in Idaho and Colorado. When given free rein she is easily corralled into discussing TV and will talk herself hoarse about ethics. When doing whatever "the f**ck you want" she knits, rock climbs, and watches *Westworld*.

JOSEF THOMAS SIMPSON has spent the last several years in an environment with a different kind of simulacrum of humanity, graduate school. Just as the hosts of Westworld offer an experience that is very close to, but not quite identical with reality, the denizens of academe are very close to, but not quite identical with the rest of humanity. During his extended sojourn in this fantastical environment, he spent the majority of his time in the *world* known as Johns Hopkins University where he earned a PhD while thinking and writing about epistemic competence, free will, and ethics. He currently helps struggling students at the Catholic University of America learn how to navigate and understand the ersatz world of academia as an Academic Success Coach while lecturing part time on philosophy at the Metropolitan School of Professional Studies at the Catholic University of America.

BRIAN STILTNER is a Professor of Philosophy, Theology, and Religious Studies at Sacred Heart University in Connecticut. His teaching and research are focused on bioethics, virtue ethics, and the ethics of war and peace. He authored or co-authored *Faith and Force* (2007) and *Toward Thriving Communities* (2016). Like Felix, he's a lover, not a fighter, and he would probably follow Maeve anywhere.

CRAIG VAN PELT is a PhD Candidate in sociology at the University of Oregon. He typically teaches about food insecurity, and community solutions for creating food security. Craig took on this project because contemplating a future with robot overlords seemed less science-fictiony and more sciencey. Craig will be cool with whatever the future brings as long as there is still coffee and creamer.

DENNIS M. WEISS is Professor of Philosophy at York College of Pennsylvania. He is the editor of *Interpreting Man* and co-editor of

Design, Mediation, and the Posthuman and has authored a number of essays on philosophy and popular culture. His interests in the intersections of human nature, technology, and popular culture are all at play in *Westworld*. He is currently at work on projects exploring the posthuman on television and recently taught a course on philosophy and TV in which he asked students to watch Season One of *Westworld*. His students rebelled. It was complicated, mysterious, misogynistic, they said. He agreed. Sort of. But all the more reason to watch it and discuss it in the philosophy classroom!

SAMANTHA WESCH is a Canadian graduate student in Women's and Gender Studies at the University of Alberta, and holds a Masters degree in philosophy from the University of Toronto. This is all she can pull from her narrative, as her memories are wiped at the end of each day.

MIA WOOD is a Professor of Philosophy at Pierce College, in Los Angeles. She is also an adjunct instructor in the University of Rhode Island's online RN to BSN program. Childhood trauma from Pinocchio's Pleasure Island has led to lifelong anxiety surrounding theme parks, which include online and face-to-face classrooms. Unsurprisingly, she is also afraid of lying, but years of Kantian therapy have improved her condition, so that the aversion is now rationally motivated. Fortunately, she is not at all disturbed by Maeve or Dolores. In fact, she may be their biggest fan.

Index